LONDON'S CITY

A Guide Through the Historic Square Mile

LONDON'S CITY

A Guide Through the Historic Square Mile

by

SIDNEY LAURENS

Marmot Publishing

Snoqualmie, WA
U.S.A.

LONDON'S CITY

A Guide Through the Historic Square Mile

by Sidney Laurens

Published by:

Marmot Publishing

P.O. Box 725
Snoqualmie, WA 98065
U.S.A.

Library of Congress Catalog Card Number: 94-75991

ISBN 0-9641263-0-3

10 9 8 7 6 5 4 3 2 1

The happiness of London is not to be conceived but by those who have been in it. I will venture to say there is more learning and science within the circumference of ten miles from where we sit, than in all the rest of the kingdom. Why, sir, you find no man, at all intellectual, who is willing to leave London. No, Sir, when a man is tired of London, he is tired of life; for there is in London all that life can afford.

— Dr. Samuel Johnson

TABLE OF CONTENTS

LIST OF MAPS

INTRODUCTION

There has been a City of London for nearly 2000 years. If we were to dissect it layer by layer, we would find remnants of the old city of Londinium from the Great Fire of 1666, followed by relics from Tudor London, the Plantagenets, the Normans, the Angles, the Saxons, the Celts and finally the Romans.

The City was officially established in the 11th century after the Norman Conquest. Its 677 acres were completely walled in and guarded with seven gates from the Tower of London to Temple Bar and the Thames. The walls came tumbling down in the latter half of the 18th century.

The old expression "from Temple to Tower" was used to describe this traditional one square mile, although it is actually one and one-half miles long and seven-eighths of a mile wide. The City still covers the same approximate geographical area, and remains the financial and commercial center of modern day London.

Located within the City, or immediately adjacent to it, are the four Inns of Court: Gray's Inn and Lincoln's Inn in Holborn, and Inner Temple Inn and Middle Temple Inn on Fleet Street. These colleges of the law, formed during the 14th and 15th centuries, possess exclusive rights of conferring the title of "barrister" on a lawyer or solicitor, thus authorizing him to argue a case in the High Court or Court of Appeal.

Attached to these Inns of Court, a number of Inns of Chancery were established for young aspirants to the Bar. Such Inns of Chancery as Furnival's Inn, Barnard's Inn and Staple Inn, all in Holborn, ceased to have any legal standing by the middle of the 18th century.

The lives of Londoners have always revolved around their churches and taverns. During the 18th century, 149 parish churches in the City and suburbs attested to the great power and influence exercised by the clergy. All the great religious orders were represented in medieval London: the Black Friars near St. Paul's Cathedral, the Grey Friars on Newgate Street, the Augustinian Friars near Broad Street, the Carthusians and Knights Hospitallers of St. John of Jerusalem in Clerkenwell, the Crutched Friars near the Tower of London, and the White Friars and the Knights Templars on Fleet Street. Their magnificent monastic priories and places may well have been "the cloud-clapped towers, the gorgeous palaces, the solemn temples" that Shakespeare saw, but by that time the Friars had been dispossessed by Henry VIII.

Even some four centuries later, 108 parish churches still remained in the City at the time of the Great Fire of 1666. Of the 87 which were destroyed, 50 were rebuilt and all designed by the great architect Sir Christopher Wren. Only six churches within the City walls escaped the Great Fire and still survive: St. Ethelburga's, Great St. Helen's, St. Katherine Cree, St. Andrew Undershaft, St. Olave's Hart Street and All Hallows Barking (by the Tower).

The taverns did more than provide beer as a substitute for undrinkable water. They served as meeting places for the conduct of business, as recreational resorts and musical societies—but most of all as congenial places to spend an afternoon or evening. Most Londoners visited a tavern at least once a day.

The Mermaid Tavern on Bread Street was the jewel in Queen Elizabeth's crown. The Devil on Fleet Street was the glory of King James' reign. The Boar's Head in Eastcheap was immortalized by Shakespeare. The Cheshire Cheese still stands on the site occupied by the White Friars almost four centuries ago.

The early inns also played a crucial role in the development of theaters. Companies of strolling players frequently performed in the open inn yards. When James Burbage built the first permanent playhouse, The Theatre, in a London suburb in 1576, he used the inn yard as his model. The open courtyard, the projecting platform as stage, the dressing rooms in the rear, the balcony and the galleries all became the standard pattern for our modern theaters.

For Englishmen, life without an inn or tavern was unthinkable. It was Dr. Samuel Johnson who said:

> There is nothing which has yet been contrived by man, by which so much happiness is produced as by a good tavern or inn.

William Shenstone in the 18th century expressed his gratitude in *Written at an Inn at Henley:*

> Whoe'er has travelled life's dull round,
> Where'er his stages may have been,
> May sigh to think he still has found
> The warmest welcome at an inn

Hilaire Belloc echoed this sentiment in his 19th century collection, *This and That:*

When you have lost your Inns drown your empty selves, for
you will have lost the last of England.

This unique enclave of 1.06 square miles, known as the City, lies completely within the great metropolis of London which covers 625 square miles. The City has the authority to hold its own trials in the Lord Mayor's Court and the City of London Court at the Mansion House and the Guildhall. The reigning monarch of England must receive permission from the Lord Mayor in order to enter the City.

If the past is the priceless inheritance of each succeeding generation, nowhere is this more visible than in this ancient spot, best described by Christopher Marlowe's phrase, "Infinite riches in a little room." The City possesses the richest aggregation of historical and literary associations in the world. With the passage of time, many structures have vanished, monuments neglected and streets swept away. However, some parts of the City remain pretty much as they once were.

James Boswell said, "How different a place London is to different people." No two people may enjoy the same things but there is more than enough in Old London to satisfy everyone. Walter George Bell, an eminent 19th century writer, even wrote an entire book on the 536 yards of a single street: Fleet Street between Temple Bar and Ludgate Circus.

I have tried to breathe life into the almost forgotten history of the City's buildings, houses, churches, inns, streets and fields, even though many have long since disappeared. The use of histories, diaries, novels, plays, poems, memorable characters and exciting events have been introduced to better understand the cultural, historic and aesthetic significance of the times, and of the life of the people.

HOW TO USE THIS BOOK

I have divided the City of London into nine small areas designated by the letters A through I. Each area is provided with a detailed map and descriptions of its main attractions, arranged alphabetically and sequentially numbered. The numbers correspond to the site locations on the maps. A City of London map on pages 2 and 3 illustrates the boundaries of the nine areas and is intended to be used as an overview for planning excursions.

This arrangement permits great flexibility in selecting the particular sites according to the individual's interest and available time. All of the City is readily accessible from the London Underground System or the vast network of buslines. The maps indicate the underground stations within each area. The index is arranged to include each attractions area and number, as well as the page number containing the explanatory text.

Of course, the best way to see the City is on foot, just as Dr. Samuel Johnson stated over 200 years ago:

> If you wish to have a just notion of the magnitude of this city, you must not be satisfied with seeing its great streets and squares, but must survey the innumerable little lanes and courts. It is not in the showy evolutions of buildings, but in the multiplicity of human habitations which are crowded together, that the wonderful immensity of London consists.

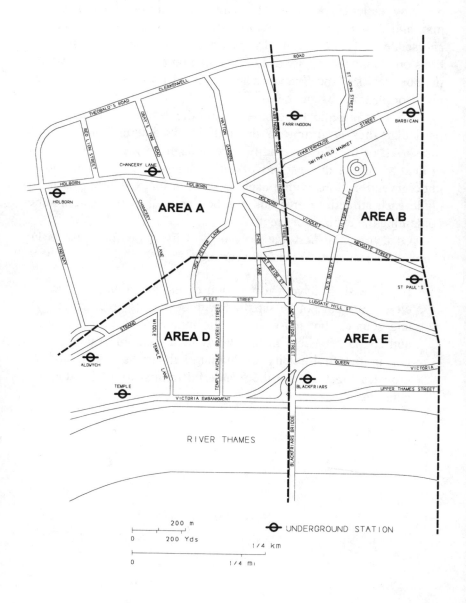

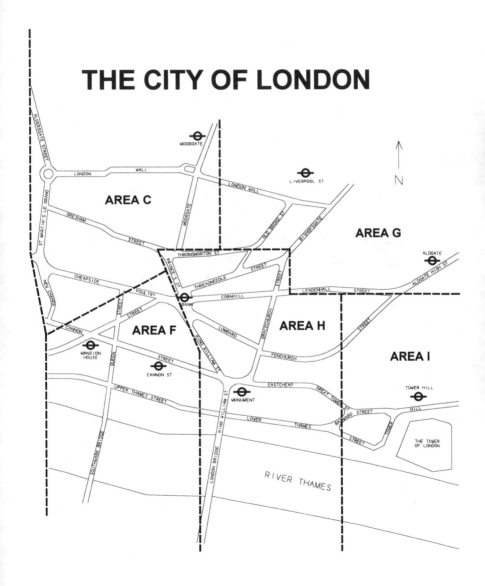

THE CITY OF LONDON

AREA A

LINCOLN'S INN FIELDS

AND

DICKENS IN HOLBORN

AREA A ATTRACTIONS

AREA A MAP

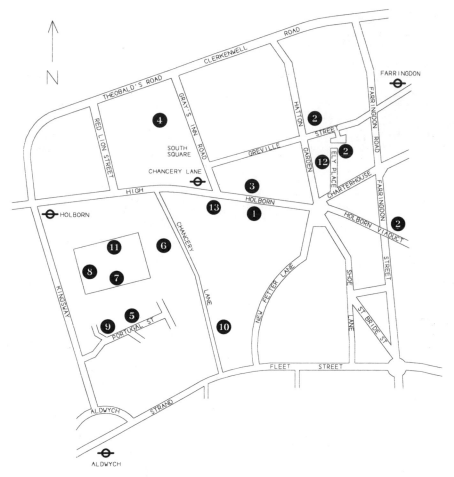

UNDERGROUND STATION

200 m

0   200 Yds

1/4 km

0   1/4 mi

BARNARD'S INN

On Holborn, to the East between Furnival Street and Fetter Lane, the only surviving relic of Barnard's Inn of the late 14th century is the Old Mall. Formerly an Inn of Chancery and, like Staple Inn, an adjunct of Gray's Inn, Barnard's Inn had over 100 students of the law during the 16th century. Rebuilt by the Mercers' Company, it was occupied by the Mercers' School from 1894-1959. The emblem of the Mercers' Company is still visible over the entrance.

Barnard's Inn had begun a long period of physical deterioration long before the Mercers' Company took over. When Dickens wrote *Great Expectations* in 1861, he had young Pip graphically describe the depressing appearance of the Inn, 33 years before the Mercers arrived:

I now found Barnard to be a disembodied spirit, or a fiction, and his inn the dingiest collection of shabby buildings ever squeezed together in a rank corner as a club for Tom-cats ... I thought it had the most dismal trees ... and the most dismal sparrows, and the most dismal cats, and the most dismal houses ... that I had ever seen ... dry rot and wet rot and all the silent rots that rot in neglected roof and cellar—rot of rat and mouse and bug and coaching-stables near at hand besides—addressed themselves faintly to my sense of smell .... I was content to take a foggy view of the Inn through the windows' encrusting dirt, and to stand dolefully out, saying to myself, that London was decidedly overrated.

BLEEDING HEART, SAFFRON HILL AND FIELD LANE

Charles Dickens has made this area his own in *Oliver Twist* (1838), following his extraordinary success with the *Pickwick Papers* (1836), and later in *Little Dorrit* (1857). Bleeding Heart Yard off Greville Street appears in *Little Dorrit*.

The legend of Bleeding Heart is told in Barham's *Ingoldsby Legends* (1840), in which a good lady is carried off by the devil, leaving nothing behind except a bleeding human heart. Was this legend the inspiration for Edgar Allan Poe's short story, *The Tell-Tale Heart*? As Barham tells it:

And still, it is said, at that "small hour" so dread,
When all sober people are cosy in bed,
There may sometimes be seen on a moonshiny night,
Standing close by the new pump, a Lady in White,
Who keeps pumping away with, 'twould seem, all her might,
Though never a drop comes her pains to requite!
And hence many passengers now are debarr'd
From proceedings at nightfall through Bleeding Heart Yard!

Dickens' version of the story in *Little Dorrit* is that

... of a young lady ... imprisoned in her chamber by a cruel father for remaining true to her own true love, and refusing to marry the suitor he chose for her ... the young lady used to be seen up at her window behind the bars, murmuring a lovelorn song of which the burden was, "Bleeding Heart, Bleeding Heart, bleeding away", until she died.

On Saffron Hill, running parallel to Hatton Garden, the Artful dodger, the murderous Bill Sykes and the evil Fagin could be found, in Dickens' *Oliver Twist*, his first attack on the heartlessness of organized charity with Oliver as the helpless pawn who dared to ask for a second helping. This street with its cobbled pavements and large warehouses is still reminiscent of Dickens and his times.

Field Lane, one of the most squalid of London's criminal dens, located near the place where Holborn and Farringdon Road now meet led to Saffron Hill. Dickens has graphically described this street in *Oliver Twist*:

> Near to the spot on which Snow Hill and Holborn meet, there opens: upon the right hand as you come out of the City: a narrow and dismal alley, leading to Saffron Hill. In its filthy shops are exposed for sale bunches of second-hand silk handkerchiefs of all sized and patterns; for here reside the traders who purchase them from pickpockets ... the emporium of petty larceny .... Here, the clothes-man, the shoe-vamper, and the rag-merchant, display their goods, as signboards to the petty thief; here stores of old iron and bones, and heaps of mildewy fragments of woollen-stuff and linen, rust and rot in the grimy cellars.

When Oliver was arrested, he was taken to a police court presided over by an unusually harsh and insensitive magistrate whom Dickens named Mr. Fang, but whose real name was Mr. Laing. The site of that unhappy confrontation with the Law has been identified as No.52 Hatton Garden.

FURNIVAL'S INN

About 100 yards east of the intersection of Gray's Inn Road and Holborn, between Brooke Street and Leather Lane, on the north side of Holborn looms an overpowering Gothic building of red brick, the Prudential Assurance Company. The building occupies the site of Furnival's Inn where Dickens had lodgings form 1834-37 and conceived and wrote the first part of the *Pickwick Papers*, creating a lovable old gentleman who founded a club of innocent lunatics.

The first monthly part of the *Pickwick Papers* appeared in print in March 1836. On April 2, Dickens married Catherine Hogarth at St. Luke's Church in Chelsea and brought her to live with him in Furnival's Inn. After his son was born in 1837 they moved to Doughty Street, Bloomsbury, where he completed the *Pickwick Papers*. The Doughty Street residence remains as the only London house in which Dickens lived that still exists; it is now a Dickens museum.

Furnival's Inn must have been a pleasant place in which to live, for Dickens has Mr. Grewgious comment in *The Mystery of Edwin Drood* that "Furnival's is fireproof and specially watched and lighted." In *Martin Chuzzlewit* it is described as:

> ... a shady, quiet place, echoing to the footsteps of the stragglers who have business there, and rather monotonous and gloomy on Sunday evenings ... his rooms were the perfection of neatness and convenience, at any rate; and if he were anything but comfortable, the fault was certainly not theirs.

GRAY'S INN

The entrance to Gray's Inn, one of the four great Inns of Court in London, is at No.22 High Holborn, through a gate dating from 1688. The site was originally part of the Manor of Portpool, the former owners being the Lords Grey de Wilton, and believed to have been inhabited by members of the legal fraternities prior to 1370. Portpool Lane, across Gray's Inn Road, still recalls the name of the ancient manor.

The Holborn Bars, or outer gates, for which the citizens received legal authority in 1222, survived to indicate the western boundary of the City until recent times. Two stone obelisks mark the spot today, one at the eastern corner of Gray's Inn road and Holborn, the other at Staple Inn, opposite.

The Gatehouse was occupied for many years by a bookshop owned by Jacob Tonson, purchaser of the copyright of John Milton's *Paradise Lost* and publisher for John Dryden (1631-1700). Dryden became so irritated over a dispute with Tonson that he described him in a caustic sketch:

> With leering locks, bull-faced, and
> freckled fair,
> With two left legs, and Judas -
> coloured hair,
> And frowzy pores that taint the
> ambient air.

The Gatehouse was still in use as a bookshop as late as 1861 when Dickens refers to "The old-established vendor of periodicals who sits alone in his little crib of a shop behind the Holborn Gate" in chapter XIV of *The Uncommercial Traveler*.

Nathaniel Hawthorne was impressed with the peaceful surroundings of Gray's Inn. In his *English Notebooks* (1853-57), he wrote that Gray's Inn

> ... is a great, quiet domain, quadrangle beyond quadrangle, close beside Holborn, and a large space of greensward enclosed within it. It is very strange to find so much of ancient quietude right in the monster city's very jaws, which yet the

monster shall not eat up—right in its very belly, indeed, which yet, in all these ages, it shall not digest and convert into the same substance as the rest of its bustling streets. Nothing else in London is so like the effect of a spell, as to pass under one of these archways, and find yourself transported from the jumble, mob, tumult, uproar, as of an age of weekdays condensed into the present hour, into what seem an eternal sabbath ....

Grays' Inn is famous for its picturesque 17th century gardens designed by Sir Francis Bacon, who became Treasurer in 1597 and lived in the Inn for almost 50 years. Of the gardens, Charles Lamb (1775-1834) wrote:

They are still the best gardens of any of the Inns of Court, my beloved Temple not forgotten—have the gravest characters, their aspect being altogether reverend and law-breathing. Bacon has left the impress of his foot upon their gravel walks.

The gardens were the fashionable promenade of the 17th century by the upper classes who wished to see and be seen. Samuel Pepys, the diarist (1633-1703), wrote:

When Church was done, my wife and I walked to Gray's Inn to observe the fashion of the ladies because of my wife's making some clothes.

The Inns of Court on various traditional occasions presented plays written and acted by their members or hired regular acting companies to stage their own productions. The most notable event at Gray's Inn occurred on December 28, 1594 with an annual revel held to celebrate the "Feast of Fool's Day", sometimes known as "Innocents' Day", presided over by a Lord of Misrule called the "Prince of Purpoole". This event was the first performance of Shakespeare's *Comedy of Errors* presented by his company, the Lord Chamberlain's Men, in the Great Hall for Queen Elizabeth I. The Hall, dating from the middle of the 16th century and restored after extensive damage sustained during the last war, enjoys the distinction of being one of the only two surviving buildings in which a Shakespeare play was originally performed, the other being Middle Temple Hall.

Numbered among the illustrious men who belonged to Gray's Inn, in addition to Sir Francis Bacon, were Thomas Cromwell, Earl of Essex (1485-1540), chief minister to Henry VIII; Sir Thomas Gresham (1519-79), financier and "king's merchant"; Lord William Cecil Burghley (1520-98), Queen Elizabeth I's trusted counselor and chief secretary of state; Sir Francis Walsingham (1530?-1590), statesman and diplomat in the Court of Queen Elizabeth I; William Laud, Archbishop of Canterbury (1573-1645) and Lord Thomas Macaulay (1800-1859), statesman.

Charles Dickens was employed as a clerk with Messrs. Ellis and Blackmore from May 1827 to November 1828, initially at No.1 South Square and later at No.1 Raymond Buildings on the west side of Gray's Inn Gardens. Thomas Traddles in Dickens' *David Copperfield* resided at No.2 South Square, and Mr. Phunky, Junior Counsel for Mr. Pickwick in *Pickwick Papers*, also had chambers there. Mr. Pickwick himself travelled to Gray's Inn to negotiate a settlement with the attorney Perker.

Between 1829 and 1834 Thomas Babington Macaulay, statesman and historian, occupied chambers at No.8 South Square in a building that was demolished to make way for the extension of the Library. Lord Bacon lived at No.1 Coney Court which burned down in 1678. The site was at the western end of Gray's Inn Square adjoining the gardens in which he took so much pleasure. Bacon is commemorated by an elegant bronze statue in South Square.

KING'S COLLEGE HOSPITAL

The hospital was built in 1852 upon the abandoned graveyard of the church of St. Clement Danes on Portugal Street just behind the Royal College of Surgeons. In that old graveyard, one Joe (Joseph or Josias) Miller who died on August 15, 1738, aged 56 years, was buried.

An actor at the Drury Lane Theatre for over 25 years, Joe Miller enjoyed a well-deserved reputation as a wit, or as we would call him today, a stand-up comedian. He was obviously very popular and well-liked for an epitaph composed by the Church Warden was engraved on a wall of the church. The inscribed stone, destroyed by enemy action during World War II, praised the deceased as a "tender husband, a sincere friend, a facetious companion and an excellent comedian" and went on to pay additional tribute to his memory:

> Could but esteem and love preserve our breath,
> And guard us longer from the stroke of death,
> The stroke of death on him had later fell,
> Whom all mankind esteemed and loved full well.

The fame of his book, *Joe Miller's Jests*, has survived to this day. Compiled by friends a year after his death to raise funds for his destitute family, it originally contained less than 300 jokes, but many more jokes were added in numerous editions of the book over the years. His name has become part of the language so that when someone cracks an old joke, we call it a "Joe Miller".

LINCOLN'S INN

Diagonally across Chancery Lane from the Public Record Office stands Lincoln's Inn, one of the four illustrious Inns of Court in London. The Inn probably derives its name from Henry Lacy, Earl of Lincoln, who built himself a large mansion on this site in the 14th century, and later bequeathed it to found a residential inn for lawyers.

For over 600 years, many of the most distinguished leaders and brilliant writers and wits have been students at one of the Inns of Court. Numbered among the famous men associated with Lincoln's Inn were Sir Thomas More (1478-1535), John Donne (1573-1631), William Penn (1644-1718), Horace Walpole (1717-97), William Pitt (1759-1806), Thomas Macaulay (1800-59), Cardinal Newman (1801-90), Benjamin Disraeli (1804-81), Herbert Asquith (1852-1928) and John Galsworthy (1867-1933).

The turreted Gatehouse on Chancery Lane dates from 1518, and it is believed that Ben Jonson worked as a bricklayer during its construction. John Aubrey (1626-97), an early historian, said in his *Brief Lives* that

> ... a knight, or bencher, walking through [Lincoln's Inn gardens] and hearing him [Jonson] repeat some Greek names out of Homer, discoursing with him, and finding him to have a wit extraordinary, gave him some exhibition to maintain him at Trinity College in Cambridge.

The Chapel, rebuilt 1620-23, has been restored again and enlarged. The crypt was once used as a meeting place for barristers and their clients. A couplet in Samuel Butler's *Hudibras* (1663-78) refers to this practice:

> Or wait for customers between
> The piller rows of Lincoln's Inn

Many great divines have been preachers in the Chapel, the most famous being John Donne, afterwards Dean of St. Paul's Cathedral. The Old Hall dates from 1492 and is noted for its linenfold paneling, splendid oak screen, outstanding roof and Hogarth's 1748 painting, *St.*

Paul before Felix. The Old Buildings are all of Tudor brickwork of 1609 and extensive gardens surround the intercommunicating courts.

The High Court of Chancery, a court of equity concerned principally with litigation involving property, sat in the Old Hall from 1733 to 1873, presided over by the Lord High Chancellor. Charles Dickens had worked as a clerk for a lawyer in offices nearby for one and a half years before he left to become a reporter. It is probable that his youthful exposure to a legal system that perpetuated a cruel penal code and inhuman conditions, especially in the indiscriminate exploitation of children, made him a life-long crusader for equality and justice.

In Dickens' *Bleak House* (1853) the fictional case of Jarndyce and Jarndyce presents a tragic exposition of the abuses of the courts and the interminable delays of the Law. More than 250 years earlier, Shakespeare had also inveighed against "the law's delay, the insolence of office."

Dickens based his case on an actual one heard in the same Court involving the estate of one William Jennings who died in 1798. Not reluctant to express his distaste for the Law and lawyers, Dickens concentrated his firepower on the Court of Chancery:

> This is the Court of Chancery; which has its decaying houses and its blighted land in every shire; which has its wornout lunatic in every madhouse, and its dead in every churchyard; which has its ruined suitor, with his slipshod heels and threadbare dress, borrowing and begging through the round of everyman's acquaintance; which gives to monied might, the means of wearing out the right; which so exhausts finances, patience, courage, hope; so overthrows the brain and breaks the heart; that there is not an honourable man among its practitioners who would not give—who does not often give—the warning, "Suffer any wrong that can be done you rather than come here."

Bleak House comes to an end "in trickery, evasion, procrastination, spoliation, botheration, under false pretenses of all sorts "

Long before *Bleak House*, Dickens was an early crusader for the oppressed and had expressed his opinion of the law and the legal system in England. In *Oliver Twist* he has Mr. Mumble saying, "If the law supposes that, the law is a ass—an idiot."

LINCOLN'S INN FIELDS

Inigo Jones conceived and laid out the largest square in the City, bordering Lincoln's Inn on the west, during the years between 1640 and 1657. Planned to duplicate the dimensions of the base of the Great Pyramid, Lincoln's Inn Fields actually covers about 12 acres, or one and one-half acres less. The square became a favorite duelling-ground, the site of a pillory and the scene of several spectacular executions.

In September 1586 Anthony Babington and 13 others were tried and condemned to death for conspiring, with the connivance of Mary, Queen of Scots, to murder Queen Elizabeth I. Caught in the net was a hapless young man of good family, one Chidiock Tichbourne, whose budding career as a poet abruptly ended before he had reached the age of 18 years. His poignant poem, *Lament*, is believed to have been written in the Tower of London on the night before his execution:

> My prime of youth is but a frost of cares;
>> My feast of joy is but a dish of pain;
> My crop of corn is but a field of tares;
>> And all my good is but vain hope of gain;
> My day is past, and yet I saw no sun;
>> And now I live, and now my life is done.
>
> My tale was heard, and yet it was not told;
>> My fruit is fall'n, and yet my leaves are green;
> My youth is spent, and yet I am not old;
>> I saw the world, and yet I was not seen:
> My thread is cut, and yet it is not spun;
>> And now I live, and now my life is done.
>
> I sought my death, and found it in my womb;
>> I looked for life, and saw it was a shade;
> I trod the earth, and knew it was my tomb;
>> And now I die, and now I am but made;
> The glass is full, and now my glass is run;
>> And now I live, and now my life is done.

A gallows was erected on the spot where it was alleged the conspirators had been accustomed to meet and plan their ill-fated scheme.
In full view of the assembled populace, the 14 conspirators were
hanged, disemboweled and quartered, seven on the first day and seven
on the second. James Anthony Froude, in his *History*, described the
ghastly execution:

> They were hanged but for a moment, according to the letter
> of the sentence, taken down while the susceptibility of ag-
> ony was unimpaired, and cut in pieces afterwards with due
> precautions for the protraction of the pain.

When Queen Elizabeth learned of this barbaric custom, she put a stop
to it and ordered that the condemned men in the future be hanged until
dead.

This public revelation of the threat from the Catholic opposition
to the Crown resulted in wide-spread demand for Mary's death. Queen
Elizabeth was reluctant to order Mary's execution, but finally signed
the warrant in February 1587. When Mary received the gloomy news,
she wrote a pathetic letter to Elizabeth asking her to "permit my poor
desolated servants ... to carry away my corpse, to bury it in holy
ground, with the other queens of France."

Mary's execution took place in Fotheringay Castle on February 8,
1587. On that morning, we are told, she wrote a Latin supplication for
heavenly release from her 19 years of imprisonment:

> O Lord God! I had hoped in Thee.
> O my dear Jesus! now free me.
> In cruel chains, in bitter pain, I desire Thee.
> Longing, moaning, and bending the knee,
> I adore, I implore, that You set me free.

In 1683 Lord William Russell was executed in Lincoln's Inn
Fields on a charge of complicity in the Rye House Plot, a plan purportedly to assassinate Charles II and his brother, Duke of York, as
they passed a farmhouse called Rye on their return from Newmarket,
along the London Road. Both Lord Russell and his father, the Earl of
Bedford, petitioned the king for mercy, but without success. Lady
Rachael Russell, the devoted wife of the accused and grand-daughter
of Shakespeare's royal patron, the Earl of Southampton, begged for the

life of her husband. David Hume in his *History of England* (1754-62) states that lady Russell

> ... threw herself at the King's feet and pleaded with many tears, the merit and loyalty of her father, as an atonement for those errors into which honest, however mistaken, principles had seduced her husband. These supplications were the last instance of female weakness (if they deserve the name) which she betrayed. Finding all applications vain, she collected courage, and not only fortified herself against the fatal blow, but endeavoured by her example to strengthen the resolution of her unfortunate lord.

Gilbert Burnet, English bishop and historian, tenderly relates Lord Russell's final moments in his *History of My Own Times* (1725):

> He was singing psalms a great part of the way, and said, he hoped to sing better very soon. When his companion asked him what he was singing, he said the beginning of the 119th Psalm. ...As he observed the great crowds of people...he said to us, "I hope I shall quickly see a much better assembly." ... As they were entering Lincoln's Inn Fields, he said, "This has been to me a place of sinning, and God now makes it the place of my punishment." ... he prayed again to himself, and then undressed himself and laid his head on the block, without the least change of countenance; and it was cut off at two strokes.

A tablet commemorating Lord Russell's execution has been placed in the center of the shelter.

During the 17th and 18th centuries, thieves boldly preyed upon people who walked in Lincoln's Inn Fields after dark. John Gay, author of *The Beggar's Opera*, wrote a book, *Trivia, or the Art of Walking the Streets of London* (1716), in which he warned the public about the dangers in the fields after dark:

> Where Lincoln's Inn, wide space, is rail'd around,
> Cross not with vent'rous step; there oft is found
> The lurking thief, who while the Day-light shone,
> Made the Walls echo with his begging Tone:

That crutch which late Compassion mov'd, shall wound
Thy bleeding Head, and fell thee to the Ground.
Though thou art tempted by the Link-man's Call,
Yet trust him not along the lonely Wall;
In the Mid-way he'll quench the flaming Brand,
And share the Booty with the pilf'ring Band.
Still keep the public Streets, where oily Rays
Shot from the crystal Lamp, o'erspread the Ways.

Two decades later, the situation had not improved. The preamble to an Act of 1735 stated that "Lincoln's Inn Fields had become a receptacle for rubbish and nastiness of all sorts."

On the southern edge of Lincoln's Inn Fields stands the Royal College of Surgeons. A tennis court on this site was turned into a playhouse for the Duke of York's company in June 1661, headed by Sir William Davenant. Shakespeare had been a close friend of the family when Sir William's father, John Davenant, owned a tavern in Oxford. Sir William was only ten years old when Shakespeare died in 1616, but he was not above hinting that he was actually Shakespeare's son. After many changes of management, the playhouse finally closed after 1737.

The Lincoln's Inn Theatre was a favorite of Samuel Pepys, who attended so often as to make Mrs. Pepys "as mad as the devil." The playhouse had the distinction of producing two memorable premieres during its relatively short existence.

The popularity of William Congreve, the brilliant exponent of the comedy of manners, reached its greatest height with the first presentation of his *Love for Love* at the theater on April 30, 1695. Anne Bracegirdle, one of the period's leading actresses, played the role of Angelica which proved to be her best known success. In the epilogue to the play she points out the background of the playhouse's site:

And thus, our audience, which did once resort
To shining theatres to see our sport,
Now, find us tossed into a tennis-court.
These walls but t'other day were filled with noise
Of roaring gamesters, and your "damn-me" boys;
Then bounding balls and rackets they encompast,
And now they're filled with jests, and flights, and bombast!

The last proprietor of the Lincoln's Inn Fields Theatre was John Rich, the first theatrical producer to introduce pantomime to the English stage. His claim to well deserved distinction rests however upon his original production of John Gay's *The Beggar's Opera* in January 1728. The play achieved an unexpected success by running for 62 performances, a record at that time. The lovely Lavinia Fenton, who played the part of Polly Peachum, so bewitched the Duke of Bolton that she became his Duchess.

The play also cast a spell over Fleur in Galsworhy's *Forsyte Saga* for she

> … sang with Polly Peachum, mimed with Filch, danced with Jenny Diver, postured with Lucy Lockit, kissed, trolled, and cuddled with Macheath ….

The Beggar's Opera is a classic and still performed from time to time. It was adapted on its 200th anniversary by Kurt Weill and Bertolt Brecht as a musical, *The Three Penny Opera*.

NO.58 LINCOLN'S INN FIELDS

Inigo Jones built some distinguished houses on the western edge of Lincoln's Inn Fields. John Forster, friend and biographer of Charles Dickens, lived at No.58 from 1834-56. Dickens, a regular visitor, introduced the house in his novel, *Bleak House* (1853), as the home of the suave lawyer, Tulkinghorn:

> Here in a large house, formerly a house of State, lived Mr. Tulkinghorn. It is let off in streets of chambers now; and in those shrunken fragments of its greatness lawyers lie, like maggots in nuts. But its roomy staircases, passages and ante-chambers still remain; and even its painted ceiling, where Allegory in Roman Helmet and Celestial linen sprawls among balustrades and pillars, flowers, clouds and big-legged boys, and makes the head ache, as would seem to be Allegory's object always, more or less.

In that same house on December 2, 1844, Dickens read aloud his *The Chimes* to a group of friends. Forster in his *Life of Charles Dickens* (1872-74) commented that the occasion "was the germ of those readings to larger audiences, by which, as much as by his books, the world knew him in his later life." During the years 1867-68 Dickens had made a highly successful tour of the United States in similar readings for the public from his own works.

THE OLD CURIOSITY SHOP

Next door to the Royal College of Surgeons stands the new extension of the Imperial Cancer Research Fund, projecting into Portsmouth Street.

An adjoining old house bears the inscription: "The Old Curiosity Shop, Immortalized by Charles Dickens." A shop with that name appeared in Dickens' 1840 novel, *The Old Curiosity Shop*, in which the plot called for the death of Little Nell. An unprecedented torrent of letters begged Dickens to spare the life of the "angel child" who was "too good to live". Flattered by this public reaction, he prolonged her sufferings even beyond the limits of Victorian sentimentality, but failed to give in to the entreaties of his readers.

The house is believed to be one of the oldest in London, probably dating back to the 16th century, but the original shop in the novel actually stood near Leicester Square. The novel was written in 1839 but the inscription on the house appeared much later, specifically in 1868. Furthermore, the concluding paragraphs in the novel stated that "the old house had been long ago pulled down."

PUBLIC RECORD OFFICE AND MUSEUM

Chancery Lane begins at Fleet Street. About 100 yards to the north on Chancery Lane, on the east side of the street, stands a Tudor-like building of the mid-19th century. This is the repository of Britain's historic documents dating back to the Norman Conquest of the 11th century. The search rooms are open only to those with a Reader's Ticket. The Public Record Museum, however, is open to the public every afternoon.

Nowhere is there a better description of the one room cornucopia of treasures than Marlowe's phrase from his *The Jew of Malta*: "infinite riches in a little room." The most valuable documents are the *Domesday Book*, the census of taxable properties in England made for William the Conqueror in 1085-87, and the Magna Carta of 1215, the keystone of English liberty and foundation of constitutional government.

Famous historical documents are exhibited. Battle dispatches include Drake's report of the defeat of the Spanish Armada, Marlborough's announcement of victory at Blenheim, Nelson's log of the Battle of Trafalgar and Wellington's dispatches from Waterloo. The wills of Shakespeare, Emma Hamilton and Jane Austen and numerous documents including the indictment of Sir Thomas More, Captain Bligh's record of the mutiny on the Bounty and the treaty guaranteeing the neutrality of Belgium which the Germans rejected as a "scrap of paper" are also on view. In addition, letters from famous persons, such as Catherine the Great, Marie Antoinette, Napoleon, the anonymous letter betraying Guy Fawkes' plot to blow up the Houses of Parliament, Cardinal Wolsey's plea of mercy to Henry VIII—and even a preaching license issued to John Bunyan, author of *The Pilgrim's Progress*, are displayed.

The Americana collection includes a sketch map of the Ohio River drawn by George Washington in 1753, the Olive Branch Petition addressed to George III from the Continental Congress of July 8, 1775, and a letter of August 25, 1795 from George Washington to George III, his "great and good friend".

SOANE'S MUSEUM

On the north edge of Lincoln's Inn Fields at No.12 and No.13 an unpretentiously beautiful early-19th century building served as both the home and museum of Sir John Soane (1753-1837), distinguished architect of the Bank of England. A man of great taste and discrimination, Sir John gathered together a variegated collection of Roman, Egyptian, Greek and Italian Antiques, furniture and stained glass, Napoleon's pistol, Christopher Wren's pocket watch, Soane's own architectural designs, and paintings by Turner, Canaletto, Hogarth and Lawrence. Unique and not to be missed: the Sarcophagus of Seti I, King of Egypt in 1370 BC and father of Rameses the Great and the two series of paintings by William Hogarth (1637-1764) of *The Rake's Progress* (eight scenes) and the *Election* (four scenes). Maximum usage of many small spaces has been accomplished through the practice of employing mirrors, and by the clever device of hanging paintings on window shutters.

ST. ETHELDREDA'S / ELY CHAPEL

On the northeast side of Holborn Circus in the cul-de-sac of Ely Place stands a 13th century treasure, Ely Chapel, now St. Etheldreda's, the only relic remaining of the great townhouse of the Bishops of Ely, the noblest ecclesiastical residence in London after 1290. Henry VIII first met his future Archbishop of Canterbury, Thomas Cranmer, in the cloisters of the palace. John Evelyn, the diarist, attended the marriage of his daughter in the chapel in 1693. By Queen Elizabeth's time, the palace covered an extensive area containing an immense garden noted for its fruits and flowers but best remembered for its strawberries, which Shakespeare mentions in *Richard III* when Richard says to the Bishop of Ely:

> My Lord of Ely, when I was last in Holborn,
> I saw good strawberries in your garden there:
> I do beseech you send for some of them.

After the Savoy Palace was burned down by Wat Tyler and his rebels in 1381, John of Gaunt, father of Henry IV, made his home in the Bishop's townhouse until his death in 1399. His death scene is set in "a room in Ely-house" by Shakespeare in *Richard II* where he delivers his stirring patriotic eulogy of England:

> This royal throne of kings, this sceptered isle,
> This earth of majesty, this seat of Mars,
> This other Eden, demi-Paradise;
> This fortress built by Nature for herself
> Against infection and the hand of war;
> This happy breed of men, this little world;
> This precious stone set in the silver sea,
> Which serves it in the office of a wall,
> As a moat defensive to a house,
> Against the envy of less happier lands;
> This blessed plot, this earth, this realm, this England.

In 1576 Queen Elizabeth I ceded most of the church property to Sir Christopher Hatton, her favorite dancing partner and chancellor.

He erected a sumptuous house and immense garden on part of the grounds, but his heirs became debt-ridden and sold the property to commercial interests, only the name being retained. Hatton Garden, next street to the west running parallel to Ely Place, is the center of the diamond and jewelry trade today.

The place and chapel began to slowly deteriorate. In time, the Hall and Church became a hospital, the palace a prison and the crypt a saloon. All the buildings were demolished in 1772 except for the Chapel which was purchased by the Catholic Church in 1874, and consecrated as the Church of St. Etheldreda by Cardinal Manning in 1879. The west window memorializes Catholic martyrs, principally Thomas á Becket and Sir Thomas More. The chapel has the unique distinction of being the only building now used for Catholic worship which had been originally erected for that purpose before the Reformation.

The vaulted crypt of 1252 has masonry walls eight feet thick and blackened beams standing on roman pavement. Ancient carved wood relics, stained glass windows, chestnut roof—all serve to create a mystical affirmation of London's medieval world.

A word about St. Etheldreda. Ely Cathedral, regarded as one of the great cathedrals of Europe, stands on what was once a marshy island known as the Isle of Ely. Etheldreda, daughter of an East Anglian king, founded a nunnery on the island in 673 and was its first abbess. After her death it was discovered that her tomb had great healing powers. In honor of this miracle, William the Conqueror had the present cathedral built in Ely and consecrated to St. Etheldreda or her English name of St. Awdrey.

The Saint attributed her fatal illness as divine punishment for wearing necklaces of fine silk. Since her English name was Awdrey, the necklaces sold at the fair in Ely were called Sain Tawdrey's laces. The quality of the laces began to decline and by the 17th century they became, by a process of slurring her name to S'tawdry, known as tawdry products. Thus a saint has ironically contributed her name to the language to designate cheap showy finery.

STAPLE INN

Leaving Soane's Museum, walk left to Great Turnstile and left again to High Holborn. On the right hand side, opposite Gray's Inn Road, a row of gabled and oak timbered shops dating from 1586 mark the entrance to a courtyard surrounded by Staple Inn. This Elizabethan survival has endured fires, bombings and the ravages of time and progress to remain an oasis of peace and quiet. Nathaniel Hawthorne described it in his *English Notebooks* written during the period 1855-57 while he was occupying the post of American Consul at Liverpool:

> I went astray in Holborn through an arched entrance over which was Staple Inn, and here likewise seemed to be offices; but in a court opening inwards from this there was a surrounding seclusion of quiet dwelling-houses, with beautiful green shrubbery and grass plots in the court and a great many sunflowers in full bloom .... There was not a quieter spot in England than this, and it was very strange to have drifted into it so suddenly out of the bustle and rumble of Holborn and to lose all this repose as suddenly on passing through the arch of the outer court. In all the hundreds of years since London was built, it has not been able to sweep its roaring tide over this little island of quiet.

Charles Dickens was equally impressed with the peaceful atmosphere when he described Staple Inn in *The Mystery of Edwin Drood* (1870):

> Behind the most ancient part of Holborn ... is Staple Inn. It is one of those nooks, the turning into which, out of the clashing street, imparts to the relieved pedestrian the sensation of having put cotton in his ears and velvet soles on his boots.

In that same novel, Mr. Grewgious had chambers in Staple Inn.

The wool staplers, dealers in the wool commodity, conducted their business in Staple Inn as early as 1375. When the merchants moved out about the beginning of the 15th century, the Inn became an

Inn of Chancery under the legal jurisdiction of Gray's Inn where law students would spend their first year of study. Staple Inn passed out of its legal dependence on Gray's Inn into commercial ownership in 1884. It received severe damage in World War II and was rebuilt in 1950 using much of the old material, so that its Elizabethan charm and atmosphere have been retained. The Inn is now occupied by the Institute of Actuaries.

Samuel Johnson moved from Gough Square to Staple Inn in 1759 where he wrote his *Rasselas, Prince of Abyssinia* in one week. According to Boswell, Dr. Johnson received 100 pounds for his book with which to defray the expenses of his mother's funeral and pay some little debts which she had left.

AREA B

SMITHFIELD

AND

NEWGATE PRISON

AREA B ATTRACTIONS

AREA B MAP

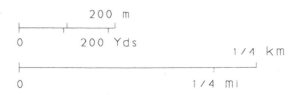

UNDERGROUND STATION

ALDERSGATE

This gate, opposite No.62 Aldersgate Street, was in place as early as the 10th century. In 1335 the gate was covered with lead and a small house constructed under it for the gatekeeper.

John Day, a 16th century printer, had his workshop over the gate. There he printed *The Folio Bible* (1549), Foxe's *Book of Martyrs* (1563), Roger Aschan's *Scholemaster* (1570) and Tyndale's *Works* (1573).

James I first entered into London by this gate in 1603 to receive the crown after the death of Elizabeth I. On October 20, 1660, Samuel Pepys "saw the limbs of some of our new traitors set upon Aldersgate, which was a sad sight to see."

A metal representation of the gate is fastened to a wall of St. Botolph's Churchyard in Little Britain. The gate was removed in 1761.

THE CHARTERHOUSE

To the east of the intersection of St. John and Charterhouse Streets stands the 16th century gatehouse of the Charterhouse, an almost unknown building of London. The Charterhouse (a corruption of Chartreuse) began as a Carthusian monastery in 1371. Henry VIII dissolved the Priory after he had John Houghton, the last rector, executed in 1535 for refusing to acknowledge him as head of the church.

Elizabeth I lived at the Charterhouse for a time in 1558 while her coronation ceremony was being prepared. In 1611 Thomas Sutton, an Elizabethan soldier-merchant, purchased the property and founded the Charterhouse School as well as a hospital and almshouse. The school developed into one of the most famous public institutions of learning in London until 1872, when it moved to Godalming in Surrey. From 1875 to 1933, the Merchant Taylor's School occupied the quarters before it moved to Moor Park. A few of the structures still serve as lodgings for 40 "poor gentlemen". The remaining buildings, expanded and modernized, serve as a medical school for St. Bartholomew's Hospital.

Famous writers educated at Charterhouse School include: Richard Crashaw (1613?-49), Richard Lovelace (1618-58), Joseph Addison (1672-1719), Sir Richard Steele (1672-1729), William Makepeace Thackeray (1811-63) and Francis Palgrave (1824-97). John Wesley (1705-91), the founder of Methodism, was educated at the Charterhouse School before he went to Oxford in 1720. He believed that much of his good health was the result of taking his father's advice to run around the Charterhouse grounds three times every morning.

Thackeray memorialized the school, which he called Grey Friars in his novel, *The Newcomes* (1853-55):

Mention has been made once or twice in the course of this history of the Grey Friars school, —where the Colonel and Clive and I had been brought up, —an ancient foundation of the time of James I, still subsisting in the heart of London city. The death-day of the founder of the place is still kept solemnly by Cistercians. In their chapel, where assemble the boys of the school, and the fourscore old men of the Hospital, the founder's tomb stands, a huge edifice, embla-

zoned with heraldic decorations and clumsy carved allego-
ries. There is an old Hall, a beautiful specimen of the architecture of James's time; an old Hall? many old halls; old
staircases, old passages, old chambers decorated with old
portraits, walking in the midst of which we walk as it were
in the early seventeenth century. To others than Cistercians,
Grey Friars is a dreary place possibly. Nevertheless, the
pupils educated there love to revisit it; and the oldest of us
grow young again for an hour or two as we come back into
these scenes of childhood.

Thackeray also reflected the sentimentality of the Victorian
reader with his description of the Colonel's death-bed scene in the
Charterhouse:

At the usual evening hour the chapel bell began to toll, and
Thomas Newcome's hands outside the bed feebly beat a
time. And just as the last bell struck, a peculiar sweet smile
shone over his face, and he lifted up his head a little, and
quickly said, "Adsum!" and fell back. It was the word he
used at school, when names were called; and lo, he, whose
heart was as that of a little child, had answered to his name,
and stood in the presence of The Master.

The buildings mentioned by Thackeray may still be visited by arrangement with the master or registrar.

CHRIST CHURCH / CHRIST'S HOSPITAL

The Post Office buildings on Newgate Street, opposite Warwick Lane, occupy the ancient site of the great church of the Grey Friars, also known as the Franciscans.

After the dissolution of all the monasteries and abbeys by Henry VIII in the 1530s, Edward VI rededicated the church in 1552 and made it the head of a new parish to be called Christ Church. Destroyed in 1666 by the Great Fire and rebuilt by Sir Christopher Wren during 1667-91, it was finally obliterated in the fire bomb raids of Christmas week in 1940. It was not rebuilt, although the steeple was re-erected in 1960. The garden is all that remains now.

Christ's Hospital, just to the north of Christ Church, was established in 1552 by Edward VI as a refuge for orphans and children of the poor. As a school supplying food, clothing, lodging and education, it was called Christ's Hospital and became famous as the "Blue Coat School", a reference to the dress worn by the students.

London lost one of its most interesting buildings when Christ's Hospital moved to West Horsham, Sussex in 1902. Celebrated writers who attended the school include Samuel Richardson (1689-1761), Samuel Taylor Coleridge (1772-1834), Charles Lamb (1775-1834) and Leigh Hunt (1784-1859).

Ben Jonson's play, *Every Man in his Humour* (1598), contained the following reference to Christ's Hospital:

> I took him of a child up at my door,
> And christ'ned him, gave him my own name, Thomas;
> Since bred him at the Hospital ...

Leigh Hunt has given us a vivid description of the school's exacting way of life in his *Autobiography*, published in 1860 after his death:

> Our routine of life was life. We rose to the call of a bell at
> six in the summer, and seven in winter; and after combing
> ourselves, and washing our hands and face, we went to the
> call of another bell to breakfast. All this took up about an
> hour. From breakfast we proceeded to school, where we
> remained till eleven, winter and summer, and then had an

hour's play. Dinner took place at twelve. Afterwards was a little play till one, when we went again to school, and remained till five in summer and four in winter. At six was the supper. We used to play after it in summer till eight. On Sundays, the school time of other days was occupied in church, both morning and evening; and as the Bible was read to us every day before every meal, beside prayers and grace, we rivalled the monks in the religious part of our duties.

In October 1782 at seven years of age, Charles Lamb was admitted to Christ's Hospital and put into the dark blue gown, red leather belt, knee breeches and yellow stockings of the Blue Coat School. During the seven years Lamb was a student there, he met the poet Coleridge, who was to become his life-long friend. Lamb's loving recollection of those years glorifies the school in his celebrated essay, *Christ's Hospital Five and Thirty Years Ago* (1820). It calls to mind William Hazlitt's observation in *The Spirit of the Age* that "Mr. Lamb has the very soul of an antiquarian ... the film of the past hovers forever before him."

Lamb's nostalgic images of the past did not prevent him from excoriating his former Upper Master, the Reverend James Boyer:

J.B. was a rabid pedant. His English style was cramped to barbarism ... J.B. had a heavy hand .... In his gentler moods ... he had resort to an ingenious method ... of whipping the boy, and reading the Debates, at the same time; a paragraph, and a lash between ... a paragraph, and a lash between ...

Coleridge entered the Blue Coat School on July 18, 1782, at ten years of age. In his *Table Talk* (1835) he told the story of the school's basic philosophy of education:

The discipline of Christ's Hospital in my day was extra Spartan. All domestic ties were to be put aside. "Boy," I remember Boyer saying to me once when I was crying, the first day of my return after the holidays, —"boy, the school is your father; boy, the school is your mother; boy, the school is your sister, boy; the school is your first cousin, and all the rest of your relations. Let us have no more crying.

Lamb finally gave credit to J.B.'s great merits as an instructor, quoting Coleridge's praise upon hearing that his old master was on his deathbed:

Poor J.B.!—may all his faults be forgiven; and may he be wafted to bliss by little cherub boys, all head and wings, with no <u>bottoms</u> to reproach his sublunary infirmities.

A plaque commemorating Charles Lamb, formerly on the site of the school, is displayed on the east wall of St. Sephulcre's Church at Giltspur and Newgate Streets. The inscription concludes: "Perhaps the most loved name in English Literature who was a Bluecoat Boy here for 7 years."

CLOTH FAIR, BARTHOLOMEW CLOSE AND LITTLE BRITAIN

The narrow passages of these streets in Smithfield form an historic enclave—one of the last surviving areas of medieval London—around the church of St. Bartholomew the Great. Some of the celebrated men who once lived in this area included John Milton in 1660, Benjamin Franklin during 1725-26 and Washington Irving in the early 1800s.

Cloth Fair had been the resort of drapers and clothiers for centuries. At its eastern end, No.1 Middle Street, is an authentic 19th century pub, The Hand and Shears, a gathering place for French and Flemish dealers in cloth and textiles during the annual St. Bartholomew's Fair. The name of the pub originated from the custom of a group of tailors who, at the stroke of midnight, emerged with shears in hand to start the festivities in advance of the official opening by the Lord Mayor in the morning. Many such scenes are preserved in the prints on display in the pub.

Moll Flanders, in Daniel Defoe's novel of 1721, is visiting the Fair when she meets "a gentleman extremely well dressed and very rich" who begs her to "trust myself in a coach with him." At another point in the story, Moll steals a package from a maid and flees through Smithfield:

> I walked away and turning into Charterhouse Lane, made off through Charterhouse Yard, into Long Lane, then crossed into Bartholomew Close, so into Little Britain, and through the Bluecoat Hospital, into Newgate Street.

In another theft, Moll is so overcome with fear that she even contemplates murdering a child in order to hide her crime:

> Going through Aldersgate Street, there was a pretty little child had been at a dancing school and was agoing home all alone .... I took it by the hand and let it along till I came to a paved alley that goes into Bartholomew Close, and I let it in there .... The child had a little necklace on of gold beads, and I had my eyes upon that, and in the dark alley I stopped,

pretending to mend the child's clog that was loose, and took off her necklace and the child never felt it, and so let the child on again. Here, I say, the devil put me upon killing the child in the dark alley, that it might not cry, but the very thought frightened me so that I was already to drop down; but I turned the child about and bade it go back for that was not its way home; the child said she would ...

John Milton is said to have taken refuge in a friend's house in Bartholomew Close in order to avoid arrest and prosecution after the return of the Stuarts in 1660.

During the 18th century, Little Britain was an important center of the bookselling and printing trades. Benjamin Franklin relates his experiences there in 1724 in his *Autobiography*:

Ralph (James Ralph) and I were inseparable companions. We took lodgings together at Little Britain, at three shillings and sixpence a week, which was all we could afford .... I then got work at Palmer's, a famous printing house in Bartholomew Close, and here I continued near a year ...

Pip searches for Mr. Jaggers in these same streets in Dickens' *Great Expectations* (1861):

Mr. Jaggers had duly sent me his address; it was Little Britain, and he had written after it on his card, "just out of Smithfield, and close by the coach office" .... I made the tour of Little Britain, and turned in to Bartholomew Close ... as I was looking out at the iron gate of Bartholomew Close into Little Britain, I saw Mr. Jaggers coming across the road towards me.

Samuel Johnson, at three years of age, lived with his mother in Little Britain, and Charles Wesley underwent his evangelical conversion in 1738 at No.13, the home of John Bray. *The Spectator*, a periodical written by Joseph Addison and Richard Steele, was published in Little Britain during 1711-12.

THE MAGPIE AND STUMP

The pub, The Magpie and Stump, still doing business at No.18 Old Bailey, became very popular because of its location immediately behind Newgate. Its rooms on the top floor were in great demand on execution days because they commanded an excellent view of the gallows. The pub plays a part in Dickens' *Pickwick Papers* (1837) when Mr. Pickwick and Sam Weller set out to find Mr. Lowten:

The object of Mr. Pickwick's visit was to discover Mr. Lowten, and on enquiry, found him presiding over a sing-song and actually engaged in obliging with a comic song at the moment. After a brief interview with that worthy, Mr. Pickwick was prevailed upon to join the festive party.

Dickens' ingenious explanation of the pub's name deserves mention:

When we add, that the weather-beaten sign-board bore the half-obliterated semblance of a magpie intently eyeing a crooked streak of brown paint, which the neighbours had been taught from infancy to consider as the "stump", we have said all that need to be said of the exterior of the edifice.

NEWGATE PRISON — ST. SEPULCHRE'S CHURCH

The Central Criminal Court, popularly known as the Old Bailey, stands on the corner of Old Bailey and Newgate Street. The name, Old Bailey, probably derives from the Latin "Ballium", the outer or base court of a feudal castle: its position lay behind the ancient Bailey of the City Wall between Lud Gate and New Gate.

The Court occupies the grim, tragic and unholy site of Newgate Prison, the most notorious of all English jails. Newgate was London's chief prison for felons from the 13th century, when the original gate was used as a place of detention, to 1903 when it was finally demolished to make way for the Central Criminal Court. Its forbidding walls embraced such well known prisoners as William Penn, Daniel Defoe, Lord William Russell, Jonathan Wild and Jack Sheppard. The latter two were notorious highwaymen and the subjects of books by Henry Fielding and Daniel Defoe.

Conditions in the prison were appalling; cruelty, extortion and torture were widespread. One of the most revolting methods of torture was called "the press-yard". Heavy weights would be placed on a prisoner's body that would finally press him to death. The warden or governor of the prison was leaseholder of the building, and his income was derived from fees paid by the prisoners for food, quarters and certain privileges.

A man with money could live well, but life for the poor was miserable. Those without financial resources were housed in damp and filthy dungeons, with 15-20 men confined in a space of only 25 by 23 feet. To obtain food, many of these prisoners had no alternative but to thrust their hands through the holes in their cell walls and appeal for food or money from passers-by. Those who did not die from disease, wasted away from the effects of slow starvation.

The prison had such an evil reputation that an official inquiry in 1334 found that:

> ... prisoners detained on minor charges were cast into deep dungeons, and there associated with the worst criminals. All were alike threatened, many tortured, till they yielded to the keeper's extortions, or consented to turn approvers and swear away the lives of innocent men. These poor prisoners

were dependent upon the charity and good will of the benevolent for food and raiment.

The horrors of Newgate influenced the work of leading writers for centuries. Contemporary playwrights recorded the pleas of the prisoners or relatives and friends begging up and down the streets:

> Bread, bread, one penny to buy a loaf
> Of bread, for the tender mercy of God.
> Bread, bread, some Christian man send back
> Your charity to the poor prisoners of Newgate,
> Four-score and ten poor prisoners.

A unique collection of prints, *Begging Bread for the Prisoners*, may be seen at the Huntington Library and Art Gallery in San Marino, California, USA.

Sir Thomas Malory, who popularized the vision of Camelot, died in Newgate in 1471, having been jailed for murder and other crimes. He is believed to have written *Le Morte d'Arthur* in prison to relieve the boredom of the many years he was confined there. His legendary account of King Arthur was posthumously printed by William Caxton in 1485.

Public executions were considered great sporting events with as many as 20,000 spectators gathering at the scene in high holiday spirits. A cynical observation on the public's enthusiasm for such hideous exhibitions made by Oliver Cromwell (1599-1658), the great Protector, is quoted in *Hogarth's Complete Works* by J. Ireland and John Nichols:

> When Oliver Cromwell ... once went to dine in the city, the populace rent the air with their gratulations. "Your highness," said the secretary, "may see by this that you have the voice of the people as well as the voice of god."—"As to God," replied the Protector, "I will not talke about Him here; but for the people, they would be more noisy, and more joyful too, if you and I were going to be hanged."

For centuries the inhumane conditions of English prisons had saddened the hearts and consciences of numerous Englishmen. Few

felt more intensely than Thomas Dekker as long ago as 1606 in his
The Seven Deadly Sinnes of London:

> There are in London ... thirteen strong houses of sorrow,
> where the prisoner hath his heart wasting away sometimes a
> whole prenticeship of years in cares. They are most of them
> built of freestone, but none are free within them; cold are
> their embracements, unwholesome is their cheer, despairful
> their lodgings, uncomfortable their societies, miserable their
> inhabitants. O what a deal of wretchedness can make shift
> to lie in a little room!

George Wither, an early English poet, spent three years in Newgate Prison, from 1660 to 1663, because his manuscript, *Vox Vulgi*,
was considered seditious by the authorities.

Daniel Defoe's pamphlet, *The Shortest Way With Dissenters*
(1702), led to his imprisonment in Newgate. He started *The Review*, a
political journal, while in prison and continued to publish it until 1713.

Defoe had been pilloried earlier but such was his popularity that
he was greeted with cheers and showered with flowers instead of the
usual rubbish. After his release on November 3, 1703, he used that
incident as the basis for his *Hymn to the Pillory* (1704).

His experiences in Newgate proved useful when he came to write
Moll Flanders (1721). Moll is born in Newgate and her career in
crime leads her back there and almost to the gallows. Her description
of Newgate and some of its inmates is so chillingly authentic that it
deserves a full quote:

> That horrid place! my very blood chills at the mention of its
> name; the place where so many of my comrades had been
> locked up, and from whence they went to the fatal tree; the
> place where my mother suffered so deeply, where I was
> brought into the world, and from whence I expected no re-
> demption but by an infamous death: to conclude, the place
> that had so long expected me, and with so much art and suc-
> cess I had so long avoided.

> I was now fixed indeed: 'tis impossible to describe the terror
> of my mind, when I was first brought in, and when I looked
> round upon all the horrors of that dismal place. I looked on

myself as lost, and that I had nothing to think of but of going out of the world, and that with the utmost infamy: the hellish noise, the roaring, swearing, and clamour, the stench and nastiness, and all the dreadful crown of afflicting things that I saw there, joined together to make the place seem an emblem of hell itself, and a kind of entrance into it.

Moll discovers that the prisoners eventually become reconciled to their almost certain fate and defiantly sing:

> If I swing by the string,
> I shall hear the bell ring,
> And then there's an end of poor Jenny.

The bell referred to was that of the church of St. Sepulchre, across from Newgate, at the corner of Giltspur Street. On May 8, 1605, John Dow, a London citizen and merchant taylor, gave a bequest to the church to provide that "on the night before the execution of such as were condemned to death, the clerk of the church was to go in the night-time, and also early in the morning, to the window of the prison in which they were lying." After ringing his hand bell (still preserved in the church) he was required to recite this verse:

> All you that in the condemned hold do lie,
> Prepare you, for tomorrow you shall die!
> Watch all and pray, the hour is drawing near
> That you before the almighty must appear.
> Examine well yourselves, in time repent,
> That you may not to eternal flames be sent.
> And when St. Sepulchre's bell tomorrow tolls,
> The Lord above have mercy on your souls.

The parade of convicts on its way to Tyburn (the modern Connaught Place) would pause at St. Sepulchre's to receive a nosegay and a blessing while the bells tolled.

Samuel Johnson's biographer, James Boswell, described his visit to Newgate Prison on May 3, 1763 in his *London Journal*:

I stepped into a sort of court before the cells. They are surely most dismal places. There are three rows of 'em, four in a row, all above each other. They have double iron windows, and within these, strong iron rails; and in these dark mansions are the unhappy criminals confined .... Paul, who had been in the sea-service and was called Captain, was a genteel, spirited young fellow. He was just a Macheath. He was dressed in a white coat and blue silk vest and silver, with his hair neatly queued and a silver-laced hat, smartly cocked .... He walked firmly and with good air, and his chains rattling upon him, to the chapel.

The Macheath referred to by Boswell was the hero of John Gay's *The Beggar's Opera* (1728), the handsome leader of a band of thieves and highwaymen. In the last act of the play, he is shown in chains in Newgate Prison where he hears "the toll of the bell" announcing his coming execution. However, the play ends happily with his reunion with Polly Peachum, his true wife, whom he had secretly married.

Plate 11 of the William Hogarth engravings, *Industry and Idleness*, graphically presents the size and conduct of the motley mob witnessing the execution of the idle apprentice at Tyburn.

In 1783 the new Newgate Prison was completed and executions were transferred from Tyburn to Newgate. They took place in front of the prison until 1868, and then within its walls until 1901. The brutality that characterized these exhibitions persisted and are vividly described by Richard H. Barham in his *Ingoldsby Legends* (1837):

> And hark!—a sound comes, big with fate;
> The clock from St. Sepulchre's tower strikes—Eight!—
> List to that low funeral bell:
> It is tolling, alas! a living man's knell!—
> And see!—from forth that opening door
> They come—He steps that threshold o'er
> Who never shall tread upon threshold more!
> —God! 'tis a fearsome thing to see
> That pale wan man's mute agony,—
> The glare of that wild, despairing eye,
> Now bent on the crowd, now turn'd to the sky,

As though 'twere scanning in doubt and in fear,
The path of the Spirit's unknown career;
Those pinion'd arms, those hands that ne'er
Shall be lifted again,—not even in prayer;
That heaving chest!—Enough—'tis done!
The bolt has fallen!—The spirit is gone—
for weal or for woe is known but to One!—
—Oh! 'twas a fearsome sight!—Ah me
A deed to shudder at,—not to see.

Although prison reform was making some headway during the 19th century, little seemed to have changed by 1861 when Dickens in *Great Expectations* has Pip describe his visit to Newgate Prison:

While I looked about me here, an exceedingly dirty and partially drunk minister of justice ... was so good as to take me into a yard and show me where the gallows were kept, and also where people were publicly whipped, and then he showed me the Debtors' Door, out of which culprits came to be hanged; heightening the interest of that dreadful portal by giving me to understand that "four on 'em" would come out at that door the day after tomorrow at eight in the morning to be killed in a row. This was horrible, and gave me a sickening idea of London: the more so as the Lord Chief Justice's proprietor wore (from his hat down to his boots and up again to his pocket-handkerchief inclusive) mildewed clothes, which had evidently not belonged to him originally, and which, I took it into my head, he had bought cheap of the executioner.

Newgate Prison is a symbol of the cruelty of a system of law that had lost touch with human needs. In Dickens' *Barnaby Rudge* (1840), he vividly describes the attack on the prison by the Gordon rioters and the subsequent release of over 100 of the condemned inmates.

George Crabbe, the poet, described the assault in his journal:

I went alone to it, and never saw anything so dreadful. The prison was a remarkable strong building; but, determined to force it, they broke the gates with crows and other instruments .... They broke the roof, tore away the rafters, and

having got ladders descended .... Flames all around them
.... I stood and saw about twelve women and eight men secured from their confinement to the open air, and they were
conducted through the street in their chains. Three of these
were to be hanged on Friday.

A wooden beam, charred from the attack, can be seen in St. Sepulchre's Church.

When Newgate Prison was demolished in 1902, one of the gates
was auctioned off and moved to Buffalo, New York , USA, where it
still remains. Dickens may have referred to this gate in *Oliver Twist*.
A similar gate is now in the Museum of London.

A commemorative tablet in the Central Criminal Court is inscribed with a well-deserved tribute to a most unusual jury:

Near this site William Penn and William Mead were tried in
1670 for preaching to an unlawful assembly in Gracechurch
Street. This tablet commemorates the courage and endur-
ance of the jury, Thomas Vere, Edward Bushell, and ten
others who refused to give a verdict against them although
locked up without food for two nights and were fined for
their final verdict of not guilty.

THE SALUTATION AND CAT

A celebrated inn with this odd name once stood at No.17 Newgate Street, nearly opposite Christ's Hospital. The coaching inn which burned down in 1883, and was never replaced, engages our attention because a number of Lamb's letters nostalgically recall the many happy nights he spent in the smoky parlor of the tavern with William Hazlitt, critic, and the poets, Coleridge and Robert Southey. During many of his melancholy periods from 1794 on, Coleridge would use the tavern as a retreat for weeks on end. This is reflected in a letter Lamb wrote to Coleridge on May 27, 1796:

> Make yourself perfectly easy about May [the landlord]. I paid his bill, when I sent your clothes. I was flush of money, and am so still to all the purposes of a single life, so give yourself no further concern about it. The money would be superfluous to me, if I had it.

In another letter the following month, on June 10, he reminisces:

> I imagine to myself the little smoking room at the Salutation and Cat where we have sat together through the winter nights, beguiling the cares of life with Poesy.

A few days later, on June 14, he again indulges in tender memories of the happy days spent in the tavern:

> I have been drinking egg-hot and smoking Oronooko ... which ever forcibly recalls to my mind our evenings and nights at the Salutation.

(Egg-hot was a hot drink made with beer, eggs, sugar and nutmeg. Oronooko was a Virginia tobacco).

SMITHFIELD

Across from the Charterhouse lies Smithfield, an area of great interest and bloody history. Originally a smooth field outside the City walls and active as a cattle market as early as 1150, it is now the site of London's principal meat market.

The open space lent itself ideally to jousts, tournaments and fairs; Smithfield however is still remembered for its executions of religious martyrs. The diary of Edward VI (1537-53) duly records the execution in Smithfield of

> ... Joan Bocher, otherwise called Joan of Kent, was burnt for holding that Christ was not incarnate of the Virgin Mary.

Mary I, Tudor queen of England, reigned for only five years (1553-58). In 1555 she earned the name of "Bloody Mary" for having had some 300 Protestants burned at the stake for heresy. The executions took place at a point opposite the entrance to St. Bartholomew's Hospital "established to heal the sick". A granite slab on the outside wall of the hospital commemorates the victims of Mary's religious fervor. The last person to be executed for religious reasons was one Bartholomew Legate in 1611 as a "blasphemous heretic".

In 1196 William Fitzosbert publicly protested against the heavy taxation levied by Richard I and caused a riot. To avoid arrest, he sought sanctuary in the church of St. Mary-le-Bow in Cheapside. Unable to persuade him to give himself up, the authorities set fire to a pile of wood outside the church door and smoked him out. He was dragged through the streets to Smithfield and hanged. One historian estimated that the crown witnessing the execution numbered over 50,000—this is doubtful, for the entire population of London then probably numbered less than that.

One evening in June 1381 Wat Tyler, leader of the Peasant's Revolt, marched into Smithfield to demand of Richard II that the church property be confiscated and the proceeds distributed to the poor. Through a ruse, Tyler was stabbed by William Walworth, Lord Mayor of London, and carried into St. Bartholomew's Hospital where he died. The next day his lifeless body was dragged out of the hospital where his head was cut off and exhibited on London Bridge.

The 17th century was preeminently the age of witchcraft in England; Smithfield being the favored ground for execution of witches. Shakespeare often refers to witches and necromancy in his plays, most strikingly in *Henry VI, Part 2*, where the king decrees that:

> The witch in Smithfield shall be burnt to ashes,
> And you three shall be strangled on the gallows.

The witch was Margery Jourdemain of Eye.

During that same century, the Protestants annually celebrated an anti-popery parade to Smithfield where they burned effigies of the Pope and the cardinals. They had not forgotten the zealous Roman Catholic Guy Fawkes' Gunpowder Plot, a conspiracy to blow up the Houses of Parliament on November 5, 1605.

Sir John Falstaff, Shakespeare's comic knight, appeared in several scenes set in Smithfield. According to the Page in *Henry IV, Part 2*, Bardolph went "into Smithfield to buy your worship a horse", to which Falstaff replies:

> I bought him in St. Paul's, and he'll buy me a horse in Smithfield: an I could get me but a wife in the stews, I were mann'd, horsed and wived.

Falstaff is later arrested in Smithfield on the complaint of Mistress Quickly, who assures the Sheriff's officers, Fang and Snare, that he (Falstaff):

> ... comes continuantly to Pie-corner—saving your manhoods—to buy a saddle .... Yonder he comes and that arrant malmsey-nose knave Bardolph with him. Do your offices, do your offices, Master Fang and Master Snare; do me, do me, do me your offices.

Pie-corner was located at what is now the junction of Giltspur Street and Cock Lane, where a gilded figure known as the "Fat Boy" commemorates the Great Fire of 1666. The disastrous fire started in Pudding Lane and was said to have ended at Pie-corner.

In the same play, Doll Tearsheet playfully calls Falstaff a "whoreson little tidy Bartholomew boar-pig." The reference is to the Bartholomew Fair held from 1133 to 1840. For several weeks each year around August 24, the Feast of St. Bartholomew was a celebrated event in Smithfield.

Originally a cloth fair, it gradually became a riotous carnival complete with markets, shows, bacchanalian feast, drunken revelry, puppet plays, ballad singers, mountebanks, wrestling matches, rouges and pickpockets. It gave its name of one of Ben Jonson's plays, *Bartholomew Fair* (1614), a robust chronicle of the bawds, cut-purses and swindlers who preyed on the stall holders as well as their customers.

Samuel Pepys (1633-1703), the diarist, frequented the Fair on numerous occasions. An entry of August 31, 1661 reports two visits on the same day:

> At home and the office all the morning, and at noon comes Luellin to me, and he and I to the tavern and after that to Bartholomew Fair, and there upon his motion to a pitiful alehouse, where we had a dirty slut or two come up that they where whores .... From hence he and I walked towards Ludgate and parted. I back again to the fair all alone, and there met with my Ladies Jemimah and Paulina, with Mr. Pickering and Mademoiselle, at seeing the monkeys dance, which was much to see, when they could be brought to do so, but it troubled me to sit among such nasty company.

On a subsequent visit of September 1, 1668 he:

> ... saw several sights; among others, the mare that tells money, and many things to admiration; and among others, come to me, when she was bid to go to him of the company that most loved a pretty wench in a corner. And this did cost me 12d. to the horse, which I had flung him before.

This was not the only learned horse: Shakespeare mentions "the dancing horse" in his *Love's Labour's Lost* (1594-95).

Charles Lamb (1775-1834) took William and Dorothy Wordsworth to Bartholomew Fair in 1802 after their return from France. In *The Prelude* (1850), Wordsworth remembered the "chattering monkeys ... the hurdy gurdy ... and the children whirling in their roundabouts at The Fair holden where martyrs suffered in past time."

In his *Essays of Elia* (1823), Lamb has a charming dissertation in "The Praise of Chimney-Sweepers" describing a celebration held in Smithfield during Bartholomew's Fair:

> My pleasant friend Jem [James] White ... to reverse the wrongs of fortune in these poor changelings, he instituted an annual feast of chimney-sweepers, at which it was his pleasure to officiate as host and waiter. It was a solemn supper held in Smithfield, upon the yearly return of the fair of St. Bartholomew .... The place chosen was a convenient spot among the pens, at the north side of the fair, not so far distant as to be impervious to the agreeable hubbub of that vanity, but remote enough not to be obvious to the interruption of every gaping spectator in it.

Lamb joyfully relates the hearty eating and drinking, the toasts, ceremonies and comfort afforded the young orphans by this unselfish act of his friend. The happy day comes to a close, and Lamb pays a sad farewell to their benefactor:

> He carried away with him half the fun of the world when he died—of my world at least. His old clients look for him among the pens; and, missing him, reproach the altered feast of St. Bartholomew, and the glory of Smithfield departed for ever.

The Fair continued as an amusement center until 1855 when it was abolished due to the complaints of the inhabitants of Smithfield that it "not only encourages profligacy and violations of the law, but also obstructed business for six weeks."

ST. BARTHOLOMEW THE GREAT

The oldest parish church in London, and one of the oldest in England, St. Bartholomew the Great is an incomparable example of the unpretentious strength of Norman church architecture.

Rahere, a Canon of St. Paul's Cathedral, founded the Augustinian Priory in 1123 and became its first prior. The interesting story of the creation of the church relates that Rahere, while on a pilgrimage to Rome, became seriously ill. In his delirium he saw a creature with huge wings and claws about to cast him into the boundless void. Rahere was terrified and vowed that he would dedicate himself to aid the poor people of London if his life were spared. The image changed to that of a man who stated that he was Bartholomew, one of the 12 disciples of Jesus, come to save him. Rahere then resolved to build a church and a hospital for the poor once he reached home safely.

At the Reformation in the 16th century, the monastic buildings were sold and for years many parts of the various church structures were demolished or neglected. The Lady Chapel became a tenement, the choir a factory for the manufacture of wool and silk fringes, the north transept a blacksmith's forge, the bays of the cloisters a stable and the crypt a coal and wine cellar. The Lady Chapel later became a print shop where Benjamin Franklin worked as a printer when he first arrived in London from Philadelphia in 1725.

William Hogarth (169701764), printer and engraver, born in Bartholomew Close, was baptized in the church in 1697, as were two of his sisters in 1699 and 1707.

ST. BARTHOLOMEW'S HOSPITAL

In furtherance of his vow, Rahere also founded this hospital, adjacent to the Church, in 1123. Familiarly called "Bart's" today, it sits on the original site and is the oldest teaching hospital in London. In 1609 William Harvey (1578-1657) was chief physician at St. Bart's Hospital. He served in that capacity from 1609 to 1643, during which time he made public his revolutionary discovery of the circulation of the blood.

Robert Bridges (1844-1930), poet laureate of England, studied medicine at Bart's. He became a student in 1869 and had medical appointments there until he retired in 1882 and devoted himself to writing. While practicing medicine at Bart's, he published three volumes of poetry.

St. Bartholomew's Hospital should have a warm place in the hearts of the "Baker Street Irregulars" for it was there that Sherlock Holmes came to meet a prospective roommate for the first time, Dr. John Watson, recently invalided home from India. There is even a plaque to prove it!

ST. JOHN'S GATE

Down St. John's Lane, two blocks east of Turnmill Street, the sole remains of the great Priory St. Johns of Jerusalem unexpectedly looms: a 1504 turreted gatehouse bordered by lofty towers. Its wide vaulted interior still retains the arms of the ancient order on the ornamental bosses. The Knights Hospitallers were suppressed and their property confiscated by Henry VIII in 1530. During the reigns of Elizabeth I and James I, an apartment over the Gate became the Office of the Revels. For almost 100 years, all plays had to be licensed by the Master of the Revels before they could be performed. It is not difficult to visualize Shakespeare, Jonson, Marlowe and the other playwrights of that period being summoned to the Gate to explain various passages in their plays prior to approval.

During the first half of the 18th century, the rooms above the Gate were occupied by Edward Cave, editor of the *Gentleman's Magazine*, one of the first to publish the writings of Samuel Johnson, who became the greatest literary figure of the century. James Boswell, in his *Life of Samuel Johnson* (1791), tell us that

> ... when he [Johnson] first saw St. John's Gate, the place where ... *Gentleman's Magazine* ... was originally printed, he "beheld it with reverence" ... he has given it still greater lustre by the various admirable Essays which he wrote for it.

Dr. Johnson, during that period, was sometimes in such extreme poverty that he could not pay for a lodging and wandered all night through the streets. His clothes were obviously not very presentable, his person unkempt. His appearance was so strikingly incongruous that even 150 years later, George Gissing in his novel *The Nether World* (1889), described a pathetic episode which occurred between Johnson and Cave at St. John's Gate:

> There it was that the said Samuel once had his dinner handed to him behind a screen, because of his unpresentable costume, when Cave was entertaining an aristocratic guest. In the course of the meal, the guest happened to speak with interest of something he had recently read by an obscure Mr.

Johnson: wherat there was joy behind the screen, and probably increased appreciation on the unwonted dinner.

Of St. John's Gate itself, Gissing went on to say:

After a walk amid the squalid and toil-infested ways of Clerkenwell, it impresses one strangely to come upon this monument of old time. The archway had a sad, worn, grimy aspect. So closely is it packed in among buildings which suggest nothing but the sordid struggle for existence, that it looks depressed, ashamed, tainted by the ignobleness of its surroundings. The wonder is that it has not been swept away, in obedience to the great law of traffic and the spirit of the time.

Several notable taverns were located on St. John Street. The Three Cups was mentioned in Defoe's Moll Flanders, and the Bottle of Hay was visited by Samuel Pepys. Oliver Goldsmith, Samuel Johnson and Tom Paine were frequent customers of the Old Red Lion, still at No.418. Taverns with the same name have occupied that site since the beginning of the 15th century.

TURNMILL STREET

A sign on the wall at the exit from the Farringdon Street Underground Station directs one to "Cow Cross Street, Leading to Turnmill
Street." Turnmill Street, though much changed, was once called
Turnbull Street, one of the most disreputable places in London, the
haunt of thieves and prostitutes.

Shakespeare must have been well acquainted with that unsavory
section of London for he had Falstaff, speaking about Justice Shallow
in *Henry IV, Part 2* (1597-98), say:

> Lord, Lord, how subject we old men are to this vice of ly-
> ing! This same starved justice hath done nothing but prate
> to me of the wildness of his youth, and the feats he hath
> done about Turnbull-street; and every third word a lie.

One of the most infamous resorts in Turnbull Street was
"Pickthatch". The name refers to a half-door surmounted by spikes,
often used in brothels. We have Falstaff again, in *The Merry Wives of
Windsor* (1600-01), berating Pistol with:

> —go: —a short knife and a throng; —to your manor of
> Pickthatch, go.

The short knife was used to cut purses in a crowd; Falstaff is thus
calling Pistol a cut-purse.

Turnmill Street ends at Clerkenwell Road. The one time village
of Clerkenwell grew up around the Priory of the Knights Hospitallers
of the order of St. John of Jerusalem, founded about 1130. The name
was derived from the well of the parish clerks. Arnold Bennett mentions performances of miracle plays at the well during the Middle
Ages in his *Riceyman Steps* (1923). The Original buildings were
burned down in 1381 by Wat Tyler's rebels, but later rebuilt.

AREA C

CHEAPSIDE

AND

THE MERMAID TAVERN

AREA C ATTRACTIONS

AREA C MAP

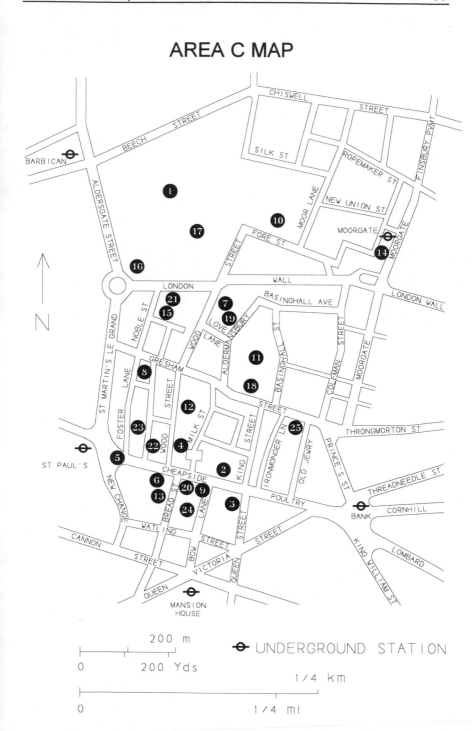

THE BARBICAN CENTRE

The name "Barbekan" was applied to an outer fortification of the City, usually a tower erected over a gate. At this location, it was a tower on the north side of Barbican Street. It was leveled in 1267 by Henry III during the war with the barons, but references were made to it in later years so it must have been rebuilt. It is not known when it was finally demolished but John Milton, the eminent poet, lived on Barbican Street from 1645-47.

The area was almost completely destroyed by enemy bombing in World War II. The authorities took the opportunity to plan a completely new area called a "City Within the City", or the Barbican Project. The 60 acre area of bombed out land was purchased in 1958 by the City Council and officially opened in 1982 as the Barbican Center for Arts and Conferences on London Wall.

Shops, offices and towering blocks of flats to accommodate over 6,000 people were built to bring people back to the City to live. As an Arts Centre, it engulfed a new Guildhall School of Music and Drama; a new Museum of London; the base of operations of the London Symphony Orchestra; the new home of the Royal Shakespeare Company; the City of London School for Girls; the Halls of the Ironmongers' Company and the Barbers' Company; a concert hall, two theaters, three cinemas, an art gallery, a public library, conference and exhibition halls, an open air sculpture court, two public restaurants, a conservatory, a pond and several fountains.

St. Giles, Cripplegate, in the Middle of the development, is the parish church for the Centre.

BENNETT'S CLOCK SHOP

A little west of Bird-in-Hand court, Bennett's Clock Shop used to stand at No.65 Cheapside. Its figures of Gog and Magog, the two medieval giants guarding the Guildhall, made the shop one of London's most picturesque frontages.

When the building was demolished in 1929, Henry Ford purchased the figures for his Edison Institute in Greenfield, Michigan, USA.

BIRD-IN-HAND COURT

At No.76 Cheapside, on the second floor over the Bird-in-Hand Court opposite Ironmonger Lane, John Keats, the poet, lodged in 1815. While living there he wrote one of his immortal sonnets, *On First Looking Into Chapman's Homer*:

> Much have I travelled in the realms of gold,
>> And many goodly states and kingdoms seen;
>> Round many western islands have I been
>
> •   •   •   •   •   •   •
>
> Yet did I never breathe its pure serene
> Till I heard Chapman speak out loud and bold:
> Then felt I like some watcher of the skies
>> When a new planet swims into his ken;
> Or like stout Cortez when with eagle eyes
>> He stared at the Pacific—and all his men
> Look'd at each other with a wild surmise—
>> Silent, upon a peak in Darien.

THE CAT AND THE FIDDLE

On Cheapside, between Milk Street and Bread Street, once stood a tavern with the familiar name of The Cat and the Fiddle. It appears that the well known nursery rhyme referred to that eating house:

> Hey, diddle, diddle!
> The cat and the fiddle,
> The cow jumped over the moon.
> The little dog laughed
> To see such sport,
> And the dish ran away with the spoon.

CHEAPSIDE

The name of the old marketplace derives from the Old English "chep"—to barter or market. Each craft guild lived and worked in a special area nearby:

Bakers: Bread Street
Goldsmiths: Goldsmith Row (between Bread and Friday)
Fishmongers: Friday Street
Shoemakers: Cordwainer Street
Grocers: Sopers Lane
Poulterers: Poultry
Dairymen: Milk Street
Mercers (small wares dealers): Between Poultry and Sopers Lane

The widest street in Old London, Cheapside has been one of the City's principal commercial streets since medieval times, and the axis on which the life of the City revolved. Crowded with booths and stalls, the picturesque street of gabled houses hummed with the usual commotion of a busy marketplace. On holidays, the street was cleared and used for jousts, pageants, tournaments—even public executions.

Cheapside was infamous for its brawling apprentices. Geoffrey Chaucer (1340-1400) describes one of these lusty young men in "The Cook's Tale" in his celebrated *The Canterbury Tales* (as adapted):

> There was a prentice living in our town,
> Worked in the victualling trade and he was brown.
> At every wedding he would sing and hop
> And he preferred the tavern to the shop.
> Whenever any pageant or procession
> Came down Cheapside, goodbye to his profession.
> He'd leap out of the shop to see the sight
> And join the dance and not come back that night!

For centuries Cheapside, not Fleet Street, was the heart of literary London.

THE CHEAPSIDE CROSS

The famous Cheapside Cross once stood in the middle of Cheapside, in front of the Church of St. Peter, Cheap. It was one of a series of 12 memorial crosses erected by King Edward I in 1291 to mark the stages in the funeral procession of his Queen, Eleanor of Castile, from Lincolnshire to her tomb in Westminster Abbey.

The structure underwent numerous changes and indignities. It had been renovated with new lead work and frequently regilded as a showpiece for visiting dignitaries. By the second half of the 16th century, however, it had become a symbol of idolatry as well as an obstruction to traffic. All proposals for its removal were unavailing.

One night in June 1581, the Cross was severely damaged, the Resurrection scene completely destroyed. This was later replaced by a small shrine containing an alabaster figure of Diana, with water, according to John Stowe, "prilling from her naked breast." Shakespeare included a reference to the statue in *As You Like It* (1599). Rosalind sets forth the contrariness and inconsistency of her sex when she says to Orlando:

> I will weep for nothing, like Diana in the fountain, and I will
> do that when you are disposed to be merry.

After many more vicissitudes, the battered old monument was at last demolished in 1643.

THE CROSS KEYS TAVERN

A few yards from the tower of St. Alban's, Wood Street, built by Sir Christopher Wren in 1698, stood a tavern familiar to the readers of Charles Dickens. The Cross Keys Tavern, which disappeared by the end of the 19th century, was the destination of young Dickens when he first came to London, as described in his *The Uncommercial Traveller*:

> I call my boyhood's home ... Dullborough. Most of us come from Dullborough who come from a country town. As I left Dullborough in the days when there were no rail-roads in the land, I left it in a stage-coach. Through all the years that have since passed, have I ever lost the smell of the damp straw in which I was packed—like game—and for-warded, carriage paid, to the Cross Keys, Wood-street, Cheapside, London? There was no other inside passenger, and I consumed my sandwiches in solitude and dreariness, and it rained hard all the way, and I thought life sloppier than I had expected to find it.

The incident must have made an indelible impression, for he has Pip in *Great Expectations* (1861) repeat his own youthful arrival in London:

> The journey from our town to the metropolis, was a journey of about five hours. It was a little past mid-day when the four-horse stage-coach by which I was a passenger, got into the ravel of traffic frayed out by the Cross Keys, Wood-street, Cheapside, London.
>
> We Britons had at that time particularly settled that it was treasonable to doubt our having and our being the best of everything. Otherwise, while I was scared by the immensity of London, I think I might have had some faint doubts whether it was not rather ugly, crooked, narrow, and dirty.

Charles Dickens was born in Portsea, but Dullborough was his name for the town of Rochester, "the birthplace of his fancy".

GOLDSMITHS' HALL

The Goldsmiths' Company was empowered by Edward III in 1327 to assay and stamp gold and silver plate. The king ordered that the genuine goldsmiths "sit in their shops in the high street of Cheap"; the trade was prohibited from operating any place but at this exchange.

The present Hall, on Foster Lane at Gresham Street, the fourth on the site, opened in 1835 and is the most magnificent of all the Company Halls. In 1871 the hall and staircase were lined with costly marble. There are numerous statues and busts: four statuettes of the *Seasons* by Samuel Nixon are positioned on the staircase. Candles are still used in the chandeliers in the court room.

A large display of silver plate illustrates the changes of style and fashion during the past four centuries. A collection of the best silver work of the present day has been exhibited in England as well as overseas.

The Company has established numerous charities including pensions, grants for the poor, donations to convalescent homes and orphanages, subsidies for libraries and museums, training and education of young persons in trouble, and funds for general charitable purposes.

GOLDSMITHS' ROW

On the south side of Cheapside, between Bow Church and Bread Street, once stood a magnificent series of houses and shops known as Goldsmiths' Row. Built in 1491 by Thomas Wood, a goldsmith, almost 200 goldsmiths were plying their trade along this row. John Stow, in his *Survey of London* (1618), described Goldsmiths' Row as:

> ...the most beautiful frame of fair houses and shops that be within the walls of London, or elsewhere in England. It containeth in number ten fair dwelling-houses and fourteen shops, all in one frame, uniformly built four stories high, beautified towards the street with the Goldsmith's arms and the likeness of woodmen, in memory of his name, riding on monstrous beasts, all of which is cast in lead, painted over and gilt ...

This fabulous setting of mystical splendor served as an appropriate showcase for public promenades by people of fashion. The opening scene of George Chapman's play, *Eastward Hoe* (1605), takes place in Goldsmiths' Row.

By 1630 many of the younger goldsmiths had moved to other parts of London, and Goldsmiths' Row could not continue to function as a centralized showcase of the goldsmith's art. The Goldsmiths' Company, incorporated in 1327, still has the responsibility of assaying and stamping gold and silver plate.

GRUB STREET

Grub Street used to lead north from Fore Street, where Daniel Defoe was born in 1660, and was known early in the 17th century as the haunt of needy writers and literary hacks. Samuel Johnson defined Grub Street in his *Dictionary of the English Language* (1755) as "much inhabited by writers of small histories, dictionaries and temporary poems, whence any mean production is called Grubstreet."

Oliver Goldsmith (1730?-74), Johnson's contemporary, also a hack writer in his early years, expressed his sympathetic understanding of the sufferings borne by another Grubstreeter in an epitaph he wrote:

> Here lies poor Ned Purdom, from misery freed,
> Who long was a bookseller's hack;
> He led such a damnable life in this world,
> I don't think he'd wish to come back.

George Gissing named his novel *New Grub Street* (1891) for its vigorous condemnation of the compromised standards that some writers make in order to achieve popularity and success.

Grub Street was renamed Milton Street in 1830 but much of it disappeared in the Barbican redevelopment. The term "Grubstreet" lasted even after the street name was changed and is still defined in our current dictionaries as "of or like literary hacks or their work."

THE GUILDHALL

On Basinghall Street, within a stone's throw of the Cross Keys Tavern, the Guildhall was established by the combined efforts of the various guilds as a center for the City government. Built in 1411, on the site of an earlier building with the same name, it contained a vaulted undercroft and a 150 foot long Great Hall. Old Guildhall was severely damaged by the Great Fire of 1666 and the incendiary bomb raid of December 29, 1940, but the Great Hall, re-roofed and restored, still stands with its original windows on each end. The 15th century crypt survived unscathed over the centuries.

As the center of administration for the City, the Common Council and the City justices hold their sessions in the Guildhall. The Great Hall continues to be used for meetings and banquets, the most important being the pageantry and festivities attendant on the installation of the new Lord Mayor every year on November 9th. The coat of arms over the entrance reads "Domine Dirige nos"—Lord, direct us.

In earlier periods, the opinion of Guildhall could not be ignored by either the King or the Parliament. Many kings gained their thrones with the support of Guildhall; others lost their crowns largely due to its opposition. In *Richard III*, Shakespeare has Richard obtaining the Lord Mayor's support by deceiving him into believing that Lord Hastings had plotted his (Richard's) murder. Later Richard sends Buckingham to follow the Lord Mayor to Guildhall and "look for the news."

The Great Hall was long used for State trials. In 1546 Anne Askew, the Protestant martyr, was found guilty of heresy and executed. Henry Howard, Earl of Surrey, was tried on a trumped up charge and executed in the following year at the age of 29. In 1553 Lady Jane Grey, the "nine days Queen of England" and her husband, Lord Guilford Dudley, were found guilty of treason and beheaded in the Tower of London six months later. In the same year, Thomas Cranmer, Archbishop of Canterbury, was found guilty of treason, but his life was spared by Queen Mary. Three years later, he was burned at the stake as a heretic.

In February 1594, the Queen's Jewish physician was tried on a dubious charge of attempting to poison Queen Elizabeth. He was convicted and hanged at Tyburn on June 7, 1594. Many Shakespearean scholars and critics have advanced the theory that the Physician, Dr. Roderigo Lopez, was the model for Shakespeare's Shylock in *The Merchant of Venice*.

The last State trial held in the Great Hall was that of a Jesuit, Dr. Garnett, in 1606 accused of complicity in the Gunpowder Plot (a scheme to blow up the Houses of Parliament led by Guy Fawkes, later executed). Dr. Garnett was found guilty and executed in St. Paul's Churchyard.

Dick Whittington, according to the legend, was called back by the sound of Bow Bells to be thrice Mayor of London (though he actually served four times as Mayor), made substantial contributions towards the building of Guildhall. His money paid for a floor of Purbeck marble, glass windows embellished with his coat of arms and half the construction costs of the library in 1423.

The Guildhall Library is justly proud of its magnificent collection of prints, maps and manuscripts which chronicle the development of London and the City from its earliest beginnings: Ralph Agas' *Plan of London* (1591); John Stow's *The Survey of London* (1618), *Annales, or a General Chronicle of England* (1631) and John Ogilby's *Map of London* (1676). Other priceless treasures are: the indenture prepared for the purchaser in the sale of a house in Blackfriars on March 10, 1613, by Henry Walker to William Shakespeare; registers of City churches and four editions of the Folios of Shakespeare's plays.

The Worshipful Company of Clockmakers has created a unique collection of clocks and watches in the Clock Museum in the East Lobby. Ranging from grandfather clocks to miniature watches from the 15th to the 20th centuries, these one of a kind timepieces were created by expert and imaginative craftsmen.

The Guildhall is still guarded by the carved limewood images of two medieval giants known as Gog and Magog, each over nine feet tall. They are replacements for the two statues destroyed in the last war. The origin of the giants is obscure, through undoubtedly of pagan mythology; they have guarded Guildhall since the 15th century.

THE HOLE IN THE WALL

Situated in Mitre Court, a pub aptly named The Hole in the Wall, stands on part of the site of the old Wood Street Compter or Counter, a debtor's prison. The City fathers built a prison in 1555 on land which had once belonged to the fabled Dick Whittington, four times Lord Mayor of London and hero of the legend of Dick Whittington and his Cat. Obliterated in the Great Fire of 1666 and rebuilt in 1670, it was finally removed in 1790.

Falstaff, in Shakespeare's *The Merry Wives of Windsor*, says:

Thou mightst as well say I love to walk by the Counter-gate, which is as hateful to me as the reek of a lime kiln.

The Compters or Counters were run strictly as a profit making venture, the inmates accommodated according to their ability to pay. The Master's section was the best and most expensive, next best was the Knight's ward, then the two-penny area, and finally "The Hole", the cheapest and darkest underground vault with only straw mattresses to cover the cold and damp stone floor. In this squalid quarter, a hole in the wall permitted fresh air to enter and the poor inmates to beg for food from passersby:

Good, gratious people, for the Lord's sake pity the poor women! We lie cold and comfortless night and day on the cold boards in the deep, dark dungeon!

The name of the pub preserves the melancholy memory of the cruel prison system of the day. Mitre Court itself is used to accommodate the overflow from the pub. The center of the Court contains some underground wine vaults well worth seeing.

THE MERMAID TAVERN

The chief glory of Cheapside, "identified with more talent and genius than ever met before or since", the Mermaid Tavern stood in Bread Street, a house or two down from the western corner of Cheapside.

Mentioned as early as 1464, the tavern became famous during the Elizabethan Age when English literature rose to glorious heights. Sir Walter Raleigh founded the illustrious Mermaid Club in 1603, which met at the tavern on the first Friday of every month. Its members, in addition to Raleigh, included such literary figures as William Shakespeare, Ben Jonson, John Selden, John Donne, Thomas Heywood, Thomas Carew, Michael Drayton, Thomas Lodge, Thomas Dekker, George Chapman, Thomas Fuller, Thomas Campion, Tom Coryat and a pair of rising young dramatists, Francis Beaumont and John Fletcher.

An account of the well-known battles of wits between Shakespeare and Jonson at meetings of the Mermaid Club was reported by Thomas Fuller in his *Worthies of England* (1662):

> Many were the wit combats betwixt Shakespeare and Ben Jonson, which two I behold like a Spanish great galleon and an English man-of-war. Master Jonson (like the former) was built far higher in learning, solid but slow in his performances. Shakespeare, lesser in bulk but lighter in sailing, could turn with all tides, tack about, and take advantage of all winds by the quickness of his wit and invention.

Shakespeare's connection with the famous tavern is officially documented. When he bought a house in Blackfriars in 1613, he named as one of the three trustees of the property a William Johnson, vintner. This William Johnson was the landlord of the Mermaid Tavern.

Ben Jonson, in his poem *Inviting a Friend to Supper* (1616), celebrated the tavern and its delicious wine:

> But that, which most doth take my Muse, and mee,
> Is a pure cup of rich Canary-wine,
> Which is the Mermaids, now, but shall be mine:

> Of which had Horace, or Anacreon tasted,
> Their lives, as doe their lines, till now had lasted.

Francis Beaumont (1584-1616), in a famous letter to Ben Jonson, rhapsodized about the tavern:

> ... In this warm shine
> I lie and dream of your full Mermaid wine ...
> What things have we seen
> Done at the Mermaid! heard words that have been
> So nimble and so full of subtile flame
> As if that every one from whence they came
> Had meant to put his whole wit in a jest,
> And had resolved to live a fool the rest
> Of his dull life ...

The tavern was destroyed in the Great Fire of 1666, and nothing exists today at that spot to remind us of its illustrious history. The memory of that hallowed corner, however, haunts the imagination with "such stuff as dreams are made on."

In a later day, long after the Mermaid Tavern had vanished from sight, John Keats nostalgically asks in *Lines on the Mermaid Tavern* (1820):

> Souls of poets dead and gone,
> What Elysium have ye known,
> Happy field or mossy cavern
> Choicer than the Mermaid Tavern?
> Have ye tippled drink more fine
> Than mine host's Canary wine?

A lapse of almost three centuries has failed to dim the mystique of that celebrated tavern. Walter Theodore Watts-Dunton, in his *Christmas at the Mermaid* (1897), recreated an imaginary scene at the Mermaid on a wintry night after Shakespeare had retired to Stratford. The phantoms of the past include many members of the Mermaid Club: Jonson, Raleigh, Lodge, Dekker, Chapman, Drayton and Heywood. After the battles of wit and story-telling are over, and the evening draws to a mellow close, Heywood reflects the mood of the visionary company:

More than all the pictures, Ben,
  Winter weaves by wood or stream,
Christmas loves our London, when
  Rise thy clouds of wassail-steam:
Clouds like these that, curling, take
Forms of faces gone, and wake
Many a lay from lips we loved, and make
  London like a dream.

THE MOORGATE

Directly south of the Moorgate Underground Station, at No.85 Moorgate, stands a pub simply called The Moorgate. A blue plaque on the outside of the building announces that John Keats, the poet, had been born on the site in August 1795. At that time the inn was known as The Swan and Hoop where Keats' father was employed as a stable-man in the livery stable.

John Keats died in 1821. In his brief 25 years, he wrote poetry distinguished by pure enchantment which had not been seen since Marlowe and Shakespeare. His immortal odes and sonnets remain as some of the most beautiful poems in the English language.

THE MOUNTJOY HOUSE

Sometime between 1602 and 1604, William Shakespeare found lodgings above the shop of one Christopher Mountjoy, a French Huguenot refugee and maker of wigs and women's headdresses. He may have been living there as late as May 11, 1612, when he appeared at the Court of Requests as a witness in a dispute between Mountjoy and Belott over Mountjoy's daughter's marriage dowry, and stated that he had been intimate with the family some "ten years more or less."

The Mountjoy house was located on the northeast corner of Monkwell and Silver Streets. Monkwell Street ran south from the front of St. Giles Cripplegate church to Silver Street, and then parallel to the Wall. It is thought to have derived its name from a hermitage with a well that stood at the north end of the street. Silver Street ran east, ending at Wood Street. This is the only place we know for certain in which Shakespeare lived in London. This information was unearthed by an American scholar, Professor William Wallace, at the Public Record Office in 1909.

During the years that Shakespeare lived in the Mountjoy house, he wrote some of his greatest plays: *Othello*, *Macbeth*, *King Lear*, *Anthony and Cleopatra*, *The Winter's Tale* and possibly his last complete play, *The Tempest*. The house was destroyed by the Great Fire of 1666. For a time that corner was occupied by a tavern, The Cooper's Arms, but that too has long disappeared. Nothing now remains to mark that historic site, completely built over by modern office blocks. Silver Street no longer exists.

MUSEUM OF LONDON

The Museum of London, opened in 1976, incorporates the Guildhall and London Museums.

A chronological history of London is traced by exhibits, tableaux and dioramas from prehistoric times through Roman, Saxon, Viking, Medieval, Tudor, Early Stuart, Commonwealth, Late Stuart, Georgian, 19th century, Imperial London, and Ceremonial London to the present.

Highlights of the exhibition include an audio-visual representation of the Great Fire of 1666, the Lord Mayor's Ceremonial Coach, marble models of English warships, the head of the god Mithras, Roman and medieval relics, an 18th century prison cell and replicas of shops and residences of various periods.

The total effect is a brilliant social history of the great City.

ST. GILES, CRIPPLEGATE

One of the few Gothic churches still standing in London, the parish church of St. Giles was built in 1390 on the site of a Norman church of 1090. Many alterations and restorations followed over the years as the result of fires and other disasters. The latest rebuilding took place in 1960 after the church had suffered a direct hit during the blitz on August 24, 1940, and further damaged in the fire storm of December 29 in the same year. The stone tower and nave are all that remain of the original 1390 church.

John Stow, in his *Survey of London* (1598), suggests a romantic basis for the name Cripplegate. He stated that cripples used to stand at the gate to beg. When the body of King Edmund the Martyr was brought to London and carried through the gate, several cripples were miraculously cured and regained the ability to walk. The more likely explanation is that the name derived form the Anglo-Saxon "creple", meaning the "covered way into the Roman fort".

Lancelot Andrewes, the most learned scholar and divine of his time, was vicar from 1588 to 1605. Among the celebrated Englishmen buried here are: John Foxe (died 1587), author of *The Book of Martyrs* (1563); Sir Martin Frobisher (died 1594), navigator and seaman and John Bunyan (died 1688), non-conformist preacher and author. The church, however, is best remembered as the burial place of John Milton (died 1674), the blind poet. A bust of Milton made for the church in 1793 was paid for by Samuel Whitbread, a leading brewer, whose company provides the picturesque horses which pull the Lord Mayor's coach during the annual Lord Mayor's Show.

Milton's tomb was desecrated in that same year (1793) in a sad example of irreverence and greed. A contemporary writer reported the shameful incident:

A journeyman named Holmes procured a mallet and chisel, and forcing open the coffin so that the corpse (which was clothed in a shroud, and looked as if it had just been buried) might be seen. Mr. Fountain, one of the overseers, then endeavoured to pull out the teeth but, being unsuccessful, a bystander took up a stone and loosened them with a blow. There were only five in the upper jaw but they were quite

white and good. They, together with some of the lower
ones, Mr. Fountain (and two other men) divided between
them. A rib bone was also taken and the hair from the head
which was long and smooth was torn out by the handfull.
After this the caretaker Elizabeth Grant took the coffin under her care charging sixpence to anyone who wished to
visit it. Later she reduced her fee to threepence and finally
to twopence before the corpse was reinterred.

Milton's tomb appears in Thomas Hardy's novel, *The Hand of
Ethelberta* (1876), where Ethelberta and her friends are grouped
around the tomb:

Ethelberta drew from her pocket a small edition of Milton,
and proposed that she should read a few lines from *Paradise
Lost*. She stood with her head against the marble slab just
below the bust, and began a selected piece ... the passage
containing the words:

> Mammon lead them on;
> Mammon, the least erected spirit that fell
> From heaven.

The signatures of many famous persons are recorded in the
church registers, attesting to the fact that William Shakespeare attended the baptism of his nephew in 1604 while lodging nearby in Silver Street, Oliver Cromwell's marriage was solemnized in 1620 and
that Ben Jonson married Hester Hopkins in 1623.

A plain marble tablet dedicated to one Margaret Lucy who died
in 1634 has been almost completely ignored over the centuries. The
inscription states that to all her friends "she was very deare, but especially to her old grandmother, the Lady Constance Lucy." The Lucy
family of Charlecote in Warwickshire, of which these two were members, achieved questionable fame as possibly responsible for William
Shakespeare's flight from Stratford-on-Avon while still a young man,
to later earn immortality on the London stage.

The first printed biography of William Shakespeare was written
by Nicholas Rowe in 1709 as a preface to his edition of Shakespeare's
plays. In that biography, Rowe repeated various stories about Shakespeare, without any way of judging whether they were true or false.

The most popular story was the deer stealing episode which still flourishes, mainly because it is both colorful and scandalous. Rowe's version of that episode was that:

> He [Shakespeare] had, by a misfortune common enough to young fellows, fallen into ill company, and, among them, some, that made a frequent practice of deer-stealing, engaged him with them more than once in robbing a park that belonged to Sir Thomas Lucy of Charlecote near Stratford. For this he was prosecuted by that gentleman, as he thought, somewhat too severely; and, in order to revenge the ill-usage, he made a ballad upon him, and through this, probably the first essay of his poetry, be lost, yet it is said to have been so very bitter that it redoubled the prosecution against him to that degree that he was obliged to leave his business and family in Warwickshire and shelter himself in London.

The law of Shakespeare's day punished deer stealers with three months imprisonment and the payment of triple damages.

The legend concludes that Shakespeare revenged himself by caricaturing Sir Thomas Lucy (1532-1600) as the addlebrained Justice Shallow in *Henry IV, Part 2* and *The Merry Wives of Windsor*.

Referring again to Thomas Hardy's novel, *The Hand of Ethelberta*, Ladywell asks, "What is this round tower?", and is informed "That's a piece of the old city wall." The bastion was built to the south of the church shortly after the 13th century. Portions of the northern guardroom and the central supports of the gate are still visible. The west gate's entrance is on London Wall. Old tombstones have been set in to the paving outside the church.

ST. LAWRENCE JEWRY

Near the entrance to the Guildhall on Gresham Street, stands the church of St. Lawrence Jewry. Built in 1196, it perished in the Great Fire of 1666, but was rebuilt by Sir Christopher Wren during the decade of 1670. It was again almost completely destroyed by enemy action in 1940 and subsequently restored. The descriptive adjective in the name derives from the fact that many Jews inhabited the area at one time.

As the official church of the City of London, before electing the new Lord Mayor, Michaelmas Day services are held here annually, attended by the Lord Mayor and the Corporation,. Sir Thomas More, famed martyr and the author of *Utopia* (1516), lectured in the medieval church. He is commemorated with a stained glass window in the south wall. The piano owned by Sir Thomas Beecham, the celebrated conductor and founder of the London Philharmonic Orchestra, has been bequeathed to the church.

ST. MARY ALDERMANBURY

A few blocks east of the Mountjoy house, at the corner of Aldermanbury and Love Lane, stood the church of St. Mary Aldermanbury (St. Mary the Virgin). The Wren church was bombed during the last war and its stones removed to the United States in 1968. The structure was rebuilt at Westminster College in Fulton, Missouri, as a memorial to Winston Churchill after his celebrated Iron Curtain speech at the College.

A charming garden is all that remains with a tablet chronicling the history of the church:

THE ORIGINAL CHURCH ON THIS SITE IS BELIEVED TO HAVE BEEN SAXON ALTHOUGH THE FIRST RECORDED MENTION IS IN 1181. IN 1633 THE CHURCH WAS RESTORED BUT WAS THEN DESTROYED BY THE GREAT FIRE OF 1666. SIR CHRISTOPHER WREN DESIGNED A NEW CHURCH WHICH WAS COMPLETED IN 1677/8.

THE CHURCH WAS GUTTED DURING THE SECOND WORLD WAR AND THE SHELL SUBSEQUENTLY RE-ERECTED AT FULTON, MISSOURI. AFTER ITS REMOVAL, IN 1966, THE CITY CORPORATION PURCHASED THE SITE FOR USE AS A PUBLIC OPEN SPACE. THE LAYOUT RETAINS THE EXISTING FOOTINGS OF THE CHURCH AND INCORPORATES A KNOT GARDEN AND A FORMAL GARDEN AS A SETTING FOR THE MEMORIAL TO HEMINGE AND CONDELL.

The memorial was erected in 1896 as the gift of Charles Clement Walker of Lilleshall Old Hall, Shropshire. It is crowned by a bust of Shakespeare and a bronze reproduction of the First Folio of 1623 open to the title page's dedication:

WE HAVE BUT COLLECTED THEM ... AND DONE AN OFFICE TO THE DEAD ... WITHOUT AMBITION EITHER OF SELF PROFIT OR FAME ONLY TO KEEP THE MEMORY OF SO WORTHY A FRIEND AND FELLOW ALIVE AS WAS OUR SHAKESPEARE.

The inscription at the base of the structure reads:

TO THE MEMORY OF JOHN HEMINGE AND HENRY CON-
DELL, FELLOW ACTORS AND PERSONAL FRIENDS OF
SHAKESPEARE. THEY LIVED MANY YEARS IN THIS PAR-
ISH AND ARE BURIED HERE. TO THEIR DISINTERESTED
AFFECTION THE WORLD OWES ALL THAT IT CALLS
SHAKESPEARE. THEY ALONE COLLECTED HIS DRA-
MATIC WRITINGS REGARDLESS OF PECUNIARY LOSS
AND WITHOUT THE HOPE OF ANY PROFIT GAVE THEM
TO THE WORLD. THEY THUS MERITED THE GRATITUDE
OF MANKIND.

Prior to 1623, when Heminge and Condell published the First
Folio, it was not known how many of the plays attributed to Shakespeare were actually written by him. Of the 37 plays in the First Folio,
over half had not been printed previously and thus might have been
lost forever. Heminge and Condell were the sole survivors of Shakespeare's old company, The Chamberlain's Men, and in the preface to
the First Folio give us a rare glimpse of Shakespeare himself.

In his last will and testament, Shakespeare remembered his
friends: "To my fellows, John Heminge, Richard Burbage and Henry
Condell 26s 8d a piece to buy them rings." Burbage, leading actor,
shareholder and builder of the Globe Theatre, died in 1619 before
publication of the First Folio. Condell died in 1627, Heminge in 1630.

ST. MARY-LE-BOW

On the south side of Cheapside at the corner of Bow Lane, the Church of St. Mary-le-Bow (originally St. Mary de Arcubus), was built during the reign of William the Conqueror (1027-87). The name is believed to derive from the vaulted arches on which the church was built. Another theory suggests that the crypt originally served as the seat of the ecclesiastical court known as the Court of the Arches. As a result, arches or bow became part of the church's name.

An unusual incident involving the church in the time of Richard I (1157-99) centered around one William Fitzosbert, a citizen with a passion for justice. He publicly urged the citizens to resist the oppressive and ruinous taxations levied by the Lord Mayor and the wealthy Aldermen. Not unexpectedly, he found himself in mortal danger from the authorities. He and some of his followers barricaded themselves in Bow Church. The sanctuary of the church protected them from forcible seizure.

A bishop with little sympathy for nonconformists ordered the church to be set on fire. When Fitzosbert and his supporters tried to escape the flames, they were seized and hustled to the Tower of London. After a hasty trial and an equally hasty verdict, they were dragged by the heels through the streets and hanged at Smithfield.

In front of the church along Cheapside, Edward III (1312-77) had built a stone pavilion from which the kings and queens used to watch the numerous tournaments, pageants and processions taking place on Cheapside. The structure disappeared when the church was destroyed in the Great Fire of 1666. Wren placed a replica in the steeple to commemorate the royal balcony, known as the Crown Sild.

According to the romantic story about Dick Whittington (1358-1423)and his cat, Bow Bell summoned him back to London to be "Thrice Lord Mayor of London" (though he actually served an extra term). Until 1874, a curfew bell rang at 5:45 A.M. and at 9:00 P.M.. The work day of the apprentices began with the morning peals and ended with the ringing of the evening curfew. In an old rhyme, the apprentices complain:

> Clerke of the Bow Bell with the yellow locks,
> For thy late ringing thy head shall have knocks.

To which the Clerke replies:

> Children of Chepe, hold you all still,
> For you shall have Bow Bell rung at your will.

A well known saying has it that a Londoner is a genuine Cockney only if born within "the sound of Bow Bell". This adage was current even in the Elizabethan period, for Shakespeare used the expression in *Twelfth Night* and *King Lear*.

When the church was destroyed in 1666 its replacement, built by Sir Christopher Wren in 1673 on the same site, was the most costly of all his churches. It was again severely damaged in the great firebombing of May 1941. Laurence King rebuilt the exterior according to Wren's plans. Although Wren had originally left space for a peal of 12 bells, the Great Bell of Bow was the first to be hung.

In 1914 an ancient stone from the crypt was removed and placed in Trinity Church in New York City. This was done because King William III granted to the vestry of the Trinity Church the same privileges as given to St. Mary-le-Bow.

ST. OLAVE, SILVER STREET

Directly south of the church of St. Giles, Cripplegate, on London Wall at the corner of Noble Street, the forlorn remnant of the churchyard is all that remains of St. Olave, Silver Street, originally called St. Olave de Mocwelle (Monkwell). The church in which William Shakespeare may have worshipped was across from the house in which he lived for a number of years after 1602.

Shakespeare acted as an intermediary in arranging the marriage of the Mountjoy daughter, Mary, to the apprentice, Stephen Belott. The wedding took place in the church on November 4, 1604. The records do not show that Shakespeare attended, but since he was instrumental in promoting the marriage and living with the Mountjoys at that time, it is a reasonable assumption that he was present at the ceremony.

The church was destroyed in the Great Fire of 1666 and not rebuilt. Only the steps survived and stone blocks inscribed with the following legend record the destruction:

THIS WAS THE PARISH CHURCH OF ST. OLAVE, SILVER STREET, DESTROYED BY THE DREADFUL FIRE IN THE YEAR 1666.

ST. PETER, CHEAP

The old church of St. Peter, Cheap, stood on the west side of Wood Street at Cheapside. Destroyed in the Great Fire of 1666, it was not rebuilt.

All that remains of the church is a tiny courtyard in which a great plane tree, familiar to all Londoners, overhangs the old parish ground. The song of a thrush singing in that tree inspired William Wordsworth, made Poet Laureate in 1843 to write his poem, *Reverie of Poor Susan* (1797):

> At the corner of Wood Street, when daylight
> appears,
> Hangs a thrush that sings loud, it has sung for
> three years.
> Poor Susan has passed by the spot, and
> has heard
> In the silence of morning the song of
> the Bird.

ST. VEDAST CHURCH

The earliest mention of this church on Foster Lane, Cheapside was in the 13th century. A victim of the Great Fire of 1666, it was rebuilt by Sir Christopher Wren from 1670-73. Heavily damaged in World War II, it has been faithfully restored.

Perhaps the most significant event in the old church was the baptism of Robert Herrick on August 24, 1591. The seventh son of a Cheapside goldsmith, he was twice vicar of Dean Prior in Devonshire. But he was also a typical Cavalier writer of over 1,200 poems, including some of the loveliest lyrics in the English language.

His inspired choice of words is evident in one of his miniature lyrics in *To the Virgin to Make Much of Time*:

> Gather ye rose-buds while ye may,
>   Old Time is still a-flying;
> And this same flower that smiles today,
>   To-morrow will be dying.
>
> The glorious lamp of Heaven, the sun,
>   The higher he's a-getting;
> The sooner will his race be run,
>   And nearer he's to setting.
>
> That age is best, which is the first,
>   When youth and blood are warmer;
> But being spent, the worse, and worst
>   Times, still succeed the former.
>
> Then be not coy, but use your time;
>   And while ye may, go marry:
> For having lost but once your prime,
>   You may for ever tarry.

WILLIAMSON'S TAVERN

Behind Bow Church in Grovelands Court off Bow Lane, stands Williamson's Tavern in a 17th century house which has seen many alterations over the years. The original house, a victim of the Great Fire of 1666, was rebuilt in 1688, and served as the official residence of the Lord Mayors of London until the Mansion House was built in 1752. A stone in the parlor marks the center of the City.

The historical importance of this old structure is that it once belonged to Sir John Falstaff, immortalized by William Shakespeare as one of the world's great comic characters.

THE WINDMILL TAVERN

The Windmill on Old Jewry was originally a synagogue in 1262. When Edward I banished all the Jews from England in 1290, it became a house of friars, then a nobleman's house, followed by the Lord Mayor's house and finally a wine tavern in the early 1500s.

This old tavern played a role in 1628 which contributed to an unfortunate incident. John Lambe, an astrologer and fortune teller, was very disliked because of his close connections with the unpopular Duke of Buckingham. Many people felt that Mr. Lambe was the cause of some strange disturbances in the weather. Upon leaving the Fortune Theatre one evening, he was attacked by an angry mob and sought refuge in the Windmill Tavern. The frightened landlord refused and pushed him out into the street where he was beaten to death by the mob.

Cromwell permitted the Jews to return in 1657; they settled in Jewry Street, formerly Poor Jewry.

AREA D

FLEET STREET

AND

THE TEMPLE

AREA D ATTRACTIONS

AREA D MAP

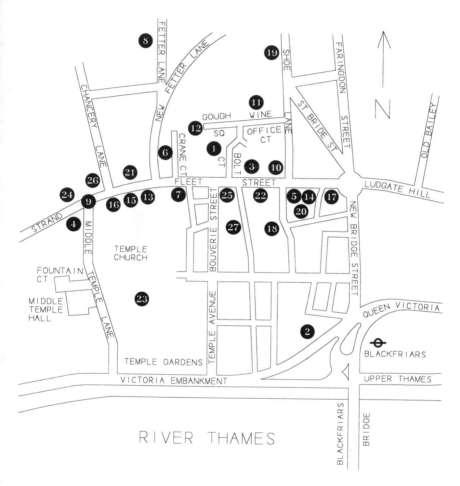

UNDERGROUND STATION

BOLT COURT

Bolt Court on Fleet Street derives its name from the old coaching inn, The Bolt-in-Tun, on the opposite side of the street. The inn provided hospitality for travelers from the 15th century to 1883, when it was demolished.

In 1776, Dr. Johnson took up residence at No.8 on the far corner and remained there until his death in 1784. The house was destroyed by fire in 1819. Johnson was doubly honored in death with burial in Westminster Abbey and a commemorative statue in St. Paul's Cathedral.

A Quaker physician, Dr. John Coakley Lettsom, lived at No.3 Bolt Court which still remains. He always signed his prescriptions with the initial "J" but in the old-fashioned form suggesting an "I". A waggish rhymer circulated this epigram:

> If any folk applies to I,
>   I blisters, bleeds and sweats 'em;
> If after that they pleased to die,
>   Well, then I Lettsom.

BRIDEWELL PRISON

The Unilever House, a modern 1931 stone building, on the Victoria Embankment across New Bridge Street from the Blackfriars Underground Station, stands on part of the site of Bridewell Palace and later the infamous Bridewell Prison. The name was derived from the nearby St. Bride's Well, a spring of reputed healing powers.

Here, Henry VIII built a "stately and beautiful house" in 1522 as his royal residence. Henry invited Catherine of Aragon to dine with him in the palace on November 30, 1529, while their divorce proceedings were taking place in the nearby Blackfriars Priory. That was probably the last time Catherine saw her husband before her marriage was declared invalid by Thomas Cranmer, Archbishop of Canterbury, thus enabling Henry to marry Anne Boleyn. In his play, *Henry VIII*, Shakespeare places the two scenes of Act III in Bridewell Place.

Henry's dissolution of the monasteries and many of the hospitals during the 1530s exacerbated the problems of poverty. The streets were teeming with the unemployed, cripples and beggars. Young Edward VI, who succeeded Henry as king, was greatly moved by the situation. In 1553 he granted possession of Bridewell Palace to the Lord Mayor "to be a workhouse for the poor and idle persons of the City", a Hospital for moral, not physical, deformities.

Thus, Bridewell on December 16, 1556, became "A House of Correction and House of Occupation" to punish wrongdoers, protect neglected children and place vagrants and beggars in profitable employment. In 1557 it was placed under the same management as Bethlehem Hospital (Bedlam) and also became a house of correction for "heresies".

In 1663 a whipping post with the inscription "The Reward of Idleness", and a ducking stool with the message "Better to Work Than to Stand Idle", were installed. Twice each week crowds of Londoners flocked to Bridewell to enjoy the public floggings. With a fine sense of proportion, the floggings took place after the church service.

In addition to solitary confinement, a number of onerous tasks were added to the list of punishments. William Hogarth, the English painter and engraver, depicted the shameful horrors of Bridewell in Plate IV of his *The Harlot's Progress*.

William Congreve, Thomas Shadwell and Alexander Pope, noted English writers, all referred to the place and its pitiful occupants. A contemporary poet described the misery of the wretched females confined in that horrible prison:

> With pallid cheek and haggard eye,
> and loud laments, and heartfelt sigh,
> Unpitied, hopeless of relief,
> She drinks the bitter cup of grief.
> In vain the sigh, in vain the tear,
> Confession never enters here;
> But justice clanks his iron chain,
> And calls forth shame, remorse, and pain.

The children of prostitutes were called Bridewell Orphans.

William Shakespeare denounced the shameful abuse of authority in the fourth act of his *King Lear*:

> Thou rascal beadle, hold thy bloody hand!
> Why dost thou lash that whore? Strip thine own back;
> Thou hotly lusts to use her in that kind
> For which thou whipst her.

In 1842 over 1300 persons were confined in Bridewell, of which less than 500 were known or suspected thieves. Hepworth Dixon, in his *London Prisons*, gives a dismal picture of the conditions at that time:

> As a House of Correction for criminals, it would hardly be worse. The building itself is bad and, as it stands upon a cold, damp soil, it is far from healthy. In wet weather the doors have water trickling down them, and the air is quite humid.

This nightmare of "justice" finally came to a merciful end when the prison was closed in 1855.

THE CHESHIRE CHEESE

The present tavern, at No.145 Fleet Street, was erected in 1667, one year after the Great Fire had destroyed its predecessor. King Charles II visited the tavern accompanied by Nell Gwynn. The list of those who frequented it would include Herrick, Pope, Congreve, Steele and Addison, Johnson, Goldsmith, Garrick, Burke, Boswell, Sheridan, Reynolds, Dickens, Thackeray, Tennyson, Lamb and many others.

A rather small armchair is the seat of honor in what is called "Dr. Johnson Corner". The chair came from the Mitre Tavern, "his place of frequent resort where he loved to sit up late", according to Boswell.

A copy of Joshua Reynolds' portrait of Johnson hangs on the wall of Johnson's Corner with the following inscription beneath it:

The Favourite Seat of
DR. SAMUEL JOHNSON
Born September 18, 1709. Died
December 13, 1784.

In him a noble understanding and a
masterly intellect were united to great
independence of character and unfailing
goodness of heart, which won the
admiration of his own age, and remains
as recommendations to the reverence
of posterity.
    "No Sir! there is nothing which has
yet been contrived by man, by which so
much happiness has been produced as
by a good tavern."

It must be noted here that Boswell does not mention the tavern in his definitive biography of Johnson.

The fame of the Cheshire Cheese Tavern may be due not only to its antiquity, but to the fact that it still remains much as it existed in earlier times. Entering the tavern is like stepping back in to the past when "a tavern chair was the throne of human felicity."

In Dickens' *A Tale of Two Cities* (1859), Sidney Carton takes Charles Darney "down Ludgate Hill to Fleet Street and so up a covered way, into a Tavern" just after Darney had been acquitted of the charge of High Treason in the Old Bailey. The tavern mentioned is said, almost without doubt, to be the Cheshire Cheese. There is even a plaque there to show where they ate. Dickens allegedly used to sit at the table to the right of the fireplace, opposite the bar, on the ground floor.

In 1891 William Butler Yeats formed the "Rhymer's Club" which met in a second floor room of the Cheshire Cheese. Members included the leading poets Edward Dowson, Arthur Symons and Richard Le Gallienne. Oscar Wilde and other poets attended some of the meetings but were not regular members.

They would dine in the restaurant downstairs before adjourning to read their poetry to each other. One evening, Yeats scrutinized the company and mused: "None of us can say who will succeed or even who has or has not talent. The only certain thing about us is that we are too many."

Yeats was wrong on both counts.

In the *Forsyte Saga* (1906-28) by John Galsworthy (recipient of the Nobel Prize for Literature in 1932), Soames takes Winifred to the Cheshire Cheese for lunch.

A notice outside the tavern lists the 15 reigns during which it has been in existence, beginning with the reign of Charles II. Another sign proclaims its celebrated visitors:

Here came Johnson's friends, Reynolds, Gibbon, Garrick, Dr. Burney, Boswell and others of his circle. In the 19th century came Carlyle, Macaulay, Tennyson, Dickens, Forster, Hood, Thackeray, Cruikshank, Leech, and Wilkie Collins. More recently came Mark Twain, Theodore Roosevelt, Conan Doyle, Beerbohm, Chesterton, Dawson, Le Gallienne, Symons, Yeats and a host of others in search of Dr. Johnson's "The Cheese".

CHILD'S BANK / THE DEVIL

Child's Bank now occupies the site of the Devil Tavern which was demolished in 1788 when the bank was enlarged. A blue plaque marks the location.

The Devil Tavern at No.1 Fleet Street was one of the oldest and most famous inns on Fleet Street. It is mentioned as early as 1563. The original name was The Devil and St. Dunstan, with the signboard showing the saint holding the devil by the nose with his pincers. The devil may have been victorious because St. Dunstan was eventually dropped from the name of the tavern.

Ben Jonson began frequenting the tavern as early as 1616, when the death of Shakespeare ended the wit-combats between Jonson and Shakespeare at the Mermaid Tavern in Bread Street. Jonson wrote the play *The Devil is an Asse* after "I and my boys drank bad wine at the Devil." William Rowley's comedy, *A Match at Midnight* (1633), mentions the tavern by name. Jonson moved his residence to Fleet Street "without Temple-barre, at a combe-maker's shop" in order to be near the Devil and his beloved Apollo Club.

Jonson established the club which held its meetings at the Devil in a room called The Oracle of Apollo. The bust of Apollo presided over the room and is still preserved in Child's Bank. As late as the 18th century, Jonson's inscription hung over the door of the Apollo Club, reading in part:

> Welcome all, who lead or follow,
> To the oracle of Apollo.
> Here he speaks out of his Pottle,
> Or the Tripos, his Tower Bottle:
> All his Answers are Divine,
> Truth itself doth flow in Wine.
> Hang up all the poor Hop-Drinkers,
> Cries Old Sym, the King of Skinkers;
> He the half of Life abuses,
> That sits watering with the Muses.

("Old Sym, the King of Skinkers" referred to the landlord.)

The board on which Jonson drew up the 24 rules of the club in pure and elegant Latin is also preserved in the partner's room in Child's Bank. A few of the rules (translated) are:

12. Let the contest be rather of books than of wine;
13. Let the company be neither noisy nor mute;
14. Let none of things serious, much less of divine,
    When belly and heart's full, profanely dispute.

After Jonson's death in 1637, the Devil continued to attract such luminaries as Samuel Pepys, Sir Richard Steele, Joseph Addison, Jonathan Swift, Alexander Pope, Oliver Goldsmith, Samuel Johnson and James Boswell. The lawyers were delighted to play on the name when they left messages at their offices reading, "Gone to the Devil".

THE COGERS

This tavern, at No.9 Salisbury Court, has two claims to fame. One is that it stands on the site of Samuel Pepys' birthplace. A blue plaque attesting to this fact is on the wall of the Hindustan Times House opposite. The other is that it replaced the former tavern, The White Bear, which in 1755 was the original home of the Ancient Society of Cogers, the oldest debating society in London.

The name of the society is derived from the Latin "cotigo"—"I think", and its motto is "cogito ergo sum"—"I think, therefore I am". This became the philosophy of René Descartes (1596-1650), French philosopher and scientist, generally regarded as the father of modern philosophy.

The society was composed originally of citizens who kept an eye on political events and on their representatives in Parliament. Members are said to have included Dr. Johnson, Goldsmith, Macaulay and Dickens. A wax apple was always present on the table over which the Grand Coger presides as a symbol of discord.

The society still meets every Saturday at 7 P.M. and the subject is always the events of the week. The men only restriction was relaxed in 1968 to admit women on equal terms. Visitors are welcome and may address the group with the consent of The Grand.

CRANE COURT

From 1710 to 1780, The Royal Society met in a house at the west end of Crane Court, selected as being "in the middle of town out of the noise and very convenient for the Society." On meeting nights, Sir Isaac Newton ordered that a lamp be lit above the narrow entry from Fleet Street to welcome the members.

When The Royal Society moved to Somerset House in 1780, the Philosophical Society rented the old meeting house. Samuel Coleridge gave his course of lectures on Shakespeare there during 1819-20.

The room in which Sir Isaac Newton presided over the meetings was reverently preserved until the entire building was destroyed by fire in 1877.

EL VINO'S

A home for journalists and lawyers, El Vino's at No.47 Fleet Street maintains the atmosphere of an establishment retreat which dictates that men must wear coats and ties. The dark woods, conservative appointments, old wines and the aroma of fine cigars all serve to enhance the ambiance of a gentleman's private club.

It looks suspiciously like Pommeroy's Wine Bar frequented by Horace Rumpole and his colleagues in the television series, *Rumpole of the Bailey.*

FETTER LANE

A dull looking street today, Fetter Lane off Fleet Street was once graced by the presence of many celebrated men in history and literature. Ben Jonson and John Dryden, the playwrights, lived there for a time. Tom Paine, the American Revolutionary patriot, lived for a short period at No.77. John Wesley, founder of Methodism, held the first Watchnight services in England at the Moravian Meeting House at No.32. Charles Lamb went to school there, probably in 1871, at an academy of a Mr. Bird. Samuel Gulliver, Jonathan Swift's fictional character in *Gulliver's Travels*, was the name of the landlord of the Black Bull Tavern.

Samuel Butler, after his return from New Zealand in 1864, settled in at No.15 on the site of the oldest of the inns of Chancery. Butler wrote *Erewhon* in 1872, its sequel *Erewhon Revisited* in 1901 and the classic *The Way of All Flesh*, an embittered account of paternal tyranny in 1903.

Fetter Lane was the site of one of London's most famous gardens supervised by Dr. John Gerard, the Elizabethan naturalist. In 1596 he published a catalogue listing the 1,100 varieties of plants in his garden. William Shakespeare is believed to have been a frequent visitor to the garden where he probably gained much of the flower knowledge he so lovingly displayed in his plays. He mentions 180 different plants. In *Hamlet* he provides a blanket of flowers for Ophelia in her delirium:

> There's rosemary, that's remembrance; ... and there is pansies, that's for thoughts ... there's fennel for you, and columbines:—there's rue for you, and here's some for me;—we may call it herb-grace o' Sundays:—O, you must wear your rue with a difference.—There's a daisy: I would give you some violets, but they wither'd all when my father died.

And in *The Winter's Tale*, Perdita fashions a necklace of flowers for the king's son, Florizel:

> ... the fairest flowers o' the season
> Are our carnations, and streak'd gillyvors,

... Here's flowers for you
Hot lavender, mints, savory, marjoram;
The marigold, that goes to bed wi' the sun,
... daffodils,
That come before the swallow dares, and take
The winds of March with beauty; violets dim,
          ... pale primroses,
          ... bold oxlips and
The crown-imperial, lilies of all kinds,
The flower-de-luce being one!
          ... O, these I lack
To make you garlands of, and my sweet friend,
To strew him o'er and o'er.

FLEET STREET

The name of this "tippling street" is derived from the Fleet River, now an underground sewer. It has been synonymous with journalism since 1825, when the first newspaper was published on Fleet Street, giving it the nickname of The Street of Ink. The first great journalists were Daniel Defoe, Joseph Addison, Sir Richard Steele, Samuel Johnson and Oliver Goldsmith.

The street was the home of those who made a living by writing, publishing or selling books, plays or articles. It has a longer association with literature than any other place in London.

In a sense, Fleet Street is the most famous thoroughfare in all of London. When you walk down the street, history walks with you. If we could conjure up the great spirits that still haunt that place, we would see Dr. Samuel Johnson, its most famous resident, walking with James Boswell or Oliver Goldsmith as:

> A queer old figure, stout, stooping, ungainly in his plain brown suit with black worsted stockings and none too clean linen. He belonged to Fleet Street and it to him.

Richard B. Sheridan, the playwright, recorded a guest's description of Johnson's approach:

> I perceived him at a good distance, walking along with peculiar solemnity of deportment, and an awkward sort of measured step. At that time ... stone posts were in fashion to prevent the annoyance of carriages. Upon every post, as he passed along, I could observe he deliberately laid his hand; but missing one of them, when he had got some distance, he seemed suddenly to recollect himself, and immediately returning back, carefully performed the accustomed ceremony, and resumed his former course.

G.K. Chesterton (1874-1936) with the same burly figure, wearing his flamboyant cloak and swordstick, followed in Johnson's tradition by visiting one tavern after another, from The Cock to El Vino and The Cheshire Cheese.

Fleet Street's numerous inns and taverns were a necessary feature. They were the meeting places for all sorts and conditions of men to gossip, to read the news sheets, to write letters, or indite dedications to lordly patrons. Many of the taverns and coffee houses had a literary flavor and were cherished havens for the leading men of letters. Some of them, like the celebrated Cheshire Cheese, have preserved, almost unaltered, the external characteristics of an earlier day.

THE GLOBE

An interesting old tavern, The Globe, used to stand at No.134 Fleet Street, close to Shoe Lane. It existed from early in the 17th century until recent times. In the 18th century, it was the headquarters for many clubs such as the Wednesday Free And Easy Club, one of Oliver Goldsmith's favorites. Washington Irving, in his *Life of Goldsmith*, writes:

Another of those free and easy clubs met on Wednesday evenings at The Globe. It was somewhat in the style of the three Jolly Pigeons; songs, jokes, dramatic imitations, burlesque parodies and broad sallies of humor formed a contrast to the sententious morality, pedantric casuistry, and polished sarcasm of the learned critic .... Johnson used to be severe upon Goldsmith for mingling in the motley circles, observing that, having been originally poor, he had contracted a love for low company. Goldsmith, however, was guided not by a taste for what was low, but what was comic and characteristic.

Edward Purdon, a regular customer of the tavern, was the subject of one of Goldsmith's best known epigrams:

Here lies poor Ned Purdon, from misery freed,
    Who so long was a bookseller's hack;
He had led such a damnable life in this world
    I don't think that he'll wish to come back.

GOLDSMITH'S HOUSE

Irish born Oliver Goldsmith (1730-74), one of the great literary figures of the period, was in turn a strolling player, an actor, a bookseller's clerk, a chemist's assistant, a medical practitioner and a hack writer before he finally found success with his book, *The Vicar of Wakefield*. This was followed by a number of celebrated works, principally *The Good-Natured Man, The Deserted Village* and *She Stoops to Conquer*.

In 1760 Goldsmith moved to No.6 Wine Office Court, a place memorable for the completion of *The Vicar of Wakefield*. No.6 is gone, but Nos.1-3 of the same period still stand. Dr. Johnson paid his first call on Goldsmith on May 31, 1761, and succeeded in getting the book published by coming to his rescue when Goldsmith was on the verge of financial ruin and despair. Johnson wrote:

> I received one morning a message from poor Goldsmith that he was in great distress, and it was not in his power to come to me, begging that I would come to him as soon as possible. I sent him a guinea, and promised to come to him directly. I accordingly went as soon as I was drest, and found that his landlady had arrested him for his rent, at which he was in a violent passion. I perceived that he had already changed my guinea, and had got a bottle of Madeira and a glass before him. I put the cork to the bottle, desired he would be calm, and began to talk to him of the means by which he might be extricated ... . He then told me that he had a novel ready for the press, which he produced to me [*The Vicar of Wakefield*]. I looked into it, saw its merit; told the landlady I should soon return, and having gone to a book seller, sold it for sixty pounds ... . I brought Goldsmith the money, and he discharged his rent, not without rating his landlady in a high tone for having used him so ill.

Goldsmith was a happy go lucky and improvident man. Destitute until his first success with *The Vicar of Wakefield*, he was overly generous in sharing his good fortune, with the result that he knew poverty more often than affluence. Although described as "in wit a man, in

simplicity a child", and characterized by Horace Walpole as " the inspired idiot", he had faith in human nature which, though often
abused, was never shaken.   While on a grand tour of Europe, he
quickly lost all his money gambling in Leyden. He completed the tour
relying for support mainly by playing his flute on street corners for
pennies.

Goldsmith may have been no match for Johnson, who was in-
clined to be overbearing and harsh. He said "there is no arguing with
Johnson, for when his pistol misses fire, he knocks you down with the
butt end of it."   However, he often gave as good as he got.   When
Johnson laughed at him for saying that little fishes in a proposed fable
should talk like little fishes, he quickly retorted, "Why, Dr. Johnson,
this is not so easy as you seem to think, for if you were to make little
fishes talk, they would talk like whales."

Boswell quotes another example of Goldsmith's wit:

One evening, in a circle of wits, he found fault with me for
talking of Johnson as entitled to the honour of unquestion-
able superiority.   'Sir, you are for making a monarchy of
what should be a republic.'

He was an eccentric, but his innate goodness and generosity en-
deared him to many. His quaint incongruities found expression in his
clothes, his finances, his social habits, as well as his conversation.
Macaulay was a little hard on him when he wrote:

… when he [Goldsmith] talked he talked nonsense and made
himself the laughing stock of his hearers. He was painfully
conscious of his inferiority in conversation; he felt every
failure keenly; yet he had not sufficient judgment and self-
command to hold his tongue …. His first thoughts on every
subject were confused but they required only a little time to
work themselves clear. When he wrote they had that time,
and therefore his readers pronounced him a man of genius
…

Dr. Johnson admitted that Goldsmith played the fool in his conversations; nevertheless, he said, "no man was more wise when he had
a pen in his hand."

Goldsmith is probably best remembered for the song in *The Vicar of Wakefield*, describing the emotional plight of a woman betrayed, which reflects the morality of the 18th century:

> When lovely woman stoops to folly
> And finds too late that men betray,
> What charm can soothe her melancholy,
> What art can wash her guilt away?
> The only art her guilt to cover,
> To hide her shame from every eye,
> To give repentance to her love,
> And wring his bosom—is to die.

The same situation, had it occurred in the 20th century, is paraphrased by the poet T.S. Eliot in *The Waste Land*:

> When lovely woman stops to folly and
> Paces about her room again, alone,
> She smoothes her hair with automatic hand,
> And puts a record on the gramaphone.

JOHNSON'S HOUSE

From 1748 to 1759, Dr. Samuel Johnson (1709-84) lived at No.17 Gough Square off Fleet Street, one of some 13 addresses he listed as his home, most of them near Fleet Street and the Strand.

The house, double fronted and quite imposing, was probably built early in the 18th century. Badly damaged in World War II, the house was lovingly restored and reopened in 1948. It is now a museum containing some of Johnson's manuscripts and letters, a few of his personal belongings and fine portraits of Dr. Johnson, James Boswell and other contemporaries.

Dr. Johnson and his six assistants labored in the long garret at the top of the house to complete the *Dictionary of the English Language*. He had expected to finish it in three years, but it took eight years of painful toil and dogged persistence. The garret may still be seen.

Johnson had a long-running feud with Lord Chesterfield which was characterized, for example, by his statement that the Chesterfield *Letters* "teach the morals of a whore, and the manners of a dancing master." The quarrel culminated in Johnson's celebrated letter of February 7, 1755, in reply to Chesterfield's too long delayed request to be a patron on the eve of publication of the Dictionary:

Is not a Patron, my Lord, one who looks with unconcern on a man struggling for life in the water, and, when he has reached ground, encumbers him with help? The notice which you have been pleased to take of my labours, had it been early, had been kind; but it has been delayed till I am indifferent, and cannot enjoy it; till I am solitary, and cannot impart it; till I am known, and do not want it.

Johnson's well known fondness for ridiculing Scotland and its citizens furnished him with numerous opportunities for barbed witticisms. When Boswell met Johnson for the first time, he was concerned with Johnson's reaction to his Scottish heritage and apologized, "I do, indeed, come from Scotland, but I cannot help it." Johnson quickly replied, "That, sir, I find is what a very great many of your countrymen cannot help." On another occasion, Johnson said, "The noblest prospect which a Scotchman ever sees is the high road that leads him to England."

In Johnson's dictionary, he defined Oats as "A grain, which in England is generally given to horses, but in Scotland supports the people."

Johnson was the quintessential Londoner. He could not conceive of anyone wanting to live anyplace else. He said to Boswell:

> The intellectual man is struck with it [London] as compre-hending the whole of human life in all its variety, the con-templation of which is inexhaustible. ... I will venture to say there is more learning and science within the circumfer-ence of ten miles from where we now sit, than in all the rest of the kingdom. ... Why, Sir, you find no man at all intel-lectual, who is willing to leave London. No, Sir, when a man is tired of London, he is tired of life; for there is in London all that life can afford.

Famous as lexicographer, essayist, critic and king of conversa-tionalists, he was the literary dictator of his time. His classical reac-tion to English romanticism retarded the course of realism, with only Robert Burns and William Blake able to avoid his authority.

His dictionary definitions are often prejudicial and incorrect; nevertheless, it is of great historical importance as a record of the lan-guage in the 18th century. His greatest work was *The Lives of the Poets* (1779-1781), comprising 52 poets, a monument to English criticism.

No Englishman of letters is as thoroughly known as Samuel Johnson due to the idolatry of one man, James Boswell, who wrote what is considered to be the greatest biography in the English lan-guage: *The Life of Johnson*. There is much truth in Macaulay's remark that "Boswell's book had done for him [Johnson] more than the best of his own books could do."

THE MITRE

A plaque on the west corner of Old Mitre Court, at Nos.34-39 Fleet Street, commemorates The Mitre, a tavern of great antiquity, as having been located on this site. The first known reference to the tavern was in 1603, when a complaint was made in connection with the back way from the Mitre providing the patrons a way of escape from the law:

> ...that there is a door loading out of Ram Alley [now Hare Place] to the tenement called the Miter in Fleet-streete, by means whereof such persons as do frequent the house upon search made after them are conveyed out that way.

As with most memories of Fleet Street, Dr. Johnson's name springs to mind. According to Boswell, Johnson preferred the Mitre to any other tavern. Boswell's biography of Johnson contains many references to the Mitre.

It was in that venerable inn that the tour to the Hebrides was decided upon; where Johnson introduced Goldsmith into his celebrated circle; and where Johnson entertained two young ladies on the subject of Methodism. Boswell quotes Johnson saying:

> "Come my pretty fools, dine with Maxwell and me at the Mitre, and we will talk over the subject"; which they did, and after dinner he took one of them on his knees, and fondled them for half an hour together.

It was of the Mitre that Boswell wrote:

> We had a good supper, and port wine, of which he [Johnson] sometimes drank a bottle. The orthodox high-church sound of the Mitre—the figure and manner of the celebrated Samuel Johnson—the extra-ordinary power and precision of his conversation, and the pride arising from finding myself admitted as his companion, and a pleasing elevation of mind, beyond what I had ever experienced.

The Society of Antiquaries sometimes held their meetings at the Mitre. The Royal Society chose it for their annual dinner in 1772. In

1778, four years after Johnson's death, the Mitre closed its doors. Afterwards, the building became the Poets' Gallery and later the Auction Rooms. It was finally demolished in 1829 to make room for the enlargement of Hoare's Bank.

The Clachan, the modern pub on the site of the Mitre, has preserved Johnson's "corner". A copy of Nollekens' well know bust of Johnson had been given an honored place. The empty wine cellar of the old Mitre lies under the Clachan.

THE OLD BELL

From 1670-84, Sir Christopher Wren was busy rebuilding St. Bride's Church which had been destroyed in the Great Fire of 1666. To provide for his workmen, the Old Bell tavern was constructed nearby at No.95 Fleet Street.

The tavern has had a long association with the printing trade. It underwent many changes in name and ownership. When it was known as The Swan, Wynkyn de Worde, successor to William Caxton, the first English printer, published some of his books there. Part of the old cellarage still exists.

The rear entrance on St. Bride's Avenue enables customers to drink their beer in the churchyard.

YE OLDE COCK TAVERN

The original tavern, The Cock and Bottle, existed as early as 1655 on Fleet Street at No.201, where the Law Courts branch of the Bank of England now stand.

The tavern survived the Great Fire of 1666. There on April 13, 1668, Samuel Pepys entertained Mrs. Knipp, the actress, of whom his wife was not unreasonably jealous. His diary entry for that date reads:

> By water to the Temple, and thence to the Cock Ale house, and drank and eat a lobster, and sang and mighty merry.

Dr. Johnson, Thackeray and Dickens were some of the illustrious Londoners who often frequented the Cock. However, it was Lord Tennyson who made the tavern famous when he sang its praises in *Will Waterproof's Lyrical Monologues* in 1842:

> O plump headwaiter at the Cock,
> To which I most resort,
> How goes the time? 'Tis five o'clock.
> Go fetch a pint of port.

The old tavern was destroyed in 1887 to make room for a branch of the Bank of England. It was reopened on the south side of the street at No.22 in the following year, having dropped the Bottle from its name. Relics of the celebrated tavern are preserved in the present inn.

The new building includes a replica, on the first floor, of one room of the old tavern. The old sign, believed to have been carved by Grinling Gibbons, is displayed in the bar, along with one of the original Jacobean mantels. A large picture inside the entrance portrays the Fleet Street that existed before the Temple Bar was removed.

PRINCE HENRY'S ROOM

This room, constructed at No.17 Fleet Street to the left of Inner Temple Lane in 1610, was named after King James I's son. Originally a tavern, The Prince's Arms, it became the council chambers for Prince Henry.

The front room is paneled in Georgian and Jacobean oak throughout. The unique plaster ceiling, with the three-feathers emblem of Prince Henry in the middle, is enclosed in a star shaped border accented by the letter H. The beautiful stained glass windows overlook Fleet Street.

PUNCH TAVERN

The magazine, *Punch*, was known throughout the world for its irreverent criticisms of events of national importance, tempered by a high level of genuine wit and humor. In 1841, a group of free spirits first conceived the idea of a magazine to criticize events and puncture the balloons of pompous officials. Mr. Punch, who symbolized a little man fighting against unjust authority, was appropriately honored in naming the magazine after him.

Punch had offices at No.99 Fleet Street for many years before moving to Whitefriars Street. The Punch Tavern commemorates the association and is located nearby. The atmosphere in the tavern is pure Victorian, sporting the Pickwick Lounge and Saloon Bar. The *Spy* cartoons on display are alone worth a visit.

In the 1840s and 1850s, the contributors to *Punch* met at No.10 Bouverie Street and dined at a large deal table called The Mahogany Tree. Thomas Hood's celebrated *The Song of the Shirt* was first published by *Punch* in 1843.

SALISBURY SQUARE

Salisbury Court leads to Salisbury Square, where the Salisbury Court Theatre was built in 1629. A plaque nearby commemorates the theater.

From 1629-31, the King's Revels mounted plays there. They were followed by Prince Charlie's Men from 1631-35 and the Queen's Men from 1637-42. During the Commonwealth (1649-60), when the playhouses were ordered closed, plays continued to be illegally performed until the interior was destroyed by government soldiers in 1649.

Upon the re-establishment of the monarchy in 1660 under Charles II, the Salisbury Court Theatre was one of the first playhouses to reopen. On September 9, 1661, Samuel Pepys attended a play and recorded the following in his diary:

> And thence to Salisbury Court Playhouse where was acted for the first time, *'Tis a pity she's a Whore*, a simple play and ill acted, only, it was my fortune to sit by a most pretty and ingenious lady which pleased me much.

The theater was destroyed by the Great Fire of 1666 and was not rebuilt.

James Boswell, Samuel Johnson's biographer, records the first meeting of Dr. Johnson and William Hogarth, the celebrated painter and engraver, at the office:

> ... [Hogarth] perceived a person standing at a window in the room, shaking his head and rolling himself about in a strange, ridiculous manner. He concluded that he was an idiot, whom his relatives had put under the care of Richardson. To his great surprise, however, the figure stalked forward ... and all at once took up the argument .... He displayed such a power of eloquence that Hogarth looked at him in astonishment and actually imagined that this idiot had been at the moment inspired.

The house was demolished in 1896.

SHOE LANE

Richard Lovelace, Royalist poet and Cavalier, a great favorite at court, lived in abject poverty on the west side of Shoe Lane, off Fleet Street, for several years before his death in 1658.

Imprisoned several times, his biographer, Anthony à Wood, wrote:

> ... having consumed all his estate, he grew very melancholy (which brought him at length into a consumption), became very poor in body and purse, and was the object of charity, went in ragged clothes (whereas, when he was in his glory, he wore cloth of gold and silver), and mostly lodged in obscure and dirty places, more befitting the worst of beggars than poorest of servants.

Anthony à Wood also said that Lovelace was "the most amiable and beautiful person that eyes ever beheld." There is little doubt that this was so for "one of the Queen's retinue in the court of Charles I at Oxford University in 1636 was so taken by the poet's appearance, innate modesty, virtue, and courtly deportment that she persuaded the University chancellor, Archbishop Laud, to incorporate Lovelace as an M.A. two years early."

Lovelace is remembered by many for the last two lines of his poem, *To Lucasta, Going to the Wars*:

> I could not love thee, dear, so much
> Loved I not honour more.

But his best known and loved poem is *To Althea, from Prison*, which he wrote while imprisoned in 1642 in the Westminster Abbey Gatehouse because of his royalist sympathies. The last stanza reads:

> Stone walls do not a prison make,
> Nor iron bars a cage;
> Minds innocent and quiet take
> That for a Hermitage;
> If I have freedom in my love,
> And in my soul am free;

Angels alone that soar above
Enjoy such liberty.

The poem remains today, but the stone walls at the Abbey Gatehouse are long gone. Sir Richard Lovelace was buried in the old St. Bride's Churchyard across the street.

ST. BRIDE'S CHURCH

William Rich, a pastry cook in the late 1700s, modeled his wedding cakes after the steeple of St. Bride's Church on Fleet Street, and ever since bakers have followed his example. But a poet, looking through different eyes, saw the 226 foot steeple, the tallest of all the Wren churches, as "a madrigal in stone."

The original church was dedicated in 1153 to St. Bride, or St. Bridget, a sixth century Irish saint, and Abbess of Kildare, who befriended the aged St. Patrick. Wynkyn de Worde, follower of William Caxton, the first English printer, was buried before the high altar of St. Katherine in the old church in 1534. He bequeathed £36 to provide a funeral service on each anniversary of his death. That day has been long forgotten and unobserved.

Samuel Pepys, the famous diarist and son of a tailor, was born in nearby Salisbury Court overlooking the churchyard. He was baptized in the old church in 1633 as were his eight brothers and sisters.

Richard Lovelace, the poet, was buried in the churchyard in 1658. Six years later, in 1664, Samuel Pepys' brother, Thomas, was buried in St. Bride's. The entry in Pepy's diary reads:

March 18, 1663—To church, and, with the grave-maker, chose a place for my brother to lie in, just under my mother's pew. But to see how a man tombes are at the mercy of such a fellow, that for sixpence he would, as his own words were, 'I will justle them together but I will make some room for him'; speaking of the fulness of the middle aisle, where he was to lie.

The Great Fire of 1666 destroyed the church; only the marble font of 1615 survived. Sir Christopher Wren began plans for a new church in 1678, which was completed in September 1703. Samuel Richardson (1689-1761), father of the English novel, whose works are all but forgotten today, was buried in the nave in July 1761 under a flat stone merely recording his name, year of death and age. No further burials were permitted after February 1849.

In 1710, a set of ten bells were cast for the church, with two treble bells added in the following year. On January 19, 1724, a peal on 12 bells was heard in England for the first time. A writer once put his affection for the bells into a poem:

> Bells of St. Bride, wheresoever I be,
> My heart in the night-time must travel to thee;
> They may say it is Cockney, and what not besides,
> But I ne'er shall forget thee, Sweet Bells of St. Bride's.

Over and above its fascinating architecture, St. Bride's fellowship with the great names in English history and literature creates a unique appeal. John Milton, one of England's greatest poets, lodged for a time in 1639 in St. Bride's Churchyard at the house of a tailor named Russel. Thomas à Becket (1118-1170), Archbishop of Canterbury, who was murdered because of his opposition to King Henry II, was born close by. King John held parliament in the church in 1210.

Living within 100 yards or so of the church in the 17th century were Dryden, Milton, Waller, Lovelace, Walton, Aubrey, Ashmole, Pepys and Evelyn. A couple of generations later, another select company living in the immediate vicinity included Johnson, Boswell, Garrick, Reynolds, Goldsmith, Burke, Addison, Blackstone, Pope, Hogarth, Mrs. Siddons and Richardson. These were followed by still another celebrated group comprising Lamb, Hazlitt, Wordsworth, Keats, Hood and Hunt. Subsequently, Dickens was to observe the area with his journalistic eye and George Gissing would lay a depressing scene in his story, *Day of Silence*, in St. Bride's.

The Wren church was gutted by bombing in 1940 and completely restored in 1957. Within the church the American press is honored with a memorial plaque.

Glyn Jones has painted the east end of the interior in a *trompe l'oeil* style (creating the illusion of reality), simulating a high, vaulted roof.

During the excavations after the 1940 bombing, Saxon, Celtic and Roman remains were uncovered. These fragments of some 1,000 years of unrecorded history are exhibited in the Undercroft and are open to the public. Other items in the Crypt illustrate St. Bride's long association with Fleet Street and the printing trade.

ST. DUNSTAN-IN-THE-WEST

One of the three churches of Fleet Street, St. Dunstan-in-the-West is relatively modern, having replaced the previous church in 1831. Various churches have stood on this site since 1237. The name was intended to distinguish it from another church, St. Dunstan-in-the-East, dedicated to the same saint, located between Tower Street and Lower Thames Street. That church was badly damaged in 1941 and only the shell remains.

The statue of Queen Elizabeth I, modeled during her lifetime and now over the schoolhouse entrance, was originally on Ludgate before the gate was demolished in 1760. In a wooden temple on the outside of the church, a clock with wooden figures of two giants striking bells each quarter-hour became the best known clock in London. It was modeled after a similar structure in the Piazza San Marco in Venice.

Oliver Goldsmith, in his *Vicar of Wakefield* (1766), has Mrs. Thornhill saying:

Strike me ugly, if I should not find as much pleasure in choosing my mistress by the information of a lamp under the clock of St. Dunstan's.

William Cowper wrote in *Table Talk* (1782):

When labour and when dulness, club in hand,
Like the two figures at St. Dunstan's stand,
Beating alternately in measured time
The clock work tintinnabulum of rhyme,
Exact and regular the sounds will be,
But such mere quarter-strokes are not for me.

The eight bells in the tower, which belonged to the previous church, were the chimes of Charles Dickens' Christmas story, *The Chimes* (1845). He also has David Copperfield and his aunt, Betsy Trotwood, stopping to watch the jacks of the clock strike noon.

Samuel Pepys, the diarist, visited old St. Dunstan's when Reverend John Thompson was vicar. Pepys' attention was so occupied by two pretty modest maids with whom he tried to ingratiate himself, that he could hardly have paid much attention to the able sermon he professes to have heard in his diary entry of August 18, 1667:

> ... walked towards Whitehall, but being weary, turned into St. Dunstan's Church, where I hear an able sermon from the minister of the place. And stood by a pretty, modest maid whom I did labour to take by the hand and the body, but she would not, but got further and further from me, and at last I could perceive her to take pins out of her pocket to prick me if I should touch her again; which seeing I did forbear, and was glad I did espy her design. And then I fell to gaze upon another pretty maid in a pew close to me and she on me; and I did go about to take her by the hand, which she suffered a little and withdrew. So the sermon ended and the church broke up, and my amours ended also; and so took coach and home.

A tablet in the entrance porch and a stained glass window in the chapel commemorate Izaak Walton, writer and vestryman of the parish, whose first wife was buried in the churchyard. The window shows Walton standing with some of those he immortalized in his *Lives*. William Wordsworth paid a graceful tribute to him:

> The feather, when the pen
> was shaped that traced the lives of these
> good men,
> Dropped from an Angel's wing.

On the wall beneath the window is a plaque to George Calvert, Lord Baltimore (1580-1632), founder of Maryland USA, who was buried in the old church. There is also a memorial to an unusual man: one Hobson Judkin, Esq., described as "the honest lawyer."

SWEENY TODD'S

The story, as told in the old "penny-dreadful" magazines, was that Sweeney Todd, the mad barber at 186 Fleet Street, slit the throats of his customers, and his partner in crime, Mrs. Lovett, turned the corpses into meat pies that she sold along Fleet Street.

A British journalist, Peter Haining, published a book in 1979, *The Mystery and Horrible Murders of Sweeney Todd, the Demon Barber of Fleet Street*, in which he concluded that no convincing proof exists that Todd was a real person. Nevertheless, Todd has become a legend in Britain, with its roots in a murder of the mid-1780s that occurred on Fleet Street near the place where his shop is believed to have existed, across the way from the *Cheshire Cheese*.

The Sweeney Todd story first appeared as a serial in the November 1846 issue of *The People's Periodical and Family Library*, a so called "penny dreadful" read by the large mass audience of 19th century industrial England. The serial was titled, *The String of Pearls*, and delighted its readers with 37 chapters in 18 issues.

In 1847, a dramatized version, *The String of Pearls or the Fiend of Fleet Street*, was a smash hit on the stage of London's Brittanic Theatre, a haven for 19th century melodrama. According to Charles Dickens, in his *Uncommercial Traveler*, the "immense theatre was capable of holding nearly 5,000 people."

In 1973 a play by Christopher Bon, *Sweeney Todd*, opened in London's East End. That play was the basis for the Sondheim-Prince musical, *Sweeney Todd, the Demon Barber of Fleet Street*, which opened for a successful run in New York, USA, on March 1, 1979.

Sweeney Todd has taken his place alongside Jack the Ripper and the Yorkshire Strangler; serial killers who have shocked and fascinated generations of Englishmen.

THE TEMPLE

If Fleet Street had nothing to show but the Temple, it would be reason enough to immortalize it.

Entering through the 1684 gateway of the Middle Temple Lane, one of Wren's happiest efforts, the uproar of Fleet Street is dissolved and one is transported into a leafy oasis of tranquillity with the peace and quiet of long forgotten time. Almost 200 years ago, an American writer, Washington Irving, described his discovery of this magical spot in his *Sketch Book*:

> I had been buffeting for sometime against the current of population setting through Fleet Street .... The flesh was weary, the spirit faint ... when in a fit of desperation I tore my way through the crowd, plunged into a by-lane, and after passing through several obscure nooks and angles, emerged into a quaint and quiet court with a grass-plot in the centre, overhung by elms, and kept perpetually fresh and green by a fountain with its sparkling jet of water ... . I was like an Arab, who had suddenly come upon an oasis amid the panting sterility of the desert. By degrees the quiet and coolness of the place soothed my nerves and refreshed my spirit.

Charles Lamb was born in the Temple and called it "the most elegant spot in the metropolis." Thackeray, who had lived in the Temple, conjured up this vision in *Pendennis*:

> Sir Roger Coverley walking in the Temple gardens and discussing with Mr. Spectator [both fictionalized characters] about the hoops and patches who are sauntering over the grass, is just as lively a figure to me as old Samuel Johnson rolling through the fog with the Scotch gentleman at his heels, on their way to Dr. Goldsmith's in Brick Court, or Harry Fielding, with inked ruffles and a wet towel round his head, dashing off articles for the *Covent Garden Journal* while the printer's boy is asleep in the passage.

The mystic atmosphere of the Temple was never better described than by Charles Dickens in his *Barnaby Rudge*:

There are still worse places than the Temple, on a sultry day, for basking in the sun, or resting idly in the shade. There is yet a drowsiness in its courts, and a dreamy dulness in its trees and gardens; those who pace its lanes and squares may yet hear the echoes of their footsteps on the sounding stones, and read upon its gates in passing from the tumult of the Strand or Fleet Street, 'who enters here leaves noise behind.'

The Knights Templars, original inhabitants of the Temple, founded a religious and military order in Jerusalem in the 11th century to protect Christian pilgrims on their way to the Holy Land. Their first home in London, known as the Old Temple, was established in Chancery Lane early in the 12th century. Later, about 1160, they acquired the present quarters, known as the New Temple, on the banks of the Thames.

The wealth of the Knights Templars proved irresistible to the envious monarchs and the Pope dissolved the Order in 1312. The Temple passed into the hands of the crown and later to the Knights Hospitallers of St. John, who leased it to the students of the common law. It is now occupied by two of the Inns of Court, the Inner Temple and the Middle Temple, and tenanted principally by lawyers.

The Inns of Court have been the four principal non-corporate law societies of England since the 14th century. They are the Inner Temple, the Middle Temple, Lincoln's Inn and Gray's Inn, all located in close proximity. They consist of halls of learning, libraries, chambers for barristers and quadrangles of residential flats occupied, for the most part, by people in the legal profession.

After the clergy was forbidden by law to appear as advocates in the secular courts, or to lecture on law outside of the monasteries, the Inns became the great schools of law. Students training to become barristers are educated in history and music as well as law. The Inns have the exclusive privilege of admitting persons to practice at the bar, and to rent chambers to members of the bar. This practice is not only a valuable source of revenue, but serves to centralize the locations of the offices of the barristers to within the four Inns of Court. Legal study is not required for residence in the Temple.

The Temple, with its concentration of lawyers' offices, provided an irresistible subject for Dickens to show his contempt for the legal profession in *The Pickwick Papers*:

Scattered about, in various holes and corners of the Temple, are certain dark and dirty chambers, in and out of which ... there may be seen constantly hurrying with bundle of papers under their arms, and protruding from their pockets, an almost uninterrupted succession of Lawyer's Clerks ...

These sequestered nooks are the public offices of the legal profession where writs are issued, judgments signed, declarations filed, and numerous other ingenious machines put in motion for the torture and torment of his Majesty's liege subjects, and the comfort and emolument of the practitioners of the law ...

The records of the Temple include some of the most illustrious names in English history. The Inner Temple may boast that its students have been Edward Coke, John Selden, Francis Beaumont, William Wycherley, James Boswell, John Forster, Thomas Hughes and Sir Compton Mackenzie.

The Middle Temple can proudly name among its students Sir Walter Raleigh, John Ford, Thomas Carew, John Evelyn, John Aubrey, Thomas Shadwell, William Congreve, Nicholas Rowe, Henry Fielding, Sir William Blackstone, Edmund Burke, William Cowper, R.B. Sheridan, Thomas De Quincy and W.M. Thackeray.

Many other famous persons who either lived in the Temple or had close connections with it would include Thomas Middleton, Samuel Johnson, Robert Southey, Anthony Hope Hawkins, G.K. Chesterton, as well as many others. Charles Lamb's association with the Temple was almost continuous from his birth at No.2 Crown Office Row on February 10, 1775 until he finally moved away in 1817.

The Middle Temple trained many of the founders of the United States. Five of its members signed the Declaration of Independence—Edward Rutledge, Thomas Heyward, Jr., Thomas Lynch, Jr., Arthur Middleton and Thomas McKean.

Six of its members signed the Constitution in its final form: William Livingstone, Governor of New Jersey; Jared Ingersoll, Pennsylvania Attorney General; John Blair, Supreme Court Justice; John Rutledge, Governor of South Carolina; Charles Pickney, Minister to Spain; and Charles Cotesworth Pickney, Minister to France.

More than 100 additional members of the Middle Temple were instrumental in helping the Colonies achieve a free and independent country.

FOUNTAIN COURT

Fountain Court opens to the right of Middle Temple Lane and embraces the north wall of Middle Temple Hall.

The original fountain, for which the Court was named, was constructed in 1681 and fully restored to its original glory in 1919. Charles Lamb fondly recalls the fountain:

> ... which I have made to rise and fall, how many times! to the astonishment of the young urchins, my contemporaries, who, not being able to guess at its recondite machinery, were almost tempted to hail the wondrous work as magic!

In his essay, *Old Benchers of the Inner Temple*, Lamb laments the removal of fountains from numerous locations, as they are considered childish. He pleads:

> Why not gratify children by letting them stand? Lawyers, I suppose, were children once .... Why must everything smack of man, and mannish? Is the world all grown up? Is childhood dead? Or is there not in the bosom of the wisest and the best some of the child's heart left, to respond to its earliest enchantments.

(Benchers are senior members of an Inn of Court, who constitute the body charged with the management of its affairs).

Charles Dickens was also charmed by the fountain, which he described in *Martin Chuzzlewit*:

> Brilliantly the Temple fountain sparkled in the sun, and laughingly its liquid music played, and merrily the idle drops of water danced and danced, and in sport among the trees, plunged lightly down to hide themselves ...

The fountain was the setting, in the same novel, where John Westlock wooed Ruth Pinch, and Ruth blushed:

to a terrible extent beneath her brown bonnet. They had no more to do with the fountain, bless you, than they had with—with love, or any out of the way thing of that sort.

Dickens also includes the fountain in two other novels, *Barnaby Rudge* and *Great Expectations*. The water still flows in the fountain at the center of the court.

MIDDLE TEMPLE HALL

A stately example of Tudor architecture, Middle Temple Hall, "a treasure beyond price", can still be seen on the south side of Fountain Court.

Opened in 1576 by Queen Elizabeth I, the hall is 100 feet long, 40 feet wide and nearly 50 feet high. The hammer-beam roof with its numerous pendants is the finest of the period in all of England. German incendiary bombs during World War II could not ignite the ceiling's carved oaken beams.

The table, over 29 feet long, on which silver plate is displayed on special occasions, is believed to have been made from oak from Windsor Forest as a gift from the Queen. The serving table in the middle of the hall is said to have been fashioned from the timbers of Sir Francis Drake's ship, the Golden Hind. Another treasure of the hall is one of the first known pair of English globes. They bear the date of 1592.

A perfect Renaissance carved screen, stained glass windows with the arms of notable members of the Middle Temple, trophies of armor associated with the Earl of Leicester, glass lights bearing the coat of arms of Elizabeth I, Raleigh and Drake—all combine to create the ambiance of the Elizabethan period.

Above all, the hall is notable because we know that Shakespeare's play *Twelfth Night* was performed here on February 2, 1602, probably its first performance. Shakespeare himself may have played a part in the drama. The information was recorded in the diary of John Manningham, a barrister of the Middle Temple. This is especially significant because the hall is thus honored as being the only existing building in which an Elizabethan play was originally performed.

The diary was discovered at the British Museum in 1878. Under the date 2nd Feb, 1602, he wrote:

At our feast wee had a play called "Twelve Night or What You Will," much like the Commedy of Errores .... A good practice in it to make the Steward beleeve his Lady widowe was in love with him, by counterfeyting a letter as from his Lady in generall termes, telling him what shee liked best in him, and prescribing his gesture in smiling, his appairaile, & c., and then when he came to practise, making him beleeve they took him to be mad.

Shakespeare specifically mentioned the hall in one of his plays, *Henry IV, Part 1*, when Prince Hall remarks to Falstaff: "Jack, meet me tomorrow in the Temple Hall."

INNER TEMPLE GARDENS

For centuries the Inner Temple Gardens were famous for their red and white roses. According to tradition, the gardens were the location of the famous scene in Shakespeare's *Henry VI, Part 1*, (1430) when the red and white roses became the symbols for the Wars of the Roses.

In that play, the dispute as to the right of succession began in the Temple Hall and continued in the gardens between the rival partisans of York and Lancaster:

Plantagenet

Let him that is a true-born gentleman,
And stands upon the honour of his birth,
If he suppose that I have pleaded truth,
From off this brier pluck a white rose with me.

Somerset

Let Him that is no coward nor no flatterer,
But dare maintain the party of the truth,
Pluck a red rose from off this thorn with me.

The quarrel intensifies with further caustic remarks by the two protagonists:

Plantagenet

Hath not thy rose a canker, Somerset?

Somerset

Hath not thy rose a thorn, Plantagenet?

Warwick temporarily ends the quarrel with a gloomy prophecy:

> ... this brawl today,
> Grown to the faction, the Temple-garden,
> Shall send, between the red rose and the white,
> A thousand souls to death and deadly night.

And this scene in the Temple Gardens advances in its inexorable chronicle from the death of Henry V to its final resolution in Bosworth Field.

A memorial to Charles Lamb was placed in the center of the gardens in 1930. The stone figure of a boy holds a book; on the open pages are these words from Lamb's essay, *Old Benchers of the Inner Temple*: "Lawyers were children once."

In his *Pendennis*, Thackeray also reminisces about the gardens:

> Fashion has long deserted the green and pretty Temple garden in which Shakespeare makes York and Lancaster to pluck the innocent white and red roses which became the badge of their bloody wars ... fancy ... dear Oliver Goldsmith in the summer house, perhaps meditating about the next *Citizen of the World* .... Treading heavily on the gravel, and rolling majestically along in a snuff-colored suit ... one sees the great Doctor step up to him ... and ask Mr. Goldsmith to come home and take a dish of tea with Miss Williams. Kind faith of Fancy!. Sir Roger and Mr. Spectator [imaginary characters] are as real to us now as the two doctors and the boozy and faithful Scotchman.

The white and red roses still bloom in this historic garden.

THE TEMPLE CHURCH

One of London's hidden treasures, the Temple Church, is the largest of the five remaining round churches existing in England—built eight centuries ago in imitation of the round church of the Holy Sepulchre in Jerusalem. The church was given to the Inner

Temple and the Middle Temple by King James I in 1608 with the proviso that they were to maintain it and its services forever. This they have done ever since. The area known as The Temple derives its name from the church.

After Jerusalem was captured from the Mohammedans in the First Crusade in 1099, a group of knights named themselves the Knights Templars because their headquarters were on the site of King Solomon's Temple. They appointed themselves protectors of pilgrims; upon returning home to England, they built their own round churches to celebrate their triumph and dedication.

The Temple Church is primarily the lawyers' private chapel, but is normally open to the public. It has no parish, is not subject to the authority of the Bishop of London, and comes directly under the Sovereign as Head of the Church of England. An inscription inside the entrance door states that on February 10, 1185, the church was dedicated in honor of the Blessed Mary by the Lord Heraclius, Patriarch of the church of the Holy Sepulchre. This was the circular portion of the church; the oblong addition forming the choir was not completed until 1240.

Architecturally of the Transitional style, it is part Norman and part Gothic in design. The church escaped the Great Fire of 1666, but not the blitz of May 10, 1941, when it suffered considerable damage. However, painstaking restoration returned it to its former glory.

Between the arches around the aisle wall are Charles Lamb's "grotesque gothic heads that gape and grin, around the inside of the old Round Church .... They are intended to represent souls in heaven as well as in hell—but they all appear to be in hell."

The 16th Century tomb of Edmund Plowden, who died in 1584, stands at the entrance to the north aisle. He was Treasurer of the Middle Temple and supervised the building of the great Elizabethan Middle Temple Hall in 1572.

Nine medieval effigies of deceased crusaders, dating from the 12th and 13th centuries, recline in full armor on the stone floor in the round portion of the church. All lie with their heads to the East. Some of the figures are cross-legged, but historians do not agree that it necessarily denoted their presence at the Crusades.

In the northwest corner of the choir, a door leads to the gallery stair which opens to the Penitential Cell of Templar times. Two split windows look into the church. Knights who disobeyed the Master, or broke a Rule of the Temple, were subject to solitary confinement in this grim chamber measuring less than five feet long—too short to permit the penitent to lie down. Walter le Bacheler, Grand Preceptor of Ireland, was one of those unfortunates who died in that confinement.

Samuel Pepys, according to his diary, attended services at the church on at least five different occasions. He also bought the latest songs from John Playford's music shop which once stood against the porch. Sir Christopher Wren married his first wife in the church in 1669. Charles Lamb was baptized in the church in 1775.

Washington Irving, in his *Sketch Book,* was deeply affected by his visit to the Temple Church:

> I was, in fact, in the Chapel of the Knights Templar, strangely situated in the very center of sordid traffic, and I do not know a more impressive lesson for the man of the world than thus suddenly to turn aside from the highway of busy money-seeking life, and sit down among these shadowy sepulchres, where all is twilight, dust and forgetfulness.

The "sordid traffic" of the world is even more with us now than in Irving's day some 200 years ago.

The Famous Battle of the Organs played out in the Temple Church. In 1873, Father Smith and Ranatus Harris were invited to erect competing organs in the church. The contest dragged on for five years with the decision finally being made by Judge Jeffreys, as Lord Chancellor, in favor of Smith. The organ was entirely destroyed in the heavy bombing of 1941.

During the reign of James I from 1603 to 1625, the round portion of the church became a loitering ground for the unsavory inhabitants of neighboring Alsatia. To solve the problem, the door between the Inner Temple and Whitefriars was closed. The Alsations, however, attempted to remove the barrier and engaged in a pitched battle with the students, resulting in at least two deaths. The King's guards were called and many of the Alsations found themselves in prison. The leader of the rioters was executed in Fleet Street opposite Whitefriars.

The lawyers used the church for meetings with their clients, until the 17th century. This desecration of the church was specifically mentioned by Ben Jonson in *The Alchemist,* Thomas Middleton in

Father Hubbard's Tales, Samuel Butler in *Hudibras* and by Thomas Otway in *The Soldier's Fortune*.

A long, low stone on the Middle Temple side of the upper level of the churchyard is inscribed, "Here lies Oliver Goldsmith, 1728-1774." The exact place in the Temple churchyard of his burial on April 9, 1774, is unknown but probably nearby. The church was the closest burial ground to his chambers at No.2 Brick Court, where he spent the closing years of his beloved, ingenuous life.

When he lay dead in his chambers, as John Forster relates in his *Life of Goldsmith*, the staircase was filled with mourners, outcasts whom Goldsmith in his generous, large hearted life had befriended:

> women without a home, without domesticity of any kind, with no friend but him they had come to weep for, outcasts of that great, solitary, wicked city, to whom he had never forgotten to be kin and charitable …. When Edmund Burke [statesman and orator] was told that Goldsmith was dead, he burst into tears; and when the news reached Sir Joshua Reynolds in his Leicester Square painting-room, he laid his brush aside—a thing he had not been known to do even in times of great family distress—left his study and entered it no more that day.

Characteristically, in death as in life, Goldsmith died penniless and in debt. In a letter to Bennet Langton, Samuel Johnson wrote: "let not his frailties be remembered; he was a very great man."

The remains of the poet were scarcely cold, when his friends decided to honor him by a public funeral and a tomb in Westminster Abbey. This noble resolve cooled down, however, when they discovered that Goldsmith had died in debt and no money was available to pay for such expensive funeral rites. On April 9, five days after his death, he was privately interred in the burying ground of the Temple Church. None of the mourners attending the service included any of his distinguished friends.

It may have been feelings of guilt that moved Goldsmith's friends to provide an appropriate memorial. Two years after his death, the Literary Club established a fund by subscription to erect a monument to his memory in Westminster Abbey. It proved to be a simple bust of the poet in a medallion, sculpted by Nollekens, placed over the south door in Poets' Corner between the monuments of John Gay and the Duke of Argyle.

Samuel Johnson supplied a Latin epitaph which he refused to change to common English because, in his own words, "he never would consent to disgrace the walls of Westminster Abbey with an English inscription."

The Latin epitaph stands inscribed on a white marble tablet beneath the bust. In translation, it begins:

<u>OF OLIVER GOLDSMITH</u>

A Poet, Naturalist, and Historian,
Who left scarcely any style of writing
Untouched,
And touched nothing that he did not adorn.

The peace of the Temple is enhanced by centuries thick layers of age and privacy. It is astonishing how the clamor outside is dimmed within this ancient sanctuary, a fixed point in a tortuous universe.

TEMPLE BAR

The Temple Bar Memorial, with statues of Queen Victoria, Edward VII as Prince of Wales and a bronze griffin, marks the eastern end of the Strand and the official entrance to the venerable City of London. Erected in 1672, the memorial is all that remains of the last Temple Bar, which was removed in 1878 as a traffic obstacle. Charles Dickens, in *Bleak House* (1853) denounced it as "a leaden-headed old obstruction."

A barrier of some kind to identify the boundary between the City and Westminster existed as far back as the 12th century. Its purpose was to control entrance to the City by undesirables, to extract tolls and commercial fees and, most of all, to protect the City's independence and power.

After the Great Fire of 1666, Christopher Wren designed a new Bar in 1672, to replace the old wooden structure. A sturdy and large arched building completely straddled the street and its gates effectively barred the way for all travelers approaching the wall. Spikes on top of the gates exhibited the heads and limbs of executed felons and traitors. The interior was large enough to be both a prison and a storehouse.

As a memorial to the City's power, the new structure had a significance which even today is officially observed by the Crown. A reigning monarch intending to visit the City is required to obtain permission to enter. The picturesque ceremony has the Lord Mayor presenting the City sword to the sovereign who generously returns it and receives the necessary consent to pass. There is no record of any Lord Mayor refusing to honor a monarch's request, but at least once the gates were closed against the citizens themselves during the notorious Wilkes and Liberty Riots in 1769 when The Battle of Temple Bar took place.

Child's Bank, the oldest bank in London, occupied the upper story of Wren's Temple Bar. Its earliest customers included Nell Gwynn, Samuel Pepys, John Dryden and Oliver Cromwell. In 1859 Charles Dickens described the interior of Child's Bank, which he called Tellson's Bank, in his *A Tale of Two Cities* as:

an old-fashioned place, even in the year one thousand seven hundred and eighty ... very small, very dark, very ugly, very incommodious .... After bursting open a door of idiotic obstinacy with a weak rattle in the throat, you fell into Tellson's down two steps, and came to your senses in a miserable little shop, with two little counters, where the oldest of men made your cheque shake as if the wind rustled it, while they examined the signature by the deepest of windows, which were always under a shower-bath of mud from Fleet Street, which were made the dingier by their own iron bars proper, and the heavy shadow of Temple Bar.

THE TIPPERARY

The Tipperary Tavern at No.66 Fleet Street, occupies the site of an old coaching inn, The Bolt-in-Tun, which belonged to the White Friars as far back as 1443. During the early part of the 1800s, the inn was the London end of the coaching services provided to Bath. The proprietor's name was Moses Pickwick.

Charles Dickens was very observant and since he spent a great deal of time in this area, he no doubt used the name for one of his immortal characters. The old inn is commemorated across the street at Bolt Court.

WALTON'S HOUSE

The Museum of London has a model of a house which stood on Fleet Street just two doors from Chancery Lane during the years from 1624 to 1799. That house belonged to Izaak Walton, one of the most beloved of all English writers.

Izaak Walton (1593-1683) was a linen-draper as well as vestry-man at the nearby church of St. Dunstan-in-the-West, where John Donne was rector from 1624 to 1631. Donne later became Dean of St. Paul's Cathedral and Walton, his good friend, wrote his biography, *Life of Donne* (1640), as well as several other books. But his most appealing and enduring work was *The Compleat Angler*, published in 1653 at St. Dunstan's Churchyard.

Walton roamed along the rivers and streams with a fishing rod, studying the unspoiled ways of nature. His simple love of the natural scenery, including the plants and animals, is embodied in that book, considered by many to be one of the most charming and ingenuous books ever written.

Charles Lamb, writing to his friends Samuel Coleridge and William Wordsworth, calls the book

> … so old a darling of mine … the delight of my childhood. The dialogue is very simple, full of personal beauties …. It breathes the very spirit of innocence, purity and simplicity of heart. It would sweenen a man's temper at any time to read it …. Issak Walton hallows any page in which his revered name appears.

In 1922, a group of outdoorsmen interested in the conservation of woods, waters and wildlife, organized a non-profit society. They named it the Izaak Walton League, dedicated to follow his philosophy of outdoor life as expressed in his writings, notably *The Compleat Angler*. The League has working chapters in almost every state in the United States, with headquarters in Chicago, Illinois.

There are at least two inns commemorating Walton's famous book, *The Compleat Angler*. One is located at Marlow-on-Thames in England, another is at Essex in Montana's Glacier National Park in the United States.

WHITEFRIARS STREET / ALSATIA

Whitefriars Street , opposite Gough Square and off Fleet Street, takes its name from a colony of Carmelites, an order of the White Friars. In 1241 Sir Richard Grey founded a house of Carmelites on land granted by King Henry III. The large priory extended from Fleet Street, adjacent to the Temple, all the way to the Thames.

The order was dissolved in 1538, and by 1545 the church was destroyed. The right of sanctuary where fugitives from justice were immune from arrest in churches and other sacred places, had been granted by King James I in 1608. It was abolished in 1697 by an Act of Parliament.

The place abounded with criminals of every description, the haunt of thieves and murderers in one of the most vicious and depraved slums in all of London. The quarter was described by a contemporary as "filled with reeking dens and drunken bawds and every house a resort of ill-fame, men and women lost to every instinct of humanity." It was difficult and dangerous for officers of the law to attempt arrests or serve warrants. Years after sanctuary was removed, the area retained its nefarious reputation.

Macaulay said that:

> … at any attempt to extradite a criminal, bullies with swords
> and cudgels, termagant hags with spits and broomsticks
> poured fourth by the hundreds and the intruder was fortunate
> if he escaped back to Fleet Street, hustled, stripped and
> jumped upon.

This crime infested area was known as Alsatia, a slang name associated with the French Alsace, long notorious for its internal strife and political dissension. Alsatia was a prime subject for many writers: Shadwell's *Squire of Alsatia*, Scott's *The Fortunes of Nigel* and Ainsworth's *Jack Sheppard*. Macaulay wrote about Alsatia in his *History* and Scott refers to it in *Kenilworth*.

On the east side of Whitefriars Street is the strangely named Hanging Sword Alley, where Jerry Cruncher of Dickens' *A Tale of Two Cities* had lodgings and from which he made his nightly raids as a body snatcher. The street was once known as Blood Bowl Alley from the notorious tavern named the Blood Bowl House. William Hogarth, in Plate IX of his *Industry and Idleness* series, shows the Idle Apprentice being arrested in a cellar in Blood Bowl House near Fleet Street, having been betrayed by his whore.

AREA E

ST. PAUL'S CATHEDRAL

AND

BLACKFRIARS

AREA E ATTRACTIONS

AREA E MAP

APOTHECARIES' HALL

Blackfriars Lane, north of Queen Victoria Street, is graced by the charming Apothecaries' Hall, dating partly from 1670 and partly from 1786. It occupies ground which was once in the precincts of the Blackfriars Monastery. At the rear is Playhouse Yard where James Burbage, an intimate of Shakespeare and fellow actor, opened his theater in 1598.

When their charter was granted in 1617, the apothecaries dispensed and sold medicines only. Before the century ended, they were also prescribing. As would be expected, the College of Physicians strenuously objected to this practice. John Dryden, the playwright, joined in the attack:

> The Apothecary tribe is wholly blind.
> From files a random recipe they take,
> And many deaths from one prescription make.
> Garth, generous as his Muse, prescribes and gives;
> The shopman sell, and by destruction lives.

The College of Apothecaries has become one of the three great medical licensing bodies for England and Wales, as well as approving candidates to compound and dispense drugs. Distinguished members whose names are household words include Tobias Smollett, Oliver Goldsmith, Edward Jenner and John Keats.

BAYNARD CASTLE TAVERN

This tavern marks the site, at No.148 Queen Victoria Street, in what is now Blackfriars, of a fortified Norman castle originally built in the 11th century by Baynard, a nobleman and follower of William the Conqueror. The castle was rebuilt many times, until finally destroyed in the Great Fire of 1666. There is a plaque at Nos.12 and 13 and a model of the castle is on exhibit in the Museum of London.

It was in the castle that the Duke of Buckingham offered the crown to the Duke of Gloucester, later Richard III, and where Richard probably plotted the murder of his two young nephews in the Bloody Tower two months later. At the time of Henry VIII's death in 1547, Sir William Herbert was appointed Keeper of the castle and became the Earl of Pembroke, father of one of the "incomparable paire" in the dedication of the First Folio of Shakespeare. Queen Elizabeth I dined with the Earl in the castle in 1559.

Three ancient paintings in the tavern deserve mention. They represent Edward the Black Prince's entrance through Temple Bar with his royal prisoner, King John of France, in 1357; arrival of a stage at an inn in the 17th century; and the procession of Elizabeth I to St. Paul's Cathedral after the defeat of the Spanish Armada in 1588.

THE BELL TAVERN

Immediately south of St. Paul's Churchyard, stood the original Bell Tavern on Carter Lane, in the vicinity of Playhouse Yard on the river side. The tavern is important in literary history because Richard Quiney, father of Thomas Quiney, Shakespeare's future son-in-law, wrote a letter to Shakespeare "from the Bell in Carter Lane, 25 October, 1598" requesting a loan of £30 to cover losses from a fire in his home in Stratford.

This letter is the only surviving piece of correspondence addressed to Shakespeare and is preserved at Stratford-on-Avon. Nothing written in Shakespeare's own hand exists.

A tablet in Carter Lane, a few steps to the east of the Choir House adjoining the Deanery, records this event. The name plate is now on a door opening into the Faraday Building.

A pub nearby at 6 Addle Hill perpetuates the name of the Bell; another pub, The Rising Sun pub at 61 Carter Lane, is close to the original location. Legend has it that the Bell may have been the nightly rendezvous of the players from the Blackfriars Theater, and perhaps of Shakespeare himself, after the performances were over.

LA BELLE SAUVAGE

As far back as 1453 a celebrated inn stood a little west of the church of St. Martin on Ludgate Hill. The original, Savage's Inn, was probably named after the proprietor, one William Savage.

In 1529 it became known as La Belle Sauvage (the beautiful savage), dedicated to the Princess Pocahontas of Virginia, the American Indian wife of John Rolfe, an English settler. They lodged at the inn in 1616 while she was received at court by Queen Anne. Unfortunately, the Princess died in the following year.

In 1554 Sir Thomas Wyatt led a force of several hundred Kentish men in a rebellion against Queen Mary. Lord Howard, in command of the royal troops, defeated the rebels, who made their last stand just in front of the inn. Wyatt's men ran away and he "sat down upon a bench outside the Bell Sauvage Yard", where he was arrested and later executed.

In the early days of the theater, strolling players performed in courtyards. La Belle Sauvage was one of the five inn yards in the City used for this purpose. Richard Tarleton (?-1588), the famous Elizabethan clown, often appeared as a player.

The Puritans were violently opposed to these activities. William Prynne, the pamphleteer (1600-1669), announced that the Devil himself once appeared during a performance of Marlowe's *Dr. Faustus*. John Aubrey, the antiquarian (1626-1697), also said that such an apparition appeared to him. The Puritans, under Cromwell, finally prevailed when all the theaters were closed from 1642 to 1656.

Until the railroad made travel by horse-drawn vehicles obsolete, the inn was an important coach station. It was Tony Weller's headquarters in Dickens' *Pickwick Papers* (1837). Part of the inn adjoined the Fleet Prison. This circumstance may have generated Mr. Weller's scheme to smuggle Mr. Pickwick from the prison inside an empty piano. Tressilian and Wayland Smith stayed at the inn in Scott's *Kenilworth* (1821).

The inn was demolished in 1873; the grounds were turned into a garden in 1967.

THE BLACK FRIAR

Across the street from the Blackfriars Station, at No.174 Queen Victoria Street, this pub was built in 1875 on the site of a 13th century Blackfriars Priory.

As the finest example of the Art Nouveau period in London, the pub glorifies the friars with wrought iron signs, copper panels, medallions and bronze bas reliefs and tableaux. White marble stonework, bronze mottos and an open coal fire all conspire to make the customer reluctant to ever leave.

BLACKFRIARS

Between Ludgate Hill and the Thames, and extending as far as the eastern end of Carter Lane, the great priory of the Blackfriars (the Dominicans who wore black habits) occupied a considerable area of ground enclosed by walls and gates.

In 1278 the friars were granted the site of Baynard's Castle to build a church, cloister, great hall and other buildings. The church, begun in 1279, was 220 feet long from east to west, the choir measuring about 95 feet. The division between the nave and the choir is represented today by Church Entry. Houses now occupy the western portion of the site in Blackfriars Lane, originally the homes of feather makers. One of the characters in Ben Jonson's play, *Bartholomew Fair*, refers to them when he asks:

> What say you to your feather-makers in the Friars that are of
> your own fraction of faith? Are they not, with their perukes
> and their puffs, their fans and their huffs, as much pages of
> Pride, and waiters upon Vanity?

The monastery was so large that Parliament sometimes met there. The divorce trial of Catherine of Aragon took place in the Great Hall in 1529. The King states in Shakespeare's *Henry VIII* that "The most convenient place that I can think of for such receipt of learning is Blackfriars", and there accordingly is fixed the trial scene in "a hall in Blackfriars."

After Henry VIII's dissolution of the religious houses during the period 1536 to 1539, Blackfriars disintegrated. In 1596 James Burbage bought an old building on the grounds and constructed the Blackfriars Theatre. It was completed in 1597 but Burbage was unable to occupy it because the residents objected to having a private theater in the area. Burbage accordingly leased the building to a company of boy actors, The Children of the Chapel Royal, of whom Rosencrantz makes a scornful allusion in Shakespeare's *Hamlet*:

> ... there is, sir, an aery of children, little eyases, that ... are
> now the fashion; and so berattle the common stages ... that

many wearing rapiers are afraid of goos-quills [satirists], and dare scare come thither.

He also hints that the boys poke fun at the older actors in their plays.

It was not until the summer of 1608 that the King's Men, successors to the Lord Chamberlain's Men, with Shakespeare as a partner were able to take over the operation of the Blackfriars Theatre. The small, entirely roofed enclosure, lit by candles and providing benches for the pit and stools in the galleries to accommodate 700 patrons proved very successful. The theater attracted a wealthier and more sophisticated audience than patronized the Globe. This permitted the company to produce subtler productions and more lavish sets.

The King's Men continued to operate the Globe Theatre, but the smaller Blackfriars Theatre could be used in all kinds of weather for night performances illuminated by candles, and thus became the Company's winter theater. Unfortunately, all theaters were closed by the Puritans in 1642; the Blackfriars Theatre was demolished in 1655. The remains of the priory, for the most part, perished in the Great Fire of 1666. Playhouse Yard commemorates the site of that famous theater where the plays of Shakespeare, Ben Jonson and Beaumont and Fletcher were performed.

The Apothecaries' Hall (1670) now occupies the site of the guest house which once housed the Emperor Charles V. Remains of the Great Hall were discovered when The Times printing office was rebuilt on part of the site. The Faraday building stands on the site of the old Court of Chancery destroyed by the Great Fire. Ben Jonson lived in Blackfriars from 1607 to 1616 and William Shakespeare bought a house in Ireland Yard in 1613.

When Charles Dickens was 12 years old, he suffered an experience so bitter and humiliating that it haunted him all his life. When his father was arrested for debt and lodged in the Marshalsea Prison on Borough High Street in Southwark, he was put to work in Warren's Blacking Factory at Hungerford Stairs where he stuck labels on blacking bottles for six months.

Dickens relives this experience as David in *David Copperfield* but he renames the factory and relocates it in Blackfriars:

Murdstone and Grimby's warehouse was at the water side. It was down in Blackfriars ... the last house at the bottom of a narrow street, curving down hill to the river, with some stairs at the end. where people took boat. It was a crazy old house with a wharf of its own, abutting on the water when the tide was in , and on the mud when the tide was out, and literally overrun with rats ... its decaying floors and staircase; the squeaking and scuffling of the old grey rats down in the cellars; and the dirt and rottenness of the place, are things, not of many years ago, in my mind, but of the present instant. They are all before me, just as they were in the evil hour when I went among them for the first time ....

David's first day at the factory was seared forever in his memory:

No words can express the secret agony of my soul as I felt my hopes of growing up to be a learned and distinguished man crushed in my bosom .... I mingled my tears with the water in which I was washing the bottles; and sobbed as if there were a flow in my own breast, and it were in danger of bursting.

Dickens himself, writing to his biographer, John Forster, years later said:

Until Hungerford Market was pulled down, until old Hungerford Stairs were destroyed, and the very nature of the ground changed, I never had the courage to go back to the place where my servitude began. I never saw it, I would not endure to go near it.

Charing Cross Station now stands where Warren's Blacking Manufactory was located.

BLACKFRIARS STATION

If a railroad station could conceivably be called romantic, that would be Blackfriars.

The names of exotic far away places carved on the Victorian facade evoke nostalgic memories of enchanted cities of the 19th century: VIENNA, NAPLES, VENICE, MARSEILLES, BADEN-BADEN, DRESDEN, ST. PETERSBURG.

Today passengers travel to less exotic destinations in Suburbia. Opened in 1886 as St. Paul's Station, it was one of the London, Chatham & Dover Rail Group of City stations. After 1937 it became largely a through station except for a few stops during peak hours.

COLLEGE OF ARMS

Thomas Stanley, first Earl of Derby, built his mansion Derby House, on the site of the present College of Arms, on Queen Victoria Street at Godliman, about 200 yards south of St. Paul's Cathedral. Shakespeare places Scene V of Act I of *King Richard the Third* in "Lord Derby's house".

Given as a gift to the College of Arms in 1555 the building was destroyed in the Great Fire of 1666. Rebuilt on the same site in 1683, probably by Sir Christopher Wren, the imposing structure possesses the most complete and valuable collection of heraldic and genealogical records in the world.

In 1576 John Shakespeare, father of the poet and dramatist, applied to the College of Arms for a coat of arms. The request was denied. Twenty years later William, now a successful and respected citizen, filed a new application for his father. This time the grant was made and John Shakespeare was officially entitled to call himself a "gentleman".

The motto on the coat of arms was "Non Sanz Droict" or Not Without Right. Ben Jonson, William's rival dramatist, ridiculed the heraldic arms and the motto in his play, *Every Man Out of His Humor*, by paraphrasing the motto as "Not Without Mustard".

THE FLEET PRISON

This notorious prison stood just north of Ludgate Circus, near the entrance to Fleet Lane on Farringdon Street, on the site of the present Congregational Memorial Hall. A plaque has been placed on the wall.

First mentioned in 1197 as a debtors' prison and for the detention of persons committed by the Star Chamber, many distinguished Englishmen found themselves involuntary guests of the Fleet. Henry Howard, Earl of Surrey (1517-1547), was imprisoned from 1542 to 1543. The English poet was executed on a trumped up charge. Thomas Nashe and Ben Jonson landed in the Fleet because their play, *Isle of Dogs* (1597), exposed many abuses being perpetrated on the public.

In 1601, the Fleet received two important historical figures. John Donne, afterwards Dean of St. Paul's Cathedral, spent some time there for having secretly married Anne More without her influential father's permission. He sent a brief note to his bride which summed up the unhappy situation in five words:

> Anne Donne,
> John Donne,
> Undone.

In that same year William Herbert, Third Earl of Pembroke, was banished from the Court and confined in the Fleet for a short time. He had angered Queen Elizabeth I over his illicit affair with Mary Fitton, one of the Queen's maids of honor. The Earl and his brother Philip were "the incomparable pair" to whom the First Folio of Shakespeare was dedicated in 1623. Shakespeare himself dedicated his sonnets to "Mr. W. H.", believed by some scholars to have been William Herbert.

William Penn, founder of Pennsylvania, USA, found himself in the Fleet from 1707 to 1709 as a result of his troublesome activities in proselytizing the Quaker faith. John Cleland was imprisoned in the Fleet for debt from 1748 to 1752. During that time he wrote his popular pornographic novel, *Fanny Hill, Memoirs of a Woman of Pleasure*, to obtain the required amount of money to purchase his release.

As London became more and more corrupt and lawless in the 18th century, some of the clergy, in collusion with the Warden of the

Fleet, devised a racket known as the Fleet Marriages. According to law, a woman who married could not be prosecuted for debt because her husband, upon marriage, assumed responsibility for all her debts. Disreputable clergymen imprisoned in the Fleet for debt were allowed out for the purpose of uniting drunken bridegrooms to unscrupulous women, without a license or even knowledge of each other's names, in pubs, brothels or filthy cellars. When the ships were in, the prostitutes had a field day initiating drunken sailors into the bonds of "holy matrimony".

Thomas Pennant, the historian, related his own youthful experience:

> I have often been tempted by the question, "Sir, will you be pleased to walk in and be married?" Along this most lawless space was hung up the frequent sign of a male and female hand conjoined, with "Marriages performed within", written beneath. A dirty fellow invited you in. The parson was seen walking before his shop; a squalid, profligate figure, clad in a tattered plaid night-gown, with a fiery face, and ready to couple you for a dram of gin or roll of tobacco.

In one four month period 2,954 Fleet Marriages took place; a single day's record was 173. Walter Besant's novel, *The Chaplain of the Fleet* (1881), describes the abuses of the Fleet Marriages.

The voracious clergymen did not sit and wait for customers to come to them; they employed touts to drum up business in adjacent streets and pubs. As vicious as this practice was, the clandestine marriages were legal and binding. The abuse was finally abolished by law with the passage of Lord Hardwicke's famous Marriage Bill in 1753. Strange as it may seem, the bill encountered violent opposition before it was finally passed.

William Hogarth, the celebrated English painter and engraver, vividly depicts the miseries of Fleet Prison in Plate VII of his series, *The Rake's Progress* (1735). Charles Dickens set scenes in the Fleet in *The Pickwick Papers* (1837) with Sam Weller, Jingle, Mrs. Bardell and Pickwick himself all confined within its walls. Dickens' intense reaction to the inhumane conditions in the prison are spoken by the Chancery prisoner in a voice which rattled in his throat:

If I lay dead at the bottom of the deepest mine in the world; tight screwed down and soldered in my coffin; rotting in the dark and filthy ditch that drags its slime along, beneath the foundations of this prison; I could not be more forgotten or unheeded than I am here. I am a dead man; dead to society, without the pity they bestow on those whose souls have passed to judgment. Friends to see me!. My God! I have sunk from the prime of life into old age, in this place, and there is not one to raise his hand above my bed when I lie dead upon it, and say, "It is a blessing he is gone!"

Dickens, speaking for himself as the narrator, boils over with indignation:

... the miserable and destitute condition of these unhappy persons remains the same. We no longer suffer them to appeal at the prison gates to the charity and compassion of the passers-by; but we still leave unblotted in the leaves our statute book, for the reverence and admiration of succeeding ages, the just and wholesome law which declares that the sturdy felon shall be fed and clothed, and that the penniless debtor shall be left to die of starvation and nakedness. This is no fiction. Not a week passes over our heads, but, in every one of our prisons for debt, some of these men must inevitably expire in the slow agonies of want, if they were not relieved by their fellow-prisoners.

Barry Lyndon in Thackeray's novel, *Barry Lyndon* (1844), found himself in Fleet Prison. In Thackeray's *Pendennis* (1848-50), Pen and Warrington go to see Captain Shandon "in the Fleet Prison ... where he is king of the place":

They went through the anteroom, where the officers and janitors of the place were seated, and passing in at the wicket, entered the prison. The noise and the crowd, the life and the shouting, the shabby bustle of the place, struck and excited Pen. People moved about ceaselessly and restless, like caged animals in a menagerie ...

They went through a court up a stone staircase, and through passages full of people, and noise, and cross lights, and black doors clapping and banging;—Pen feeling as one does in a feverish morning dream.

The Fleet Prison was rebuilt after its destruction by the Great Fire of 1666, and again by the Gordon Riots of 1780. Lord George Gordon was the leader of the No Popery riots to protest the relaxation of restrictions on the Roman Catholics. He was acquitted on the charge of high treason due to insanity; he died insane some 12 years later in Newgate Jail. A vivid description of the riots is given in Dickens' *Barnaby Rudge* (1840).

The Fleet was closed down in 1842 and demolished in 1844. One of its more than 70 prisoners had been confined for 28 years.

THE HORN TAVERN

The Horn Tavern is one of the last of the unspoiled old inns of London. Located at Nos.31-33 Knightrider Street, Charles Dickens was a regular customer. He introduced it in *The Pickwick Papers* (1837) where wine was brought from the tavern to Mr. Pickwick, incarcerated in the Fleet Prison, to celebrate the visit of Mr. Winkle, Mr. Tupman and Mr. Snodgrass:

> To these succeeded a bottle or two of very good wine, for which a messenger was dispatched by Mr. P. to the Horn Coffee-house, in Doctors' Commons. The bottle or two, indeed, might be more properly described as a bottle or six, for by the time it was drunk, and tea over, the bell began to ring for strangers to withdraw.

The street name is derived from the knights who rode their horses in it to go from the Tower of London to the jousts in Smithfield. Thomas Linacre (1460-1524), court physician to Henry VIII, founder of the Royal College of Physicians, lived in a stone house on this street.

LUDGATE

Ludgate, one of the Roman gates, was probably erected when Londinium spread westward. King Lud was evidently a mythical figure although his head is carved in the King Lud Tavern at Ludgate Circus. The first mention of the gate was early in the 12th century; when it was repaired in 1260 it bore images of King Lud and his two sons.

Ludgate Prison was erected over the Gate during the reign of Richard II (1377-99). As a young man, Stephen Forster was imprisoned there for debt. A rich widow saw him begging at a window, paid his debt of £20 and he was released. She employed him in her household and was so impressed by his character that she eventually married him. He was elected Lord Mayor of London in 1454.

In 1586 a new gate was erected with fresh images of King Lud and his sons on the East wall, and a statue of Queen Elizabeth I on the West wall. When the gate was demolished in 1760, the statues of Elizabeth and King Lud and his sons were moved to the church of St. Dunstan-in-the-West on Fleet Street.

Ludgate Circus was constructed between 1864 and 1875. Northwest of the Circus is a tablet with a bas-relief dedicated to Edgar Wallace, critic, mystery writer and dramatist:

> Edgar Wallace
>   Reporter
> Born London 1875
> Died Hollywood 1932
> Founder member of the Company
>   Newspaper Makers
> He knew wealth and poverty
> yet he had walked with kings and kept
> his bearing, and his talents he gave
> lavishly to authorship but to Fleet Street
> he gave his heart

Ludgate Hill was first mentioned in the time of Queen Elizabeth I. John Evelyn, the diarist, lived at the Hawk and Pheasant Inn on Ludgate from 1658-59. The London Coffee House at No.42, opened in 1731, was frequented by James Boswell; it later became a meeting place for a scientific club of which Benjamin Franklin and other scientists were members. It was here that Arthur Clennam, in Charles Dickens' *Little Dorrit*, sat one Sunday evening maddened by the jangling of church bells. The ground floor of the coffee house has been rebuilt, but the upper part remains unchanged.

William Hone had a shop at No.45 where he exhibited a Cruikshank etching of an imitation bank note in his window. The £ sign was shown as a noose around the necks of 11 criminals. The note, signed "For the Govt. and Comp. of the Bank of England, J. Ketch", was a protest against the large number of executions for forging £ bank notes. This created a sensation and elicited great public protests. The bank directors prudently withdrew the notes.

MERMAID THEATRE

In 1959, the dilapidated warehouse at Puddle Dock, Upper Thames Street, was converted as the first theater to be built in the City in over 300 years. This theater is not to be confused with the historic Mermaid Tavern, Bread Street, frequented by the leading playwrights, poets and wits of the 16th and 17th centuries until the Great Fire of 1666 wiped it out of existence.

The auditorium, covered by the initial tunnel vault, seats 500 for varied presentations of classics, comedies and musicals. In addition, the large complex includes two restaurants, several bars and a bookstall.

The site is a historic one, having been part of Baynard Castle, also destroyed in the Great Fire.

YE OLDE LONDON TAVERN

Using the word "famous" in its narrowest sense, this tavern is famous because it was here that a tenor named Broadhurst first broke a wine glass with a high note.

However, the word olde is deserved because the tavern dates back to 1731 when it was called The London Coffee House. It was used to house juries at Newgate Jail trials when the cases lasted more than a day. The tavern is located at No.42 Ludgate Hill.

ST. ANDREW-BY-THE-WARDROBE

Founded early in the 13th century, the name refers to its proximity to the King's Great Wardrobe on Queen Victoria Street, an office for the keepers of the king's state apparel.

The church was destroyed in the Great Fire of 1666 and completely rebuilt by Sir Christopher Wren in 1692. It was gutted by German firebombs in December 1940 with only the tower and outer walls remaining. Restored in 1961, Marshall Sisson entirely remodeled the inside so that it still gives the feeling of a newly built church.

Its importance is that the house purchased by William Shakespeare in March 1613 abutted the church on the east. The house was demolished in 1760 during the construction of the Blackfriars Bridge.

ST. AUGUSTINE-WITH-ST. FAITH

This church on Watling Street is happily remembered because of the courage of one of its residents during the German attacks on London which destroyed it in 1941.

A cat, appropriately named Faith, which had strayed into the church four years earlier, steadfastly protected her kitten in a corner of the rectory from the incessant firebombings until finally rescued. *The Times* honored the cat's bravery by prominently printing a report by the fire brigade in 1943:

Roofs and masonry exploded and the whole house blazed. Four floors fell through in front of Faith; fire and water and ruin were all around her. Yet she stayed calm and steadfast and waited for help. We rescued her in the early morning while the place was still burning and by the mercy of God she and her kitten were not only saved but unhurt. God be thanked for His goodness and mercy to our little pet.

The People's Dispensary for Sick Animals of the Poor also issued a certificate to Faith "for steadfast courage in the Battle of Britain". This was hung in the tower along with another certificate of honor presented to Faith by the Greenwich Village Human League Inc. of New York, USA.

This Wren church of 1680-87, which replaced the 12th century original destroyed in the Great Fire of 1666, was not rebuilt. Only the tower remains as part of the new St. Paul's Choir School on the site.

ST. BENET, PAUL'S WHARF

One of Sir Christopher Wren's most charming restorations is the church now known as St. Benet Guild Welsh Church on Upper Thames Street. The earlier church stood on Bennet's Hill near St. Paul's Wharf where the ships unloaded the stones and other building materials for the reconstruction of St. Paul's Cathedral. The original church was almost 600 years old when the Great Fire of 1666 destroyed it; Wren rebuilt it in 1683.

Inigo Jones, the King's architect and builder of the Banqueting House at Whitehall, was buried in the early church in 1652. His monument was destroyed along with the church. A small tablet honoring the great architect has been placed on the east wall.

Among the famous Londoners married in the church were Elias Ashmole, the antiquary, in 1638 and Henry Fielding, the novelist, who married his second wife in 1747.

The outside appearance of the church, rather like a doll's house, is appealing in red and blue brick accented by white corners with stone carvings over the windows. The interior, one of the least modernized City churches, contains most of the original paneling, carvings, monuments, stone floors and box pews.

The ancient church is undoubtedly referred to by Shakespeare in his play, *Twelfth Night*, evidently performed at the adjacent Blackfriars Theatre. The Clown says to the Duke:

> Primo, secundo, tertio is a good play, and the old saying is, the third pays for all: the triplex, sir, is a good tripping measure; or the bells of Saint Bennet, sir, may put you in mind,—one, two, three.

There are two services each Sunday in the Welsh language at the church.

ST. MARTIN

The first mention of this church was in 1174. It was dedicated to St. Martin, Bishop of Tours, who died in 397. The old church was just within the Roman Wall on Ludgate Hill, was the first curfew gate closed at night.

There was a monument in the old church to William Sevenoke. The story was that he was a foundling on the streets of Sevenoaks. Some charitable persons apprenticed him to a City grocer. He eventually became wealthy, was elected Lord Mayor of London in 1418 and founded almshouses and a free school.

The church was destroyed in the Great Fire of 1666 and rebuilt by Sir Christopher Wren in 1684, with the west wall as part of the medieval City wall. The 1673 font of white marble bears the same inscription as that in St. Ethelburga's Church:

> Cleanse my transgressions, not my
> outward appearance only.

The Reverend Richard H. Barham, author of the *Ingoldsby Legends*, died in 1845 and is commemorated by a tablet in the church's porch.

ST. NICHOLAS, COLE ABBEY

Built in 1677, this was the first City church to be rebuilt by Sir Christopher Wren after the Great Fire. It has a recorded history that goes back to the 12th century.

The church, on Queen Victoria Street, is dedicated to the patron saint of travelers and seafarers who lived in Asia Minor in the fourth century. He is believed to have saved Richard I's fleet when it encountered a terrible storm on its way to the Third Crusade in 1189. This confirmed his interest in "those in peril on the sea".

St. Nicholas is reputed to have restored the lives of three drowned children. This may account for his becoming Santa Claus through a corruption of his name.

The church was reduced to ruin by enemy bombing in 1941. Many treasures were lost, but those that survived include: a chained commentary on the Prayer Book of 1686, a fine old candelabrum, a sword rest, an early 16th century painting of the infant Jesus, a 16th century lectern brought from Rome, and a Flemish painting of 1530 of the Madonna and Child. All the Renaissance woodwork fortunately survived.

The Reverend Henry Shuttleworth, rector of the church during the late 19th century, is believed to have been the model for James Morell, the socialist priest in George Bernard Shaw's play, *Candida*, one of the outstanding character dramas in the English language.

ST. PAUL'S CATHEDRAL

The dome of St. Paul's gleamed like a beacon of hope above the smoke and flames of a burning London during World War II. Its apparent indestructibility was seen as a symbol that strengthened the determination of the beleaguered Londoners to prevail against the threat to their beloved city.

An article in *The Times* reflected the profound feelings of the people after the terrible destruction of the Sunday night raid by the German air force on December 29, 1940:

No one will ever forget their emotions on the night when London was burning, and the dome seemed to ride the sea of fire like a great ship, lifting above smoke and flames the inviolate ensign of the golden cross.

In typical English understatement, a Londoner was quoted as saying, "It meant a lot to see it there."

The first church on this Ludgate Hill site was Saxon. Built about 604, it was destroyed by fire in 1087. The second church was Norman, begun in the same year with a gift of stone from William the Conqueror and completed in 1285. It was a very large church: 585 feet long, 104 feet wide and 101½ feet high at the choir interior. The tower was 285 feet high, the height of the spire another 208 feet. The church contained many tombs, chapels, shrines and holy relics.

In 1561 the spire was struck by lighting and burned down to the tower, leaving it only half its original height. No new steeple was built; the spire of Old St. Paul's which had been the most lofty in Europe became only a memory.

The Cathedral had been built just outside the walls of the small parish church of St. Faith's, serving the people of Paternoster Row and St. Paul's Churchyard. As the Cathedral grew, it became necessary to demolish St. Faith's and, in about 1260, the parishioners were granted the right to worship in the crypt. This meant that St. Faith's carried on under the choir of the Cathedral, often compared to the position of a child in the mother's womb.

Beaumont and Fletcher, in their play *The Knight of the Burning Pestle* (1607), made Humphrey whose "bride is gone" and who had been beaten twice swear that he would in the dark:

> ... wear out my shoe-soles
> In passion, in Saint Faith's church under Paul's.

Even after its disappearance in the Great Fire, St. Faith's was still referred to in the John Crowne's play *The Married Beau* (1694):

> Our happy love may have a secret church
> Under the church, as Faith's under Paul's

Paul's Cross, often mentioned in old London history, stood at the northeast side of the choir of old St. Paul's. The cross, in very ancient times, may have marked a public meeting place. In later times, it was a pulpit with a cross on top, used chiefly for preaching. Wooden benches were built against the Cathedral wall. This open air pulpit was similar to the present Speakers' Corner in Hyde Park. Thomas Carlyle, the historian, called it "the Times newspaper of the Middle Ages."

In 1558 Queen Elizabeth I ordered a sermon of thanksgiving to be preached at Paul's Cross for the destruction of the Spanish Armada. Some of the captured flags were flown from the cathedral wall.

The names of the streets surrounding Old St. Paul's reflected the daily activities of the early black-cowled monks. On the side of the Cathedral was Creed Lane, where the monks began their processionals by reciting the Creed. They recited the Ave Maria in Ave Maria Lane, the Pater Noster in Paternoster Row and concluded their prayers at Amen Corner. Only the street names survive today.

St. Paul's Churchyard was the home of booksellers and publishers. The names and signs of numerous publishers may be found on the title pages of hundreds of Elizabethan and Georgian volumes. Londoners bought books from stalls clustered around the churchyard, the center of London's literary life.

The increasing commercial population of London required a gathering place for merchants. The nave of the Cathedral, open to everyone, was considered suitable for the conduct of miscellaneous commerce, despite its function as a house of worship. As the Durants say in their *The Story of Civilization, Part VII, The Age of Reason Begins*:

> Business men were cramped for quarters, and some used the nave of St. Paul's Cathedral as temporary offices, confident that Christ had changed His mind since Calvin; lawyers dealt with clients there, men counted out money on the tombs, and in the courtyard hucksters sold bread and meat, fish and fruit, ale and beer. Pedestrians, peddlers, coaches and carts swarmed in the narrow muddy streets.

In the Middle Ages, people had been prosecuted from time to time for selling fish in the Cathedral. Bishop Braybroke in 1560 referred to those who:

> … expose their wares as it were in a public market, buy and sell without reverence for the holy place. Others too by the instigation of the Devil do not scruple with stones and arrows to bring down birds, pigeons and jackdaws which nestle in the walls and crevices of the building; others play at ball and at other unseemly games, both within and without the church, breaking the beautiful and costly painted windows to the amazement of the spectators.

In 1411, a proclamation was made against wrestling within the sanctuary. In 1487 reference is made to a receipt for forty mares paid for in the church "at le Rode [road] by the north door." In 1530 a deed of settlement stipulated that £200 was to be paid at the font in the Cathedral. The desecration was so deep that the Common Council intervened in 1554 to prohibit, under penalty of fine or prison, the carrying of beer casks, baskets of bread, fish, flesh or fruit, or leading mules and horses through the Cathedral. In 1569 the first State lottery was drawn at the west door of the Cathedral. A royal proclamation forbidding money payments or fighting with dagger, sword or handgun within the church was also issued. Nothing seemed to make any difference; the fanaticism spawned by the Reformation resulted in the degradation of the Nave of the Cathedral into a meeting place of "cheats, assassins, thieves and prostitutes."

The interior of the Cathedral had been steadily falling into ruin. The dilapidated Norman nave, facetiously called Paul's Walk, became a market and the haunt of undesirables. It was used as a common thoroughfare for horses and mules. The chantry chapels were transformed into warehouses and wine cellars. Bishop Pilkington described the uses of the nave as:

> South side for Popery and Usury; the north for simony; and the horse-fair in the middle for all kinds of bargains, meetings, brawlings, murders, conspiracies; and the font for ordinary payments of money.

In the midst of this Bacchanalia, religious services were held in the choir.

Thomas Dekker, the dramatist, writing in *The Gull's Hornbook* about the irreverent activities in the Cathedral, said:

> What swearing is there, yea, what swaggering, what facing and outfacing! What shuffling, what shouldering, what jostling, what jeering, what biting of thumbs to beget quarrels, what holding up of fingers to remember drunken meetings, what braving with feathers, what bearding with mustachios, what casting open of cloaks to publish new clothes, what muffling in cloaks to hide broken elbows?

The plays of the old dramatists were full of references to this sorry state of affairs. Shakespeare used this scene in *Romeo and Juliet* (1594-95) and placed it in "Verona, a public place" at the beginning of the play to establish the enmity between the Montagues and the Capulets:

Sampson (servant to Capulet)

> I will bite my thumb at them; which is a disgrace to them, if they bear it!

Abraham (servant to Montague)

> Do you bite your thumb at us, sir?

and further exchanges lead to a fight between them.

Different locations in Paul's Walk were places of rendezvous. Lawyers interviewed their clients at one pillar, while another pillar was a gathering place for laborers seeking employment. It was there that Falstaff brought the dissolute Bardolph in Shakespeare's *Henry IV, Part 2* (1597-98):

> I bought him in St. Paul's, and he'll buy me a horse in Smithfield: an I could get me but a wife in the stews, I were mann'd, horsed, and wived.

Ben Jonson describes Captain Bobadill in his play, *Every Man in His Humor* (1598), a ne'er-do-well who frequented the main aisle of St. Paul's Cathedral, as a "Paul's Man". John Earle in his *Micro-cosmographia* wrote:

> Paul's Walk might be called the land's epitome ... the noise in it is like that of bees, a strange humming or buzz, mixed of walking, tongues and feet. It is a king of still roar or loud whisper.

Thomas Dekker, again in his *Gull's Hornbook*, paints a graphic picture of the microcosmic world of Paul's Walk:

> At one time, in one and the same rank, yea, foot by foot, and elbow by elbow, shall you see walking the knight, the gull, the gallant, the upstart, the gentleman, the clown, the captain, the appel-squire, the lawyer, the userer, the citizen, the rankrout, the scholar, the beggar, the doctor, the idiot, the ruffian, the cheater, the puritan, the cut-throat, the high-man, the low-man, the true-man, and the thief. Of all trades and professions some; of all countries some. Thus, whilst Devotion kneels at her prayers, doth Profanation walk under her nose in contempt of religion.

Despite the regulations of 1556 prohibiting the purchase of drinks or playing card games in the Cathedral, the atmosphere was much like that of a private club in the Elizabethan period. The man about town would routinely stop in to hear and discuss the latest news of domestic politics, minor scandals or just plain gossip. It was in just such a morally corrupt setting, like a petty court clique with idle talk and rumor as its sole interest, that Shakespeare makes King Lear, on his way to prison with his faithful daughter imagine that they will:

... hear poor rogues
Talk of Court news; and we'll talk with them too,
Who loses and who wins who's in, who's out,
And take upon's the mystery of things
As if we were God's spies ...

The final indignity was visited on the Cathedral during the Civil Wars from 1642 to 1649. The nave was used by Cromwell's army as a cavalry barracks. The porch was left to seamstresses, peddlers and other small traders. The soldiers ravaged the Cathedral, smashing windows, mutilating effigies, burning the beautifully carved woodwork and destroying the statues of James I and Charles I on the portico. The roof fell in when the scaffolding supporting the nave roof was sold and removed. By the end of the Civil War, the Cathedral had fallen into the last stages of decrepitude.

The Great Fire of 1666, which destroyed seven-eighths of the City, mercifully delivered the death blow to the sadly misused church of old St. Paul's. Samuel Pepys, the diarist, wrote that he had seen on September 7, 1666, "a miserable sight of Paul's church, with all the roofs fallen, and the body of the quire fallen into St. Faith's." The vault of the chancel had burned down into the crypt church of St. Faith's, where the booksellers and printers of the area had stored their books for safety. Not a single volume survived the fire.

The only monument not consumed was the white marble shroud of Dr. John Donne (1572-1631), the poet and divine, who had been Dean of St. Paul's for the last ten years of his life. Donne was one of the most important literary figures of the period.

After nearly five days, the fire finally burned itself out; the medieval City lay in ruins. The Guildhall, the Royal Exchange, the Customs House, six prisons, 44 City company halls, 87 parish churches, St. Paul's Cathedral and more than 13,000 houses perished. Over 250,000 persons were homeless. John Evelyn wrote that the catastrophe was "a resemblance of Sodome ... London was, but is not more." He found "old St. Paul's a sad ruine ... that beautiful Portico (for structure comparable to any in Europe) now rent in pieces." Samuel Pepys was appalled by the destruction and was sorry for the "poor pigeons which were loath to leave their houses ... till they burned their wings and fell down."

Less than a week after the fire was under control, at least six plans were submitted to Charles II (including one by Wren) for the construction of a new City of London. No plan was officially accepted because the king feared that any plan would have infringed upon the property rights of landowners, with serious repercussions which might threaten the crown.

In 1669, three years after the fire, the 37 year old Christopher Wren, Oxford University professor of mathematics and astronomy, was appointed by Charles II, Surveyor General of Royal Works. His duties were many and various, including all royal buildings existing or to be planned. However, in view of the devastation wrought by the Great Fire, Wren had the more immediate task of rebuilding the destroyed City churches. Of the 87 destroyed churches, only 52 were to be rebuilt.

The rebuilding of St. Paul's Cathedral was the most important and the most difficult. It required Wren's closest attention and greatest skill as an architect. The foundation stone was laid without ceremony on June 21, 1675. Thirty-three years later on October 20, 1708, the architect's 76th birthday, a satisfying ceremony took place when the last stone was added to the lantern by Wren's elder son, Christopher, born in the year the new Cathedral was begun. There is a legend that Sir Christopher himself was able to witness the culmination of his long effort from a basket, slung from a giant crane, which he used for inspecting progress on the Cathedral. He was the sole surviving witness to the laying of the foundation stone.

At some time between 1703 and 1706, after 25 years of debate and uncertainty, the design of the great dome was at last decided. The majestic dome 365 feet above London, crowned on top by a stone lantern weighing 850 tons by a golden ball and cross, dominates the London skyline. Below the 24 windows in the Dome is the Whispering Gallery, 100 feet above the floor, famous for its acoustics: a whisper against the wall can be heard clearly on the opposite side 107 feet away.

The new Cathedral was begun on the traditional cruciform Gothic ground plan with a long nave and choir. Wren modified this plan so that the meeting of the nave, transept and chancel aisles is circular; but the design of the nave is conventional, having a triforium and clerestory. He also decided to build the dome instead of the planned tall steeple. When he asked a laborer to find a stone to mark the exact center of the dome, he was given a fragment of a tombstone which bore the word *Resurgam* (I shall rise again). Wren carved this motto

in the pediment above the south door beneath a representation of a
phoenix arising from the flames, the symbol of resurrection.

Old St. Paul's is gone, but Wren's Cathedral is old now and rich
in associations of its own, the scene of many notable events in the nation's history. Within its walls statues, monuments, memorials and
chapels honor England's illustrious heroes. John Donne's life-size effigy has been placed on the eastern side of the south choir aisle, almost
exactly where it had stood in old St. Paul's.

As Dean of old St. Paul's, Donne wrote hymns, devout sonnets,
and one of the most famous verses in the English language:

> No man is an island entire of itself; every man is a piece
> of the continent, a part of the main. If a clod be washed
> away by the sea, Europe is the less, as well as if a prom-
> ontory were, as well as if a manor of thy friends or of
> thine own were. Any man's death diminishes me, be-
> cause I am involved in mankind, and therefore never send
> to know for whom the bell tolls; it tolls for thee.

The Crypt contains tombs, memorials and busts of great men of
the 18th, 19th and 20th centuries. The largest tomb is that of the Duke
of Wellington and his funeral car weighting 18 tons. The best known
and revered is the tomb of Lord Nelson, who rests in a coffin made
from the main mast of the French ship *L'Orient*, encased in a sarcophagus of black and white marble originally designed for Cardinal
Wolsey. The most original monument is that of Viscount Melbourne,
Queen Victoria's first Prime Minister, which represents the gate of
death in black marble with white marble angels. The chapel at the east
end, formerly called St. Faith's, was dedicated in 1960 as the Chapel of
the Order of the British Empire.

A medallion commemorating the artist-poet, William Blake
(d.1827), is inscribed with his famous lines:

> To see a World in a grain of sand,
> And a Heaven in a wild flower,
> Hold Infinity in the palm of your hand,
> And Eternity in an hour.

The ashes of Max Beerbohm (d.1956) and Walter de la Mare
(d.1956) are buried in the crypt.

Fittingly, one of the first persons buried in the crypt was Sir Christopher Wren on February 25, 1723. Wren asked for a burial "without pomp" and was interred beneath a simple stone slab. The translation of the Latin inscription reads:

Here lieth Sir Christopher Wren Builder of This Cathedral Church of St. Paul's etc. Who died in the year of Our Lord 1723 and of his age 91.

Above it his elder son ordered the engraving of a small marble tablet carrying, also in Latin, the following wording:

Below is laid the builder of this Church and City, Christopher Wren, who lived above ninety year not for himself but for the public-good. Reader, if you seek a monument, look about you. "Lector, si monumentum requiris, Circumspice." He died 25th Feb. 1723 in the 91st year of his life.

ST. PAUL'S CHURCHYARD

The churchyard behind the Cathedral, now an open garden, was a public nuisance as early as 1285 when Edward I ordered that the wall around the Cathedral be strengthened because:

> ... by the lurking of thieves and other bad people in the night time within the precincts of the churchyard, divers adulteries, homicides, and fornications had been committed therein.

In the northeast corner are the foundations of Paul's Cross, an open air pulpit where sermons were regularly preached for at least four and a half centuries from 1194, when it was first mentioned.

In 1441, during a sermon at Paul's Cross, Roger Bolingbroke, who claimed an ability to predict the future through communication with the dead, was exposed. Shakespeare refers to the charlatan in *Henry VI, Part 2* in a conversation between the Duchess of Gloster and John Hume, a priest:

Duchess of Gloster

What says't thou, man? hast thou as yet conferr'd
With Margery Jourdain, the cunning witch,
With Roger Bolingbroke, the conjurer?
And will they undertake to do me good?

Hume

This they have promised,—to show your highness
A spirit raised from depth of under-ground,
That shall make answer to such questions
As by your Grace shall be propounded him.

Bolingbroke was afterwards drawn, hanged and quartered.

In 1469 a curse was announced at the Cross upon shoemakers who made shoes with the pointed ends more than two inches high; this made it difficult to kneel for prayer. In medieval art, the devil is shown with such shoes.

As the result of a sermon by Sir Stephan, the curate of St. Katherine Cree Church at the Cross in 1517, the maypole was taken from the Church of St. Andrew Undershaft and destroyed as a heathen idol.

Elizabeth Barton, "the Holy Maid of Kent", did penance for her "revelations" against Henry VIII's divorce at the Cross in 1534 before she was executed at Tyburn. The Long Parliament ordered Paul's Cross removed in 1643.

The literary world of London came to full flower during the Elizabethan period, with the printer-publishers concentrating in St. Paul's Churchyard and vicinity. Fleet Street had been their earlier location, but St. Paul's became clearly the focus of the trade.

It was in the churchyard that most of the plays and poetry of Shakespeare, Marlowe, Jonson, Raleigh, Greene and others were printed by shops with such names as The Greyhound, The Holy Ghost, The Gunne, The Pide Bull, The Spred Eagle, The Sunne and The Foxe. Daniel Defoe's *Robinson Crusoe* was published in Paternoster Row in 1719.

John Newbery catered to children, publishing in the churchyard *The History of Little Good Two Shoes* dedicated "To all young gentlemen and ladies who are good, or intend to be good". In 1766 Francis Newbery published Oliver Goldsmith's *The Vicar of Wakefield* which contains a genuine tribute to John Newbery's heart felt goodness:

This person was no other than the philanthropic bookseller in St. Paul's churchyard, who had written so many little books for children: he called himself their friend, but he was the friend of all mankind.

It was in the churchyard that Betsey Trotwood, in Charles Dickens' *David Copperfield* (1849-50), met the mysterious man who was later discovered to be her estranged husband. The impressive Old Deanery in Dean's Court is one of the surviving remnants of Doctors' Commons, where Dickens worked as a legal reporter in 1829. Mr. Jingle obtained a marriage license there in Dickens' *Pickwick Papers* which he never got a chance to use.

STATIONERS' AND NEWSPAPER MAKERS' HALL

Founded about 1403, the Company on Ave Maria Lane was granted its charter by Philip and Mary in 1557. A stationer was construed to be a bookseller with a station or shop—not itinerant as most booksellers were of old.

Until 1911 when the Copyright Act was passed, every work published in Great Britain had to be registered at Stationers' Hall. The register of printed books kept since the beginning of the 16th century is of inestimable value, especially to Shakespeare scholars.

The previous Hall was destroyed in the Great Fire of 1666; the new Hall on the same site was completed in 1674. In 1933 the Stationers' Company was combined with that of the Newspaper Makers.

Twenty-seven Stationers became Lord Mayors of London and the members included the most famous names in the history of English publishing. Perhaps the most distinguished member was George Bernard Shaw.

The beautiful north window of the Hall pictures William Caxton, the first English printer, and King Edward IV. Other windows depict William Tyndale, theologian and translator of the Bible; Thomas Cranmer, Archbishop of Canterbury; William Shakespeare, poet and dramatist and St. Cecilia. There are a large number of portraits of prominent persons, including that of Henry Chicheley who was the Archbishop of Canterbury in Shakespeare's play, *King Henry V* (1598-99).

The entrance screen dating from the time of William III, 1689-1702, and the paneling of the Hall are fine pieces of carving. The old 17th century silver plate includes cups, a flagon, a salver, a dish and two candlesticks. The Company's barge is represented in the north window as well as by a model in the Hall; it had been one of the finest of the old Company's barges, rowed by twenty men. The barge was still in existence in 1892 when it was mentioned by William Hazlitt; its eventual fate is unknown.

A plane tree in the courtyard to the west of the Hall marks the spot where seditious books used to be burned.

AREA F

MANSION HOUSE

AND

ST. STEPHEN, WALBROOK

AREA F ATTRACTIONS

AREA F MAP

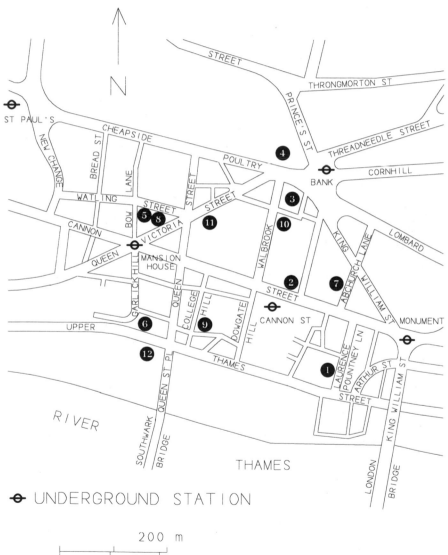

⊖ UNDERGROUND STATION

200 m

0   200 Yds

1/4 km

0   1/4 mi

LAURENCE POUNTNEY HILL

Sir John de Poulteney was Lord Mayor of London four times in the 14th century. He built his sumptuous house in the street named for him. Edward, Prince of Wales (1330-76), the Black Prince, occupied the house in 1359.

The Suffolk House stands on the site of the house known as The Rose, in which a meeting with the Duke of Buckingham takes place in Shakespeare's *Henry VIII* (1612-13). William Harvey, discoverer of the circulation of blood, came to live on the street in 1646. Nos. 1 and 2, built in 1703, are some of the finest examples of early 18th century houses in the City.

LONDON STONE

An ancient limestone relic known as London Stone, is embedded behind a grill on the outside wall of the Bank of China at No.111 Cannon Street, opposite the Cannon Street Station. Although the stone has been revered and protected for centuries, the attached plaque states that "its origin and purpose are unknown."

Some historians believe the stone to be a monolith venerated by the Celts as a sacred object. Sir Christopher Wren through it was part of a Roman building. The prevailing belief is that the stone was erected by the Romans as a miliary, or measuring point, like that in the Forum at Rome from which all distances were measured.

In maps of Elizabethan London, the stone is shown lying almost in the middle of Cannon Street. John Stow (1525-1605), the antiquarian, stated:

> ... it [the stone] was fixed in the ground very deep, fastened with bars of iron and otherwise so strongly set, that if carts do run against it through negligence, the wheels be broken, and the stone itself unshaken.

London Stone figures in Shakespeare's *The Second Part of King Henry the Sixth* when he has Jack Cade, the rebel, strike his staff on the stone and declare:

> Now is Mortimer Lord of this city. And here, sitting upon London-stone, I charge and command that, of the city's cost, the pissing-conduit run nothing but claret wine this first year of our reign.

MANSION HOUSE

Facing the south corner of the Bank of England, the Mansion House has been the official home of the Lord Mayor since its completion in 1753. Previously, the Lord Mayors conducted their affairs in their own residences.

Designed by George Dance, the Elder, the House reinforces the importance of the Lord Mayor. The principal rooms are the Egyptian Hall, which can accommodate nearly 400 guests, and the salon which displays a Waterford glass chandelier with 8,000 pieces. The House also possesses a magnificent collection of plate, swords and works of art. The Lord Mayor is the Chief Magistrate of the City and presides over a Court of Justice. Admission to the House is only by prior written authority.

Lord Mayor's Day is celebrated on the second Saturday in November when the newly elected Lord Mayor rides through the streets of the City in his gold coach, accompanied by the usual pageantry. The Lord Mayor's Banquet on the following evening in the Guildhall has the Prime Minister as one of the principal speakers.

MIDLAND BANK

The primary interest here is not the Midland Bank at No.31 Poultry, but the fact that Thomas Hood (1799-1845) was born on this site.

Of his many poems, the most celebrated was *The Bridge of Sighs* in which he mourned for the many suicides of the poor who had been exploited and dislocated by the social and industrial revolution in England:

> One more Unfortunate,
>   Weary of breath,
> Rashly importunate,
>   Gone to her death!
>
> Take her up tenderly
>   Lift her with care;
> Fashion'd so slenderly,
>   Young, and so fair!
>
> •   •   •   •   •   •
>
> Alas! for the rarity
> Of Christian charity
>   Under the sun!
> O, it was pitiful!
> Near a whole city full,
>   Home she had none.
>
> •   •   •   •   •   •
>
> Perishing gloomily,
> Spurr'd by contumely,
> Cold inhumanity,
> Burning insanity,
>   Into her rest.—

His best known poem, *The Song of the Shirt*, created a profound sensation by arousing the social conscience of the nation to the terrible living and working conditions of the poor:

With fingers weary and worn,
　With eyelids heavy and red,
A woman sat, in unwomanly rags,
　Plying her needle and thread—
Stitch! Stitch! Stitch!
　In poverty, hunger and dirt,

　　·　·　·　·　·　·　·　·　·

Work-work-work,
　Till the brain begins to swoon;
Work-work-work,
　Till the eyes are heavy and dim!

　　·　·　·　·　·　·　·　·　·

It is not linen you're wearing out
　But human creatures' lives!

　　·　·　·　·　·　·　·　·　·

Work-work-work!
　My labor never flags;
And what are its wages? A bed of straw,
　A crust of bread—and rags.
That shattered roof—this naked floor—
　A table—a broken chair—

　　·　·　·　·　·　·　·　·　·

Till the heart is sick, and the brain benumbed,
　As well as the weary hand.

　　·　·　·　·　·　·　·　·　·

And still with a voice of dolorous pitch,—
Would that its tone could reach the Rich!—
She sang this "Song of the Shirt!"

YE OLDE WATLING

Watling Street was built by the romans for free passage of their legions. This old inn at No.29 Bow Lane was destroyed in the Great Fire of 1666, but rebuilt the following year. Much of the original materials, especially the great beams, were salvaged and used in the rebuilding. The tavern was restored twice during the 20th century.

Prints of Wren's city churches and copies of old maps are displayed as a tribute to the famous architect who may have resided in the old inn while building St. Paul's Cathedral. A rule of the house is displayed, reading:

Every customer taking Alcoholic Liquor at this Counter must first be supplied with Food.

ST. JAMES GARLICKHYTHE

On Garlick Hill, on a steep cobbled street that ends at the Thames river, is the church known locally as Jimmy Garlic. The name, according to John Stow in his *Survey of London* (1598), was due to the custom that "of old time, on the bank of the river Thames, near to this Church, Garlick was usually sold."

The original church was founded in 1170 and rebuilt in 1326. It is said to be dedicated to St. James the Great, who was executed by Herod in Jerusalem. Six Lord Mayors were buried in the old church between 1341 and 1527. In 1647 the rector, Robert Freeman, was forcibly ejected by order of parliament for continuing to use the Book of Common Prayer. He regained his position at the Restoration and remained rector until his death.

The church was destroyed by the Great Fire of 1666 and rebuilt by Sir Christopher Wren in 1683, a professor of mathematics at Oxford before he became an architect. The spire is one of Wren's most graceful structures; the ceiling is the highest of the City churches.

For the last 400 years, on a Thursday in July, members of the Vintners' Company form a procession from their Hall in Upper Thames Street to the church. Preceded by two men in top hats and white smocks, carrying brooms to symbolically sweep the road, the members carry flowers as was laid down by the court in 1205:

> ... the wine porters should sweep the roads ... that the Master ... and his court of Assistants slip not on any foulness in our streets; and further, that ... each be provided with a nosegay of sweet and fine herbs that their nostrils be not offended by any noxious flavours or other ill vapours.

Other Companies, such as the Joiners', the Parish Clerks', the Painter-Stainers' and the Glass Sellers', also have their services here.

The church has some of the aspects of a museum, even possessing a perfectly preserved mummy.

ST. MARY ABCHURCH

The earliest mention of this church on Abchurch Lane was about 1198. Destroyed by the Great Fire of 1666, it was rebuilt by Sir Christopher Wren in 1681.

Some of the greatest craftsmen of the period worked on the furnishings, the font and the stonework. This is the only church with documentary evidence of the significant wood carvings by Grinling Gibbons. The painted dome is stunning, especially when lighted at night.

Harold Hutchison, author of the biography *Sir Christopher Wren* (1976), says it best:

> ... a tiny cobbled churchyard leads to an exquisite small masterpiece—a brick box with a charming lantern and delicate spire, and, inside a shallow painted dome roofing some of the finest carving in the City. The dome is 40 feet in diameter and rests on four plain brick walls without need of buttressing ...

The church is now the Guild Church of the Solicitors' Company.

ST. MARY, ALDERMARY

The earliest reference to this church on Queen Victoria Street was in 1080, which supports Stow's explanation of the name Alder that it "was older than any church of St. Marie in the City." John Milton, the renowned poet, married his third wife, Elizabeth Minshull, in the old church in 1663.

The church was destroyed in the Great Fire of 1666, except for part of the tower, and rebuilt by Sir Christopher Wren in 1681 in an unusual Tudor Gothic style. The ceiling is beautifully decorated with plaster fan vaulting consisting of saucer domes and semi-circles with a flower in the center. It is the only church ceiling comparable to that of Henry VII's Chapel in Westminster Abbey. A few carvings by Grinling Gibbons have been preserved.

Henry Gold was a rector of the church during Henry VIII's reign (1509-1547). He became entangled in the hysterical revelations of Elizabeth Barton, known as the Maid of Kent. An English tavern servant, she emerged from a mental illness declaring herself a divine prophetess. She predicted that if Henry VIII divorced Catherine of Aragon, he would not survive seven months. When this prediction proved incorrect, Barton along with six accomplices and the Reverend Gold, were executed at Tyburn in 1534.

A tablet to Percivall Pott, surgeon at St. Bartholomew's Hospital for 42 years, has been placed on the south wall of the church. He died in 1788 at the age of 75; his epitaph reads:

> He was singularly eminent in his profession, to which he added many new resources, and which he illustrated with matchless writings. He honoured the collective wisdom of past ages: the labors of the ancients were familiar to him: he scorned to teach a science of which he had not traced the growth: he rose therefore from the form to the chair. Learn reader, that the painful scholar can alone become the able teacher.

His name has been given to Pott's fracture—a type of broken ankle which he himself suffered when thrown from his horse in 1756.

ST. MICHAEL PATERNOSTER ROYAL

This church on College Hill on Upper Thames Street, dedicated to the Archangel, is inextricably bound up with the famous legend of Dick Whittington and his cat, which is still being read and enjoyed by many children.

The story goes that Dick, an orphan, decided to run away from his precarious and unpleasant existence in London. A memorial at the foot of Highgate Hill marks the reputed spot where Dick rested during his flight, wondering which way to go. He heard the bells of Bow Church begin to ring, and they seemed to be saying:

> Turn again, Whittington,
> Lord Mayor of London.

Believing it an omen, he returned to London to become a wealthy merchant, after receiving a great fortune from a Moorish king, as a reward for his cat ridding the palace of the mice and rats.

The message of the bells was indeed fulfilled when he was elected Lord Mayor of London in 1397, 1406 and 1419. He served a fourth time in 1396 by completing the term of a deceased Lord Mayor.

The name of the church requires an explanation. The word Paternoster reflects the fact that makers of rosaries lived in the immediate area. The term Royal refers to the town of La Riole, from which the local vintners imported their wine as early as 1282.

The earliest mention of the church was in 1219. Whittington provided the funds to rebuild the old church in the early 1400s. He founded an almshouse next to the church, the College of Priests a little to the north and lived in an adjoining house. He also made sizable contributions to St. Bartholomew's Hospital, Greyfriars Library and the Guildhall.

Three blue plaques are in close proximity on College Hill. One says that Dick Whittington was four times Lord Mayor of London and founded the church of St. Michael Paternoster, Royal; another states that the house next door belonged to him; and the third marks the site of the Duke of Buckingham's house in 1672.

Dick Whittington died on March 4, 1423 and was buried in the church not once, but three times. After the original burial by his executors, Stow says that Thomas Mountain, the rector in the reign of Edward VI (1547-53), had Whittington's tomb broken into to find the great riches supposed to have been buried with him. Finally, in the reign of Queen Mary (1553-59), his body was wrapped in lead and buried for the third and last time ... "and so he resteth", said Stow.

Peter Blundell, founder of the famous Devonshire School at Tiverton, familiar to readers of *Lorna Doone*, was buried in the church in 1601. John Cleveland, the Cavalier poet, was buried here in 1658.

The church was destroyed in the Great Fire of 1666 and rebuilt in 1694 by Edward Strong, Sir Christopher Wren's master mason, under Wren's supervision. In 1949 the rector, Canon Douglas, initiated a search for Whittington's tomb without success. However, a mummified cat was found.

One of the beautiful stained glass windows at the west end of the church depicts young Dick Whittington in a cap with his cat at his feet.

ST. STEPHEN WALBROOK

Behind the Mansion House, the Wall Brook ran a little west of the street bearing the name of this church. A tablet marks the site of the first church on the other side of the stream during the reign of Henry I (1068-1135), son of William the Conqueror. The church, re-erected on its present site in 1439, was destroyed by the Great Fire of 1666.

From 1672 to 1679 Sir Christopher Wren replaced the old church with what many believe to be a minor masterpiece of interior design. The exquisitely proportioned semi-circular dome is considered to have been an experiment by Wren in preparation for the greater dome of St. Paul's Cathedral. The interior with the richly coffered dome, balanced on eight arches carried by the same number of slender Corinthian columns and supported side vaultings, are an unexpected surprise.

The north wall contains a memorial tablet to Nathaniel Hodges, a physician who wrote a treatise on the Plague and worked tirelessly to arrest it. He was probably the inspiration for Daniel Defoe's Dr. Heath, so devoted to duty at such a difficult time, in his *A Journal of the Plague Year* (1722). Dr. Hodges became reduced to poverty and imprisoned in Ludgate Debtor's Prison, where he died in 1688. The tablet bears the following translation of the Latin inscription:

> Take heed of all thy days, O mortal man,
> > for time steals on
> With furtive step. Death's shadow flits
> > across the sunniest hour,
> Seeking to prey 'mong all who mortal
> > are.
> He is behind thee; and even though
> > breath be in thee
> Death has marked thee as his own.
> Thou knowest not the hour when Fate
> > shall call thee.
> E'en while this marble thou regardest,
> > time is irrevocably passing.
> Here lies in his grave Nathaniel Hodges,
> > Doctor of Medicine

Who while a child of Earth lived in hope
of Heaven.
He was formerly of Oxford, and was a
survivor of the Plague
Born, September 13 A.D. 1629
Died 10th June 1688.

Sir John Vanbrugh, dramatist and architect, was buried here in 1726 without a memorial.

TEMPLE OF MITHRAS

An authentic Roman temple occupies the forecourt of the modern Bucklersbury House in the area formed by Queen Victoria Street, Cannon Street and Walbrook.

While preparing the foundations for the Bucklersbury House in 1954, workmen uncovered the remains of a stone temple 18 feet below ground level. The original Temple of Mithras (90-350 A.D.) is believed to have been a basilica 60 feet long and 20 feet wide. It contained the heads of the gods Mithras, Minerva and Serapis, the latter the Egyptian god of the Underworld.

These heads are now displayed in the Museum of London.

THE VINTNERS' HALL

Dealers in wine had a long history prior to their incorporation in 1437, which granted them almost complete power over the wine trade. The Vintners' Company was virtually the sole licenser of inns and taverns.

For many years afterwards, the Company was harassed by numerous attempts to reduce its power. In the reign of Edward VI (1547-53), the number of inns and taverns were limited by statute, and justices were given the authority to grant and renew licenses. Further inroads were made by Queen Elizabeth I (1559-1603) who granted monopolies to court favorites. Robert Devereux, the unfortunate Earl of Essex, obtained the majority of his income from such a monopoly of sweet wines.

However, the Vintners retained the ancient privilege that 15 freemen of the Company had the right to sell wine without a license. Elizabeth complained about the increased number of irregular taverns resulting from the fraudulent exercise of this privilege by some unscrupulous freemen. Michael Sadleir refers to this practice in his novel *Fanny by Gaslight* (1940):

> There were so-called Supper Houses—every second house in Bow Street and Brydges Street and Phoenix Alley was one—which were unlicensed yet sold drinks freely. They used to pay some Free Vintner to paint his name over the door, and then, if ordered to show a licence, said they were employed by such and such a Free Vintner and need not have one.

The Vintners' Hall of the 15th century, between Thames Street and the river, was destroyed by the Great Fire of 1666. Rebuilding on the old foundations at the corner of Anchor Alley, near Queen Street Place, was completed in 1671.

Beginning in 1271, there were many notable Vintners who became Lord Mayors of London. Sir Thomas Bloodworth was Lord Mayor from 1665-66 and his conduct on September 2, 1666 during the Great Fire is criticized by Samuel Pepys in his *Diary*:

... the King commanded me to go to my Lord Mayor [Sir Thomas Bloodworth] from him, and command him to spare no houses, but to pull down before the fire every way .... At last met my Lord Mayor in Canningstreet, like a man spent, with a hand-kercher about his neck. To the King's message, he cried, like a fainting woman, "Lord! what can I do? I am spent: people will not obey me. I have been pulling down houses; but the fire overtakes us faster than we can do it." That he needed no more soldiers; and that, for himself, he must go and refresh himself, having been up all night. So he left me, and I him, and walked home; seeing people all almost distracted, and no manner of means used to quench the fire.

Sir Gilbert Heathcote, Bart., Lord Mayor 1710-11, was ridiculed by Alexander Pope in his *Imitation of Horace* for his stinginess. Brackley Kennett, Lord Mayor 1779-80, appears briefly in Charles Dickens' *Barnaby Rudge* (1840) in connection with the Gordon Riots.

The swans living on the river Thames are considered the property of the Crown, the Dyers' Company and the Vintners' Company. This division existed as early as 1509, appearing in the accounts of the Master and Wardens now in the British Museum.

During July, when the young swans or cygnets are two months old, the three Swan Markers representing the Monarch, the Vintners and the Dyers assemble at Vintry Wharf. Proceeding up the Thames on their week's journey, the markers nick the birds in the upper mandible—one nick for the Dyers' birds, two nicks for the Vintners' birds and no nicks for the Crown's birds.

The ceremony of the Loving Cup by the wine porters is an annual custom. An article in the newspaper describes the proceedings:

The ceremony of the Loving Cup is common to all City Livery Companies, but its origin is not always understood. When the loving cup passes, there must always be three standing so that the one who is holding the cup and is thus defenceless is fully protected; the one behind him should be standing back to his back, that his sword arm be free, and the one in front holds aloft the cover of the Cup in his right hand.

The custom arose from the murder nearly 1,000 years ago of Edward the Martyr, who was stabbed in the back while drinking. All good Vintners consider it the foulest crime in history.

The Hall possesses a valuable tapestry of 1466, fine plate of 1518, a hearse cloth of 1539, a Delft tankard of 1563 and a painting of St. Martin by the School of Rubens.

A statue in Coade stone of a Vintry Ward schoolboy of 1840 survives in Vintner Lane.

AREA G

BEDLAM

AND

CROSBY SQUARE

AREA G ATTRACTIONS

AREA G MAP

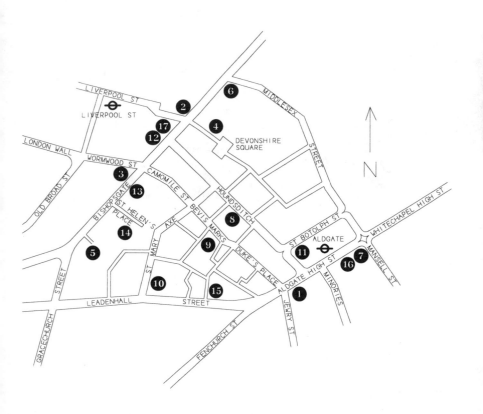

UNDERGROUND STATION

200 m

0   200 Yds

1/4 km

0   1/4 mi

ALDGATE

Aldgate, one of the four original gates of the City and probably first mentioned in 1052, was located on the present street of the same name, about 25 feet east from the corner of Jewry Street. The Anglo-Saxon *aeldgate*, meaning free or open to all, was originally a Roman gate leading to the Colchester road, now known as Whitechapel Road. Mary Tudor rode through the gate in 1553 after being proclaimed Queen.

A plaque at the post office at No.2 Aldgate High Street commemorates the gate and records that Geoffrey Chaucer lived in rooms over the Aldgate in 1374. It is believed that he wrote *The Canterbury Tales* and *Troylus and Cryseyde* while living there from 1374 to 1386.

The gate was demolished in 1761. A model is on exhibit in the Museum of London.

BEDLAM

Just outside Bishopsgate, the monastery of St. Mary of Bethlehem was erected in 1247 on the site of a Roman cemetery, now occupied by the Great Eastern Hotel and the Liverpool Street Station. A plaque on the wall of the Station marks the spot.   .

In 1377 the priory began to be used as a hospital for "distracted persons". It was the custom in the 16th and 17th centuries to send these poor wretches out begging. Most of them were harmless, but those considered dangerous wore chains—the others wore metal badges on their arms as legal proof of their right to solicit alms. These unhappy patients became known as Bedlams, and the word came to be applied to any demented person. The word continues in common usage today to describe "any noisy or confused place or situation."

The hospital was a favorite place for spectators to amuse themselves by watching the strange antics of the miserable inmates—some even provoking them into committing acts of violence. From 1380 to 1395, on every Corpus Christi Day, a brotherhood of Skinners attempted to exorcist the "possessed" inmates. The result of these efforts is unknown.

Sir Thomas More, in his *Four Last Things* (1520), describes some of the sad antics he had seen at the hospital, which was located near his residence at Crosby Hall. One R. Copland, in his *The Hyeway to the Spytel House* (1536), suggested that nagging wives "should be lodged in Bedlam." Robert Green, author and dramatist, was buried in the churchyard in 1592.

Thomas Dekker placed scenes in the hospital in many of his plays. In his *The Honest Whore* (1604), after enumerating the types of madness in Bedlam, he focuses his attention on lawyers:

Fluello: Are there no lawyers amongst you?

Sweep: Oh, no, not one; never any lawyers. We dare not let a lawyer come in, for he'll make 'em mad faster than we can recover 'em.

In *King Lear* (1605), Shakespeare must have observed the pitiable inmates of the hospital with more than a casual eye for he has Edgar cry:

> The country gives me proof and precedent
> Of Bedlam beggars, who, with roaring voices,
> Strike in their numb'd and mortified bare arms
> Pins, wooden pricks, nails, sprigs of rosemary.

Ben Jonson listed Bedlam as among the sights of London in his play, *Epicoene, or the Silent Woman* (1609). Nathaniel Lee, dramatist, died insane in a drunken fit while escaping from Bedlam in 1692. William Hogarth in 1732-33 painted a scene in Bedlam on Plate VIII of *The Rake's Progress*.

Charles Dickens (1812-70), in his essay, *Dry Rot In Men*, recounts some conversations he had with the inmates. One deluded inmate tells him, "Sir, I can frequently fly." Another says:

> Queen Victoria frequently comes to dine with me, and her Majesty and I dine off peaches and maccaroni in our nightgowns, and his Royal Highness the Prince Consort does us the honour to make a third on horseback in a Field-Marshal's uniform.

Luis Kronenberger, writing in *Kings and Desperate Men* (1942), paints a mournful picture of:

> Bedlam, that hospital for the raving mad which has become the synonym for all derangement and confusion; Bedlam, which as a four-starred item on the tourist's list of those days, was so popular that tea was served there for the crowds who on a free afternoon would gather just for fun—for good clean sport—to watch the manias rave and yell, beat on the walls, and rattle their chains.

Bethlehem Hospital was moved to another site in Moorfields in 1675-76. The two figures over the entrance carved by Cibber represented Dementia and Acute Mania. The hospital was moved again in 1812-15 to a specially designed building in St. George's Fields, Southwark, which is now the Imperial War Museum. In 1844, the criminal patients were transferred to Broadmoor; the remaining patients were taken to a new building at West Wickham in 1931.

The original buildings on Liverpool Street were sold to the Great Eastern and Metropolitan Railways Companies between 1865 and 1870 and demolished. A tablet on the peak of a tavern at the corner of Bishopsgate and Liverpool Streets commemorates the founding of the priory of St. Mary of Bethlehem. The date shown is 1240; that is incorrect as it should be 1247.

BISHOPSGATE

One of the Roman gates mentioned in the Domesday Book (1085-87), Bishopsgate stood at the junction of Camomile and Wormwood Streets. Its position is marked by plaques in the wall at Nos. 105 and 108 Bishopsgate Street on each side of the intersection.

The name of the gate refers to the Bishops of London, who had a traditional right to one stick of wood from every cartload entering the gate. In 1260 King Henry III granted an exemption from the toll for certain merchants in exchange for keeping the gate in good repair. After several repairs and rebuildings, the gate was demolished in 1760.

Reproductions of the gate appear over Dirty Dick's Tavern at Nos.202/204 Bishopsgate Street and over the entrance to the National Provincial Bank at the junction of Bishopsgate and Threadneedle Streets. The old gate is still represented in the coat of arms of the National Westminster Bank. A model of the gate may be seen at the Museum of London on London Wall.

THE BULL INN

The original inn at Nos.49-53 Bishopsgate Street was destroyed in the Great Fire of 1666, rebuilt and then finally demolished in 1866. The present pub, at No.4/6 Devonshire Row, covers only a small part of the original structure which, in the 16th century, occupied the entire Bishopsgate corner.

In the central courtyard of the original galleried inn, James Burbage and his company of players, which included Shakespeare, established the first playhouse within the walls of the City by virtue of a patent under the seal of Queen Elizabeth I. Richard Tarleton, the famous clown, performed there as did Burbage in Shakespeare's *Henry V* and *The Merchant of Venice*.

The inn is best known today for the expression "Hobson's Choice". In coaching days, Thomas Hobson had extensive stables at the inn where he enforced his rule that each horse must be hired in its proper turn, and thus bequeathed his name to posterity. Thomas Ward, is his *English Reformation*, epitomized that rule in verse:

Where to elect there is but one,
'Tis Hobson's choice,—take that or none.

The name of The Bull has a number of possible explanations. The most likely one is that it is a contraction of the Latin *bulla* or seal of a monastic establishment—Bethlehem Priory (Bedlam) in this case.

CROSBY SQUARE / HALL

On this site on Bishopsgate Street in 1466 Sir John Crosby, a wealthy grocer, alderman, wool merchant, soldier and sheriff, built his magnificent City mansion. The house was "very large and beautiful, of stone and timber, and the highest at that time in London."

Several buildings occupied three sides of a courtyard fronting on Bishopsgate Street and running back to extensive gardens and a bowling green. Its crowning glory was the Great Hall with its marble floor, beautiful roof with carved pendants supported by unique timber arches, tall oriel windows rising in three tiers from floor to roof and terminating in a fine piece of stone vaulting with the Crosby crest.

The Crosby house was occupied through the centuries by a strange mix of tenants. After Sir John Crosby's death in 1475, Richard, Duke of Gloucester, later King Richard III, made it his headquarters until 1483. William Shakespeare refers to the house several times in his play *Richard III*.

In the second scene of Act I, Richard stops the bier of Henry VI in the street and after making brutally indecent protestations of violent love to Anne, widow of Henry VI's murdered son, urges her to "repair to Crosby-place" where he would meet her later. In the next scene he orders the executioners to "repair to Crosby-place" after they have murdered Clarence. Several more scenes are laid in Crosby Palace, but the most tragic and grievous scene occurs in Act IV in the street in front of the Crosby Palace.

Queen Margaret, widow of Henry VI, seats herself in despair upon the ground and addresses the Duchess of York, mother of Richard III, with a litany of the bitter wrongs suffered by her from the evil deeds of her son:

> From forth the kennel of thy womb hath crept
> A hell-hound that doth hunt us all to death:
> That dog, that had his teeth before his eyes,
> To worry lambs, and lap their gentle blood;
> That foul defacer of God's handiwork;
> That excellent grand tyrant of the earth,
> That reigns in galled eyes of weeping souls,—
> Thy womb let loose, to chase us to our graves.—

After Richard's death at Bosworth Field in 1485, the Crosby place was occupied by a number of important persons, the most distinguished being Sir Thomas More (1478-1535), Henry VIII's Lord Chancellor. He was followed by Sir William Roper, More's son-in-law; Sir John Spencer, Lord Mayor in Shakespeare's day; the Countess of Pembroke, Sir Philip Sidney's sister; and two Russian ambassadors.

From 1621 to 1638, the East India House rented the building for its offices. From 1642 to 1672 it was leased by Sir John Langham, a Presbyterian, and after him by his son, Sir Stephen Langham. It was then turned into a Presbyterian meeting house until a fire two years later severely damaged the main structure. Fortunately, the Hall was spared. In 1676 the ground floor was used as a grocer's warehouse but the Presbyterian assembly remained until 1769 when the Hall was used by another dissenting body for nine more years.

In 1831 the Hall was vacant and in need of rehabilitation. After a Restoration Committee made the necessary repairs, it became the headquarters of the Crosby Hall Literary and Scientific Institute. In 1862 a company of wine merchants converted it into a storehouse. In 1867, the Hall became a restaurant until sold to new owners in 1907 who intended to dismantle the building. A Crosby Hall Preservation Committee was quickly formed and raised enough money to buy the Hall and prevent its demolition.

The historic and much abused Hall was moved to Chelsea in 1910 and rebuilt on the site of Sir Thomas More's old garden near the Chelsea Old Church which he had often attended. The Hall now serves as the headquarters of the British Federation of University Women.

Overlooking the Thames and in front of the More Chapel, which he had restored in 1528, stands a modern sculpture of Sir Thomas More wearing his chain of office and the red crucifix he carried in his hands as he left the Tower for his execution on Tower Hill in 1535.

More is famous as the author of *Utopia* (1516), which describes an ideal commonwealth where social life is regulated according to the dictates of natural reason. But he is remembered and revered over the centuries for his martyrdom in opposing Henry VIII on the question of his divorce from Catherine of Aragon and refusing to recognize the king as head of the English church.

More was canonized by the Roman Catholic Church in 1935.

DIRTY DICK'S

The sign, as you enter at Nos.202/204 Bishopsgate, states that this is "one of the sights of London." The interior is kept artificially dirty in order to support the story behind the tavern's name.

The hero of the strange 18th century story was not Dirty Dick, but one Nathaniel Bentley. His father was a wealthy man who died in 1761 and left all his property to his son. Nathaniel was a well educated young man whose life was completely changed by a devastating incident. About to be married, he arranged a banquet to celebrate the engagement. On that very evening, he received news of his financee's death. Grief stricken, he shut the dining room permanently, leaving everything in it to decay. He led a solitary life, going around unkempt and dirty, and died in 1809.

Although this story is believed to be true, it is likely that Bentley's home was not in Bishopsgate at all, but above the hardware business at No.46 Leadenhall Street that he inherited from his father. The begrimed contents were probably purchased by the owner of the tavern and moved to its premises as an attraction for tourists to stare at mummified cats, rat skeletons and the purported accumulations of dirt over many years.

Charles Dickens may have used the story as the basis for the abandoned wedding feast in *Great Expectations*. In the journal *Household Words*, edited by Dickens, a poem *Dirty Old Man* (1852) bears witness to the sad history of Dirty Dick's:

> The guests for whose joyance that table was spread,
> May now enter as ghosts, for they're every one dead.
> 'Through a chink in the shutter dim lights come and go,
> The seats are in order, the dishes a-row;
> But the luncheon was wealth to the rat and the mouse,
> Whose descendants have long left the dirty old house.
> 'Cup and platter are masked in thick layers of dust,
> The flowers fallen to powder, the wine swath's in crust.
> A nosegay was laid before one special chair,
> And the faded blue ribbon that bound it is there.

YE HOOP AND GRAPES

This pub, at No.47 Aldgate High Street, may well be the oldest licensed house in London. Much of the original 13th century structure still remains.

Legend has it that at one time a tunnel from the cellar led to the Tower of London. Also a device for eavesdropping on private conversations has been preserved.

The upstairs restaurant is called the Micawber Room, named after Dickens' immortal character in *David Copperfield*.

THE RED LION

This old inn, at No.31 Houndsditch, was frequented by Dick Swiveller while working for attorney Sampson Brass in Charles Dickens' *Old Curiosity Shop*. The pub displays Thomas Shepherd's 1829 prints of the City.

SPANISH AND PORTUGUESE SYNAGOGUE

This handsome synagogue off Bevis Marks is the oldest in use in England. The previous synagogue on Creechurch Lane was opened in 1657 when Cromwell permitted the Jews to return to England. It was moved to the present building in 1701.

The birth of Prime Minister Benjamin Disraeli in 1804 is recorded in the synagogue register. His father, Issac D'Israeli, was a devout member of the Sephardic congregation.

The synagogue survived the Blitz of World War II, although the neighboring Great Synagogue was destroyed. It is an almost exact copy of the only synagogue in Amsterdam which also miraculously survived the war. The fittings are original and some of the candlesticks were brought from Amsterdam.

Bevis Marks figures in Charles Dickens' *Old Curiosity Shop* as the place of residence of Sampson Brass, and the location of The Golden Axe at the corner of St. Mary Axe which Dick Swiveller recommended. Dickens also places Pubsey & Co. on St. Mary Axe in *Our Mutual Friend*.

George Gissing, the novelist, was awed by the fame of Charles Dickens when he arrived in London as a young man. He relates an early visit to Bevis Marks in his *Charles Dickens* (1898):

... one day in the City, I found myself at the entrance to Bevis Marks! ... Here dwelt Mr. Brass and Sally, and the Marchionness. Up and down that little street, this side and that, I went gazing and dreaming. No press of busy folk disturbed me: the place was quiet; it looked no doubt, much the same as when Dickens knew it. I am not sure I had any dinner that day, but, if not, I dare say I did not mind it very much.

ST. ANDREW UNDERSHAFT

This church, on Leadenhall at St. Mary Axe, dedicated to the patron saint of Scotland, was first mentioned in 1147 as St. Andrew Cornhill. The name change was derived from the church's practice from the 15th century of erecting a shaft or maypole in the middle of Leadenhall Street to celebrate May Day. The ceremony was performed annually for 32 years. When not in use, the pole, taller than the tower, was slung on hooks under the eaves of the thatched cottages in Shaft Alley. Shaft Court still exists.

In 1517 on Evil May Day, the City apprentices rioted; 300 were arrested and one was hung. The curate of St. Katherine Cree Church preached against the maypole as a heathen idol. His inflamed parishioners seized the pole, sawed it up and burned it, thus effectively terminating any further May Day celebrations.

The church contains a remarkable number of monuments, the most famous being the effigy of John Stow. Tailor, antiquary, historian and topographer, Stow in his old age was reduced to being a licensed beggar by permission of King James I.

Through research which cost in his own words "many a weary miles' travel, many a hard-earned penny and pound, and many a cold winternight's study", he produced his great *Survey of London* in 1598. He impoverished himself in his self imposed arduous task.

When he presented a copy of his book to the Merchant Taylors Company, he was granted an annuity of £4 a year; this was later raised to £10. After a lifetime of searching and recording the history of England and the antiquities of London, he died in poverty on April 5, 1605 at the age of 80 and was buried in his parish church of St. Andrew Undershaft.

His imposing statue of marble and alabaster was provided by his widow, who must have found generous contributors for the project. The inscription on the monument is translated as follows:

Sacred to the memory of John Stowe, a citizen of London who here awaits resurrection in Christ. He exercised the most careful accuracy in searching ancient monuments, English annals, and records of the City of London. He wrote excellently and deserved well both of his own and subsequent ages. The contest of a good and honest life being completed, died in the year of our Lord on the day 5th April 1605. His sorrowing wife Elizabeth erects this as a perpetual witness of her love.

The life size figure of John Stow shows him as an old, bald headed man writing with a quill pen, surrounded by his other books. Every April, on a Sunday nearest the anniversary of his death, a commemorative service, arranged by the London and Middlesex Archeological Society, is held at the church and attended by the Lord Mayor of London and the Sheriffs. After the service and a tribute to his memory, a new quill pen is placed in the statue's hand and a copy of Stow's great work is awarded as a prize for the best student essay on London. The discarded quill pen is presented to the headmaster or headmistress of the winning school.

There is little doubt but that without Stow's lifetime of selfless devotion to his survey, a great deal of information about old London would have been lost forever.

ST. BOTOLPH, ALDGATE

The first reference to this church at Aldgate High Street and Houndsditch was in 1125. Although it escaped the Great Fire of 1666, the church was so dilapidated that it had to be demolished and replaced by the present building in 1744.

The roof is noteworthy for its circular plasterwork design of petals and leaves radiating form the center. The window depicting the Agony in the Garden is the only 18th century transparency in the City. The church is predominately Victorian in character and execution, especially the yellow tiled floor.

A tablet commemorates William Symington, an engineer, who constructed the Charlotte Dundas, the first practical steamboat, in 1802. He was unable to find any support for his invention and died in poverty in 1831. In 1803, one year after Symington had built his steamboat, the American Robert Fulton successfully demonstrated a steamboat on the Seine in Paris. In 1807 his Clermont, dubbed Fulton's Folly, traveled form New York City to Albany, USA and back in 62 hours. The age of steam navigation was born.

In the northeast corner of the church, a tablet states:

> Praises on tombs are trifles
> vainly spent.
> A man's good name is his
> best monument

Daniel Defoe was married here in 1683 and Jeremy Bentham, the great English philosopher and jurist, christened in 1747. Defoe's description of the Great Plague of 1665 in his *Journal of the Plague Year* (1722) mentions that two pits were dug in the churchyard which were filled in only four months with the bodies of 5,136 plague victims.

ST. BOTOLPH WITHOUT BISHOPSGATE

Although the first recorded reference to this church on Bishops-gate at Houndsditch was early in the 13th century, it probably existed long before the Norman Conquest of 1066.

Edward Alleyn, the Elizabethan actor and founder of Dulwich College, was baptized in the original church in 1566. Stephen Gosson, author of the *School of Abuse* (1579), was the rector from 1600 until his death in 1624.

Ben Jonson's first son Nicholas, born in 1596, died of the plague in 1603 and was buried in the church. "To the child of my right hand", Jonson wrote a tender memorial:

> Rest in soft peace, and asked, say, Here doth lie
> Ben Jonson his best piece of poetry;
> For whose sake henceforth all his vows be such
> As what he loves may never like too much.

The church escaped the Great Fire of 1666 but fell into ruin early in the 18th century. It was rebuilt in 1725 as the present structure.

John Keats was baptized in the restored church on August 31, 1795. He died in Rome on February 23, 1821, and was buried in a Protestant cemetery with the following engraving on his tombstone:

> Here lies one whose name was writ in water.

Keats' poetry is unsurpassed for sheer felicity and natural magic. For him, poetry was his life's blood; his credo of poetic faith is embodied in the simple statement: "Beauty is truth, truth beauty."

ST. ETHELBURGA, BISHOPSGATE

This church is unique in that it is the smallest and possibly the most ancient in London. It measures only 60 feet by 30 feet and the height from floor to ceiling is less than 31 feet.

The present church was built in the first half of the 15th century and escaped the Great Fire of 1666. A Latin motto from the ancient temple of Aesculapius is inscribed in the pavement and translated reads: "Come in good, go out better." The old font has a Greek inscription stating in translation, "Cleanse my transgression, not my outward appearance only."

Three stained glass windows commemorate Henry Hudson (d.1611) who made his communion here in 1607 before starting out on his first attempt to find the Northwest Passage. A tiny garden with a cloister and a pond was a gift in memory of Reverend Cobb, rector of the church from 1900 to 1941. It is necessary to go through both the church and vestry to reach the garden.

ST. HELEN'S, BISHOPSGATE

This church on St. Helen's place is one of the few City churches to have escaped the Great Fire of 1666.

Legend has it that as long ago as the fourth century, a Christian church replaced a pagan temple on this site. The Emperor Constantine is believed to have erected it upon his conversion to Christianity, and dedicated it to his mother, Helena.

The priory of St. Helen's was founded about 1212 for nuns of the Benedictine Order. They wore a black habit and cloak, as well as a black cowl and veil. The northern half of the present church belonged to the convent; the rest was reserved for ecclesiastical purposes. The arched entrance from the nunnery to the choir can still be seen in the north wall.

The nuns proved to be too worldly for the clergy. New rules of conduct were promulgated in the late 14th century forbidding the nuns "from kissing secular persons", ordering the prioress to give up all but one or two of her dogs and prohibiting all dancing and reveling except at Christmas time.

The number and workmanship of the tombs in the church are such that St. Helen's has been called the Westminster Abbey of the City. The most magnificent monument is that of Sir William Pickering (d.1576), distinguished soldier and scholar under Henry VIII, Edward VI, Mary and Elizabeth I.

Other memorials include the tomb of Sir Thomas Gresham (d.1579), founder of the Royal Exchange; a memorial window to William Shakespeare, a resident of the parish, donated by Mr. H. H. Prentice, a Canadian admirer, in 1884; and a remarkable monument in memory of Sir Julius Caesar, who died in 1636. Sir Julius, a son of Queen Mary's Italian physician, devoted himself to the law and received his first appointment as Admiralty Judge from Elizabeth I. He later became Chancellor of the Exchequer and Master of the Rolls.

At the West end is a stained glass window commemorating ten notable parishioners of St. Helen's. Among them is Robert Hooke (d.1703), the City Surveyor, probably responsible for the construction of the Monument (usually attributed to Sir Christopher Wren), Bethlehem Hospital and Merchant Taylors' Hall.

ST. KATHERINE CREE

The original church was built before 1280, on part of the grave-yard of the priory of Holy Trinity, founded in 1108, and called Christ-church, later corrupted into Cree. The church, on Leadenhall Street near Aldgate, was rebuilt in 1630, on the same site, and that date is in-scribed on the keystone of an arch in the northwest corner. Inigo Jones designed it with a combination of Gothic and Classic architec-ture, resulting in a bright and attractive interior.

The large east window is constructed in the shape of a wheel, St. Katherine's traditional emblem. This design has been used to denote a particular firework as a Katherine Wheel. Tradition has it that the saint was martyred by Emperor Maximinus who ordered her to be broken on the wheel. The wheel broke apart at her touch and she was beheaded by sword. She is represented in a window on the north side. The window above the vestry door also honors her. The arms of the City of London and 17 City Companies are displayed in the north and south aisles.

A brass plate in front of the communion rails marks the site of the internment of Sir John Gayer, Lord Mayor of London in 1646. As the result of his allegiance to the executed king Charles I, he was impris-oned in the Tower of London where he died. A legend grew around Sir John's encounter with a lion while he was on a business trip to Turkey. Supposedly due to heavenly intervention, the lion did not at-tack or harm him. Some non-believers suggest that because Sir John had dropped to his knees to pray and remained motionless, he was not attacked because beasts of prey do not attack stationary creatures. At any rate, one might cynically ask what lions were doing in Turkey. Sir John left a bequest for the preaching of an annual sermon on his deliv-erance, called the Lion Sermon. The sermon is still preached every October 16th.

The church organ of 1686 was constructed by Father Smith, the famous organ builder, and has been played by Purcell, Handel and Wesley. The original 17th century entrance gate from Leadenhall has been rebuilt against the northeast wall of the garden in the back, which can only be reached through the church. The plane tree in the garden is said to be the oldest and tallest in the City.

THE STILL AND STAR

This pub, at No.1 Little Somerset Street, was dispensing drinks long before the Great Fire of 1666 which, fortunately, missed it. It continues, uninterrupted by the centuries, to cater to its customers at its over 400 year old site.

The street at one time had a slaughterhouse and was occupied by numerous butchers, thus giving it the nickname Blood Alley. Many believed that Jack the Ripper was a local butcher because of his expertise in dissection.

The pub's real significance lies in the probability that Daniel Defoe wrote *Robinson Crusoe* (1719) while living at the inn. An English mariner named Alexander Selkirk (1676-1721) joined a privateering expedition in 1703. In the following year, after a quarrel with the Captain, Selkirk asked to be put ashore at Juan Fernandez, an island off the coast of South America. He lived there alone for four years and four months. After his deliverance from the island in 1709, he published a record of his experiences which ten years later was transformed by Defoe into *Robinson Crusoe*.

THE WHITE HART INN

The Bishopsgate area originally abounded with inns to accommodate travelers who arrived after the gate was closed for the night. The White Hart Inn, standing just outside the walled City at No.121 Bishopsgate Street, was the oldest of all the Bishopsgate inns. With only a gateway separating it from the Bethlehem Priory (Bedlam), the inn housed and entertained the pilgrims in the days of English monasticism.

The Great Fire of 1666 destroyed the adjacent St. Botolph's Church, but left the White Hart Inn miraculously untouched. It underwent considerable alterations in 1787; the present tavern replaced the venerable structure in 1829. The date 1246 is cut in stone on the facade and the tavern claims to possess the oldest spirits license in London. It is better known as The 199, headquarters of Whitehead & Sons, which was its old number before it was renumbered to 121.

In the Elizabethan period, the large courtyard was often used as a theater. Part of the area is preserved as White Hart Court.

AREA H

THE MONUMENT

AND

THE BOAR'S HEAD INN

AREA H ATTRACTIONS

AREA H MAP

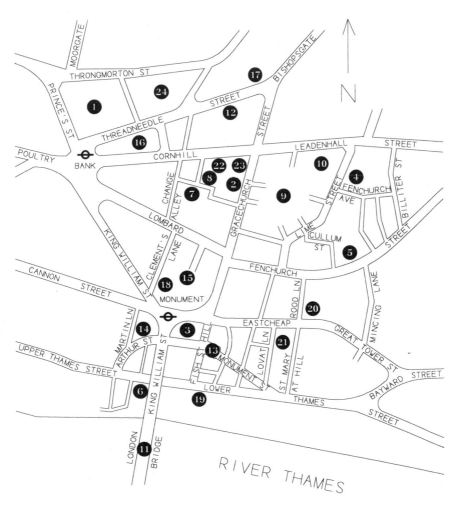

UNDERGROUND STATION

BANK OF ENGLAND

The massive building on the huge central block bounded by Threadneedle, Prince's and Lothbury Streets and Bartholomew Lane is occupied by "the old lady of Threadneedle Street", also known as the Bank of England.

The exact derivation of the well known nickname is obscure. The pediment of the building contains a modern representation of Britannia which Sheridan, the playwright, may have referred to in a speech in the House of Commons as "The Lady of Threadneedle Street."

One story concerns a young bank clerk executed for forgery. His sister lost her sanity and continually appeared at the Bank demanding to see her brother. As the years passed, she was dubbed "the old lady of Threadneedle Street."

Another version attributes the name to a political cartoon depicting William Pitt the Younger, as Chancellor of the Exchequer, seizing a chest of gold from an old lady with the heading, "Political Ravishment, or the Old Lady of Threadneedle Street in Danger."

The Bank of England was founded in 1694, but the first building to house the government's banker, the Banker's Bank, was erected in 1732-34 and modified in 1788 by Sir John Soane, the architect, who later established Soane's Museum. Sir Herbert Baker rebuilt the bank during the 1920s and 1930s; only the outer walls remain. At the northwest corner, an architectural feature known as the Temple was copied by Soane from the Temple of the Sibyl at Tivoli near Rome.

The site was previously occupied by the church of St. Christopher-le-stocks, the first Wren church to be demolished. The name derived from the fact that the Lord Mayor's stocks, in which wrongdoers were imprisoned by their arms and legs, stood in front of the church. The graveyard became the Fountain Court of the Bank.

The Bank of England is the cornerstone of British finance. It prints money and safeguards the country's gold reserve. The phrase, "Safe as the Bank of England", found its expression after the Gordon Riots of 1780 resulted in a military guard being mounted to protect the bank at night. A vivid description of the riots is given in Dickens' *Barnaby Rudge*.

Kenneth Grahame (1859-1932) wrote one of the most enduring and best loved children's stories, *The Wind in the Willows* (1908), while working at the Bank from 1879 until ill health forced his retirement in 1908. He first read it to his sickly son as a series of bedtime stories. His other child fantasy classics, *Golden Age* (1895) and *Dream Days* (1898), were also immediate successes.

Entrance to the bank's museum is from Bartholomew Street. It has video tape programs explaining the complex workings of the bank, a reconstruction of the first stocks office and an exhibition featuring the original charter, gold bars and bank notes.

BELL INN YARD / CROSS KEYS TAVERN

On the west side of Gracechurch Street, between Lombard and Cornhill, once stood the Bell Inn and the Cross-Keys Tavern. They were two of the five City Inns where plays were performed in the 16th century before the building of the theatres. A plaque marks the site.

These inn yard performances did not have the approval of the City authorities, who were concerned that the crowds might commit irresponsible acts; anyway, they should be doing something better with their time. But the Queen loved the theater, especially since she did not have to support private companies out of the royal treasury—so the authorities were unable to do anything about it.

The Bell Inn was owned by Sir Andrew Judd, Lord Mayor, in the 16th century. In 1560 its landlady was the subject of public condemnation for being a courtesan. Richard Tarleton, the famous Elizabethan clown, acted there. The Inn was destroyed in the Great Fire of 1666.

The Cross-Keys Tavern was patronized by Lord Strange's theater company in 1590. The Chamberlain's Company, of which Shakespeare was a member, used the tavern in the winter months from 1594, when the plague was over, until 1596 or 1597. Tarleton, playing at the nearby Bell Inn, went to see the famous performing horse, Marocco, at the Cross-Keys, and the following report appeared in Tarleton's *Jests*:

> Banks perceiving to make the people laugh, saies "Singnior," to his horse, "go fetch me the veriest fool in the company." The jade comes immediately, and with his mouth draws Tarlton forth. Tarlton, with merry words, said nothing but "God a mercy, horse!" ... Ever after it was a by-word through London, "God a mercy, horse!" and is to this day.

It was claimed that the horse had climbed the tower at St. Paul's Cathedral. Eventually both the showman, Banks, and the horse, Marocco, were burned at the stake in Rome after being accused of witchcraft.

The Cross-Keys inn was also consumed by the Great Fire.

THE BOAR'S HEAD TAVERN

This historic tavern, one of the largest and most famous of the 16th century taverns, once stood on the south side of Eastcheap where it intersects King William and Gracechurch Streets. Mentioned in old tracts as the Boreshead near London Stone, the earliest known record of its existence was in the reign of Richard II (1377-99). It was also one of the 40 taverns permitted to furnish food and drink by order of Edward VI (1537-53).

The tavern was made famous by William Shakespeare in both parts of *Henry IV* (1597-98) as the scene of Prince Hall's revelries, the drunken debaucheries of the disreputable old knight Sir John Falstaff and his riotous followers and the forbearance of Dame Quickly and the frailties of Doll Tearsheet and her dissolute company. In the tavern Shakespeare created his immortal comic figure, Falstaff, whose moral and physical imperfections are a microcosm whereby we can measure our own human deficiencies.

The destruction of Falstaff occurs at the conclusion of *Henry IV, Part 2*, when Prince Hall, newly crowned as King Henry V, renounces him and his jests and banishes him from his presence. Falstaff's heart is broken and he passes away, shabbily, offstage in the Boar's Head Tavern in *Henry V*. Mistress Quickly, in one of the most poignant passages in all of Shakespeare, reports his death:

He's in Arthur's bosom, if ever man went to Arthur's bosom. A' made a finer end, and went away, and it had been any christom child; a' parted ev'n just between twelve and one, ev'n at the turning o' th' tide: for after I saw him fumble with the sheets, and play with flowers, and smile upon his fingers' ends, I knew there was but one way; for his nose was as sharp as a pen, and a' babbled of green fields.

The Boar's Head Tavern was rebuilt in brick after it had been destroyed by the Great Fire of 1666. A stone with the head of a boar and the date 1668 was inset above the door. Elaborately carved vine branches of wood, with small figures of Falstaff, where placed on each side of the entrance.

A dinner honoring Shakespeare was held in the tavern every year by a club whose members assumed various characters in *Henry IV*. The last dinner was held in 1784, attended by William Pitt, Prime Minister, and William Wilberforce, the member of Parliament responsible for the abolition of slavery. Boswell mentioned to Johnson that the inn was the "very tavern where Falstaff and his joyous companions met."

Oliver Goldsmith, in his 1760 essay, *A Reverie at the Boar's-head-tavern in Eastcheap*, described a visit to the Boar's Head, "still kept at Eastcheap", and noted how he used Hal's chair and sat before the fire in the room where Falstaff told his story:

> The character of old Falstaff, even with all his faults, gives me more consolation than the most studied efforts of wisdom: I here behold an agreeable old fellow, forgetting age, and shewing me the way to be young at sixty-five .... Age, care wisdom, reflection, begone—I give you to the winds. Let's have t'other bottle: here's to the memory of Shakespeare, Falstaff, and all the merry men of Eastcheap ....

Washington Irving, author of *Rip Van Winkle* and *The Legend of Sleepy Hollow* in his *Sketch Book* (1819), also includes the essay, "The Boar's Head Tavern, Eastcheap", which had this to say:

> I was one morning turning over his pages, when I casually opened upon the comic scenes of *Henry IV*, and was, in a moment, completely lost in the madcap revelry of the Boar's Head Tavern. So vividly and naturally are these scenes of humor depicted, and with such force and consistency are the characters sustained, that they become mingled up in the mind with the facts and personages of real life .... A hero of fiction that never existed is just as valuable to me as a hero of history that existed a thousand years since.

The Boar's Head Tavern disappeared in 1831, but those moving spirits will continue to inhabit forever the tavern of Shakespeare's imagination.

EAST INDIA HOUSE

A plaque on No.15 Leadenhall at Lime Street marks the site of the East India House in which the East India Company conducted its business form 1600 to 1858. The Company was granted a charter by Queen Elizabeth I enabling it eventually to operate as the sole monopoly of the Far Eastern trade in China and India. The Company's charter was revoked in 1858 by the British government, and the building was demolished in 1924. Lloyd's Corporation later built new offices on the site when the Royal Exchange could not accommodate its increasing business.

The East India Company had considerable historic as well as literary importance. Faced by a financial crisis from the American boycott of British products, the Company received permission to ship its tea directly to the Colonies. That shipment led to the Boston Tea Party of 1773 and precipitated the War of Independence.

James Mill (1773-1836), Scottish historian, utilitarian philosopher and political economist, and his son John Stuart Mill (1806-1873), English philosopher and political economist, were clerks in East India House. James received an appointment as assistant examiner in 1819 and continued with the Company until his death in 1836. John entered his father's office in 1822 and remained with the Company until his retirement in 1858. He was the only religious heretic to have been honored by a London statute.

Thomas Love Peacock (1785-1866) obtained a post in the India Office where he remained for 38 years. However, East India's important literary alumnus was Charles Lamb (1775-1834), beloved essayist, poet and critic whose pen name was Elia. He served the Company for 33 years while hating the office work and the "merchants and their spicy drugs." When he was at last awarded his pension in 1825, he was so overcome with joy at his emancipation from the "dry drudgery at the desk's dead wood" that he exultingly wrote to William Wordsworth:

Here I am, then, after thirty-three years slavery, sitting at my own room at eleven o'clock this finest of all April mornings, a freed man, with 441 pounds a year for the remainder of my life .... I came home FOR EVER on Tuesday in last week.

The incomprehensibleness of my condition overwhelmed me. It was like passing from life into eternity.

Shortly afterwards, he sent the following letter to his friend, Bernard Barton:

> I am free, B.B.—free as air.
>> "The little bird that wings the sky
>> Knows no such liberty!"
>
> I was set free on Tuesday in last week at four o'clock. "I came home forever".
>
> B.B. I would not serve another seven years for seven hundred thousand pounds.

Lamb used his experiences at the East India House as material for his essay, *The Superannuated Man*:

> If peraventure, Reader, it has been thy lot to waste the golden years of thy life—thy shining youth—in the irksome confinement of an office; to have thy prison days prolonged through middle age down to decrepitude and silver hairs, without hope of release or respite; to have lived to forget that there are such things as holidays, or to remember them but as the prerogatives of childhood; then, and then only, will you be able to appreciate my deliverance.

THE ELEPHANT

This modern tavern at No.119 Fenchurch, twice rebuilt, stands on the site of the original inn built before the Great Fire of 1666. It was one of the few houses constructed of stone and thus survived the catastrophe.

The Elephant is included here due to its close connection with William Hogarth (1697-1764), the great English painter and engraver. He lived at the inn for several years during his youth while trying to make a name for himself. In debt to his landlord for his lodgings, he discharged his obligation by painting murals at the inn which were later recognized as masterpieces. Reproductions of two of his most famous paintings, *Gin Lane* and *Beer Street*, are still on view in the downstairs bar. A nearby street is named for him: Hogarth Court.

Whistler declared that Hogarth was "the greatest English artist who ever lived", and Hazlitt paid a glowing tribute to the dramatic life and vitality of his pictures. Lamb's evaluation of him in his essay, *The Genius and Character of Hogarth*, stated that "His graphic representations are indeed books; they have the teeming, fruitful, suggestive meaning of words. Other pictures we look at; his prints are read." He ranked Hogarth as one of the great painters and compared his paintings to the novels of Smollett and Fielding.

FISHMONGERS' HALL

The Fishmongers' Company, at the north end of London Bridge, is one of the richest and oldest of the 12 great livery companies that grew out of earlier trade guilds. The date of its founding is lost in antiquity, but was undoubtedly before the reign of Henry II from 1154 to 1189.

Earlier halls superseded the one burned in the Great Fire of 1666. Its replacement of 1671 was demolished in 1827 and the present hall dates from 1831-34. It contains many interesting mementos of England's past: A painted wooden figure of Sir William Walworth, Lord Mayor, along with the dagger he used to kill the rebel Wat Tyler in 1381; a 15th century embroidered funeral pall; some 17th century plate; two portraits by George Romney, the English painter (1734-1802); a chair made of stone and wood from the foundations of old London Bridge; and the 1955 Annigoni portrait of Queen Elizabeth II, the model for stamps and bank notes.

Since 1721 the Fishmongers' Company has managed The Watermens' Derby, known as "Doggett's Coat and Badge". Thomas Doggett, comedian and joint manager of the Drury Lane Theatre, died in 1721 and left directions in his will, along with a bequest, for an annual race to be directed by the Fishmongers' Company. Six young watermen race four and a half miles, from London Bridge to Chelsea, upstream at high tide when the current is strongest. The winner is awarded a coat and badge and £20; other lesser prizes were also given. The race is usually held in July.

Some say that Fish Street Hill, where the Fishmongers had their earlier hall, has never lost its fishy smell.

THE GEORGE & VULTURE TAVERN

The George & Vulture (formerly The George), at No.3 Castle Court, Birchin Lane, is London's oldest tavern. It is well worth searching for in a confusing maze of narrow alleys and dead end streets. It has made literary history since its founding in 1150.

The tavern played host to such literati as Addison and Steele, Jonathan Swift and Daniel Defoe. The Hell Fire Club and the Sublime Society of Beefsteaks, of which William Hogarth was a member, held their meetings at the inn. The yard was used by traveling companies of players for the presentation of mystery and morality plays.

The George & Vulture's most famous resident was Mr. Pickwick. In *Pickwick Papers* (1837), Charles Dickens wrote:

> Mr. Pickwick and Sam took up their present abode in very good, old-fashioned and comfortable quarters: to wit, the George & Vulture Tavern and Hotel, George Yard, Lombard Street.

Many of the incidents in the *Pickwick Papers* took place in the George & Vulture. The subpoenas in the case of Bardell vs. Pickwick were served on Mr. Pickwick and his friends in his sitting room. He rode from the tavern to the Guildhall on the day of the trial. Arrested while he was still in bed at the tavern and taken to the Fleet Prison, Mr. Pickwick returned to the inn after his release. The last reference to the tavern was when he joined his friends for dinner at the Adelphi Hotel before he retired to Dulwich.

Sam Weller, his cockney companion, scattered shrewd and humorous snippets of wisdom in the story:

> It's over, and can't be helped, and that's one consolation, as they always says in Turkey, ven they cuts the wrong man's head off.

Sam's father, Tony, a coachman, also contributes to the merriment with additional gems of cockneyisms:

> Tongue; well that's a wery good thing when it an't a woman's.

Wen you're a married man, Samivel, you'll understand a good many things as you don't understand now, but vether it's worth while goin' through so much to learn so little, as the charity-boy said ven he got the end of the alphabet, is a matter o' taste.

In Mr. Pickwick, Dickens had invented an ingenious, childlike and lovable old Englishman, "an observer of human nature", who founded a club of amusing simpletons. The series of entertaining episodes lightly strung together exploded on the English public with such force that the Pickwickians became national heroes, and Dickensian humor entered into everyday language. After this publication of pure humor, Dickens became the crusader for the oppressed in his subsequent novels.

Today the City Pickwick Club holds its meetings, and the Dickens Fellowship entertains its visitors, at the George & Vulture. The first edition of *Pickwick Papers* is now in the library of the British Museum, where it is known as the George & Vulture copy.

JAMAICA WINE HOUSE

Across form the George and Vulture, on St. Michael's Alley, is a blue plaque on the wall of the Jamaica Wine House attesting to the fact that in 1652 this became London's first house licensed to sell coffee.

The original establishment was known as the Pasqua Rosee Wine House, named after the Greek servant of the merchant Daniel Edwards. An early percolator is proudly displayed.

LEADENHALL MARKET

The market on Gracechurch Street off Leadenhall Street has a long history. It was originally built over a Roman basilica of 80-100 A.D. and is said to be the oldest market in London. Poultry was ordered to be sold there as early as 1257. Dick Whittington purchased the market and manor in 1411 and bequeathed it to the County Council.

Over time it contained a granary (1446), was ordained for the assay of leather (1488), added stalls for butchers (1595) and in 1622 a law was enacted that all cutlery had to be sold there. In 1663 Samuel Pepys bought "a leg of beef, a good one, for sixpence" at the market.

All was destroyed by the Great Fire of 1666, but the area continued to be used by butchers, greengrocers, fishmongers and poulterers. An official act of 1881 was designed to improve the market. Today, in an area of almost 27,000 square feet, a brisk trade is conducted in poultry, fish and many other products.

From a literary standpoint, it was in Leadenhall Market that Moll Flanders, in Daniel Defoe's novel of 1721, took the first step towards a life of crime which almost ended at the gallows:

Wandering thus about, I knew not whither, I passed by an apothecary's shop in Leadenhall Street, where I saw lie on a stool just before the counter a little bundle wrapped in a white cloth; beyond it stood a maid-servant with her back to it, looking up towards the top of the shop, where the apothecary's apprentice, as I suppose, was standing upon the counter, with his back to the door, and a candle in his hand, looking and reaching up to the upper shelf, for something he wanted, so that both were engaged, and nobody else in the shop.

This was the bait; and the devil who laid the snare prompted me, as if he had spoke, for I remember, and shall never forget it. 'twas like a voice spoken over my shoulder, "Take the bundle; be quick; do it this moment." It was no sooner said but I stepped into the shop, and with my back to the wench, as if I had stood up for a cart that was going by, I put my hand behind me and took the bundle, and went off with it, the maid or fellow not perceiving me, or any one else.

Moll became hardened to the life of theft and was eventually deported to America. She returned to England at the age of 70 with her husband, "where we resolve to spend the remainder of our years in sincere penitence for the wicked lives we have lived."

LLOYDS OF LONDON

Only a marine insurance company on Lime Street, but what exotic images that name evokes! Far away places with strange sounding names, adventure on the high seas, sailing ships loaded with precious goods—all so vividly described by the Poet Laureate John Masefield in *Cargoes*:

> Stately Spanish galleon coming from the Isthmus,
> Dipping through the Tropics by the palm-green shores,
> With cargo of diamonds,
> Emeralds, amethysts,
> Topazes, and cinnamon, and gold moidores.

The business of Lloyd's has changed very little since the days when wealthy merchants met to underwrite the insurance for sailing ships—and share in the profits or losses. They were known as underwriters because they wrote their names one under the other at the bottom of the insurance contract.

This great association of marine underwriters originated in a coffee house opened in 1688 on Tower Street by a Welshman named Edward Lloyd. He moved to larger quarters at the corner of Lombard Street and Abchurch Lane in 1692 to accommodate his increasing business. A tablet marks the site.

Ships, shipping materiel, cargoes and marine merchandise were auctioned off "by the candle". An inch of candle was lit and the auction ended when the candle burned itself out.

The coffee house must be distinguished from the tavern of that period. The tavern was frequented, for the most part, as a hangout and drinking establishment. The coffee house, on the other hand, was more a place of convenience than of pleasure, and required proper behavior. Gambling was not permitted, swearing or quarreling was an offense punishable by fines, and customers did not drink excessively of the liquor which was served along with the coffee.

There were numerous coffee houses where customers of similar interests conducted business ventures. The Baltic Coffee House in Threadneedle Street assigned a special room to the business of trade with Russia. Amalgamated to form the Baltic Exchange and later united with the London Shipping Exchange, its headquarters were located in St. Mary Axe and conducts business with many countries besides the Balkans. By the end of the 18th century, the City coffee houses had reverted to being pubs.

Lloyd's of London remains as the most important center in the world of shipping intelligence and the international insurance market. In 1774 Lloyds's moved to the Royal Exchange in Cornhill which was destroyed by fire in 1838. In 1844 Lloyd's moved back to the new Royal Exchange and remained there until their new building was erected in 1925 in Leadenhall Street on the site of the demolished East India House. Successive buildings were erected in the contiguous area, with the latest in 1986 on the spot bounded by Leadenhall and Lime Streets.

T. S. Eliot, awarded the Nobel prize for literature in 1948, was employed in the colonial and foreign department of Lloyd's Bank from 1917 to 1925. I. A. Richards, the critic, reported that he had called on Mr. Eliot at Lloyd's and found him:

> ... a figure stooping, very like a dark bird in a feeder, over a big table covered with all sorts and sizes of foreign correspondence. The big table almost entirely filled a little room under the street. Within a foot of our heads when he stood were the thick, green glass squares of the pavement on which hammered all but incessantly the heels of the passersby.

This was the human wave of pedestrians going to or coming from the Bank Underground Station at the junction of Lombard and King William Streets. The footsteps became modern versions of the damned in Dante's *Inferno* as portrayed in Eliot's *The Waste Land* (1922):

> Under the brown fog of a winter dawn,
> A crowd flowed over London Bridge, so many,
> I had not thought death had undone so many,
> Sighs, short and infrequent, were exhaled,
> And each man fixed his eyes before his feet,
> Flowed up the hill and down King William Street,
> To where Saint Mary Woolnoth kept the hours
> With a dead sound on the final stroke of nine.

The clock referred to by Eliot still keeps the hours at St. Mary Woolnoth, Lombard Street. Edward Lloyd was buried at the church in 1712; a tablet to his memory was placed there in 1931.

The memorabilia carefully guarded at Lloyd's are treasures of English history. The Lutine Bell, salvaged from the French vessel Lutine, hangs in the middle of the Underwriting Room. It rings when important announcements are to be made—once for bad news, twice for good news. On display are old policies covering the Golden Fleece on a voyage from Lisbon to Venice, and a cargo of slaves being transported in 1794, which still used the 1779 references to "pirates, rovers, etc."

The Nelson Room possesses personal correspondence belonging to Lord Nelson. The Admiral's log book contains the immortal message signaled to the fleet while the battle at Trafalgar was actually in progress: "England expects that every man will do his duty."

The Museum Room displays Roman medieval items uncovered during excavation for the building.

Underwriters continue to do business in "boxes" similar to those used in the original Lloyd's Coffee House; the attendants are still called waiters. The new premises can be visited if a waiter is available.

LONDON BRIDGE

History does not record the date of the first bridge across the Thames, but it was certainly before 43 A.D. when the German troops attacked the Britons by crossing "over a bridge a little way upstream", at a point where the Romans later founded the city of Londinium.

The bridges were made of wood and frequently destroyed by fires, insurrections, windstorms and other calamities. In 1014 the English, supported by King Olaf of Norway, tried to recapture London from the Danes, whose troops were using the bridge to throw missiles at the English ships. At King Olaf's suggestion, cables were attached to the wooden piles supporting the bridge, the other ends fastened to the ships. When the ships were rowed away, the bridge collapsed, many of the troops fell into the river and the Danes surrendered. A poem praising the bold action by King Olaf read:

> London Bridge is broken down,
> Gold is won, and bright renown,
>> Shields resounding,
>> War-horns sounding,
> Hildur shouting in the din!
>> Arrows singing,
>> Mailcoats ringing—
> Odin makes our Olaf win.

This incident may have prompted the well known nursery rhyme, but acting on the advice of the second verse:

> Build it up again with stone so strong,
> Stone so strong, stone so strong,
> Stone will last for ages long,
> My fair lady.

it was decided in 1176, during the reign of Henry II, to erect a more substantial bridge about 100 feet west of the old one.

The new bridge was 905 feet long and 20 feet wide, with fortified gates at each end. Rows of wooden houses from three to seven stories high were built on each side. A report stated that in 1358 there were 138 shops on the bridge. A chapel dedicated to St. Thomas à Becket was erected on the middle of the bridge. Becket had been murdered in 1170, and canonized in 1173. His bones were enshrined in Canterbury Cathedral where they became the holy shrine for pilgrimages as described in Chaucer's *Canterbury Tales* (1383).

In 1263 Queen Eleanor, consort of Henry III, left the Tower of London to seek protection at Windsor. As she passed under London Bridge in her royal barge, she was pelted with stones, rotten eggs and other forms of garbage by a mob of disaffected citizens on the bridge.

The unusually severe winter of 1281 formed such great blocks of ice in the river that four of the arches supporting the bridge gave way, with many resultant injuries and deaths.

The repellent practice of impaling the heads of those executed on the spikes atop the fortified gates began in 1305 with the execution of Sir William Wallace, Scottish hero and leader of the struggle for independence against Edward I of England. The head of the Earl of Northumberland was displayed on the bridge in 1403, along with part of the quartered body of his son.

Jack Cade, the defeated rebel, won the battle for the bridge but lost his head on it in 1450. The practice continued in 1540 with the heads of the saints, John Fisher, Bishop of Rochester, and Sir Thomas More, Chancellor, as well as the head of Thomas Cromwell, Henry VIII's minister. A visitor in 1602 saw "the heads of 30 gentleman of high standing, who had been beheaded on account of treason and secret practices against the Queen." In 1678 the bridge saw the last head on record, that of William Staley, a Roman Catholic goldsmith and banker, victim of Titus Oates' machinations.

In all the tragedy associated with the bridge, a little romance is welcome. In 1536 the infant daughter, Anne, of a cloth maker named William Hewet, who had a house on the bridge, accidentally fell into the river. An apprentice named Osborne plunged into the turbulent waters and saved her. When the child grew up, old Hewet said to all her suitors, "Osborne saved her and Osborne shall have her." When Anne reached 18, she and Osborne were married; he eventually became Lord Mayor of London.

In 1852 water mills were installed on the bridge, adding their clamor to the noise made by the rushing waters around the piers. Francis Beaumont's play, *The Woman's Prize* (1625), has a character saying, "The noise of London Bridge is nothing to her."

Many prominent Englishmen admired the bridge as one of the wonders of the age; foreigners praised is as being beautiful, with quite splendid, handsome and well built houses. In 1633, a fire burnt down a third of the houses. These were replaced in 1651, only to be destroyed again in the Great Fire of 1666. At a later period, Pennant, the historian, wrote:

> I well remember the street on London Bridge, narrow, darksome, and dangerous to passengers from the multitude of carriages: frequent arches of strong timber crossed the street, from the tops of the houses to keep them together, and from falling into the river. Nothing but use could preserve the rest of the inmates, who soon grew deaf to the noise of the falling waters, the clamour of watermen, or the frequent shrieks of drowning wretches.

Although written in the 19th century, a vivid description of old London Bridge is found in George Borrow's novel, *Lavengro* (1840):

> A strange kind of bridge it was; huge and massive, and seemingly of great antiquity. It had an arched back, like that of a hog, and high balustrade, and on either side, at intervals, were stone bowers bulking out over the river, but open on the other side, and furnished with a semi-circular bench. Though the bridge was wide—very wide—it was all too narrow for the concourse upon it. Thousands of human beings were pouring over the bridge. But what chiefly struck my attention was a double row of carts and wagons, the generality drawn by horses as large as elephants, each row striving hard in a different direction, and not unfrequently brought to a standstill. Oh the cracking of whips, the shouts and oaths of the carters, and the grating of wheels upon the enormous stones that formed the pavement! In fact, there was a wild hurly-burly upon the bridge which nearly deafened me. But, if upon the bridge there was a confusion, below it there was a confusion ten times confounded. The tide, which was fast ebbing, obstructed by the immense piers of the old bridge, poured beneath the arches with a fall of several feet, forming in the river below as many whirlpools as there were arches. Truly tremendous was the roar of the

descending waters, and the bellow of the tremendous gulfs, which swallowed them for a time, and then cast them forth, foaming and frothing from their horrible wombs.

Beneath the bridge, multitudes of swans swam majestically along the clear and sparkling river, filled with salmon and other fish, the royal swans identified by the nicks in their beaks (two lengthwise and three crosswise). Up and down the Thames the watermen did a brisk business, chanting "Eastward Hoe" and "Westward Hoe", as they ferried their customers back and forth on the river. The clientele consisted largely of merry makers to and from the bear gardens, theaters and brothels in Bankside.

The houses were finally removed between 1756 and 1762 and alcoves or recesses placed at intervals along the bridge. By 1789 the bridge had been repaired so many times that the *Quarterly Review* had this to say:

> This pernicious structure has wasted more money in perpetual repairs than would have sufficed to build a dozen safe and commodious bridges, and cost the lives, perhaps, of many thousand people. Had an alderman or turtle been lost there, the nuisance would have been long removed.

In 1823, construction of an entirely new bridge was authorized. Designed by John Rennie, it was begun in 1825 by his sons John and George and completed in 1831. The recesses were retained and Charles Dickens made use of them in two of his novels.

In *Oliver Twist* (1838), Dickens has Noah Claypool crouching down in one of the recesses to spy on Nancy going to her secret interview with Mr. Brownlow and Rose Maylie:

> ...he watched her ... shrinking into one of the recesses which surmount the piers of the bridge, and leaning over the papapet to conceal his figure, he suffered her to pass on the opposite pavement ...

The young hero in *David Copperfield* (1849-50) uses the recesses to linger a while, waiting for the King's Bench Prison to open so that he may have breakfast with the Micawbers:

I forget, too, at what hour the gates were opened in the morning, admitting of my going in; but I know that I was often up at six o'clock, and that my favorite lounging-place in the interval was old London Bridge, where I was wont to sit in one of the stone recesses, watching the people going by, or to look over the balustrades at the sun shining in the water, and lighting up the golden flame on the top of the Monument.

When the bridge was widened in 1905, the recesses were removed.

The present bridge was begun in 1927 and completed in 1973. The John Rennie bridge was then sold, dismantled into 10,000 granite slabs and shipped to Lake Havasu City, Arizona, USA, where it was re-erected over an artificial lake.

MERCHANT TAYLORS' HALL

The hall proper, at No.30 Threadneedle Street, is the largest of the Livery Company Halls in London, measuring 82 feet by 43 feet, and is "an accurate representation of one the 14th century."

The Company received its first charter from Edward III in 1327. Twice destroyed—first by the Great Fire of 1666 and then by air attacks in 1941—the present hall was constructed in 1959 on the site of its 1331 headquarters. It retains a 1375 crypt and a 1425 great kitchen with the original spit. The first singing of the national anthem took place in the Hall in 1607.

Since early in the 17th century, the company has had no craft functions; all its resources and activities are confined to the educational sphere. The Merchant Taylors' School was originally founded in 1561 as essentially a day school; today it accommodates some 500 boys. In 1875 it occupied the site of Charterhouse School in its handsome Gothic buildings until moving to Sandy Lodge, near Rickmansworth, in 1933.

Among the celebrated men whom it had educated were Bishop Matthew Wren, Sir Christopher Wren's uncle; Thomas Lodge and James Shirley, Elizabethan dramatists; and the great Robert Lord Clive, founder of the British Indian empire.

The company also founded schools at Great Crosby, near Liverpool, in 1618, and a new elementary school at Ashwell in 1875. Many scholarships at the universities are available to Merchant Taylors' students, and the Company contributes to the City and Guilds of London Institute. It has built churches in the East End, restored St. Helen's, Bishopsgate, its parish church, and supports a convalescent home and almshouses in Lewisham.

THE MONUMENT

Standing at the top of Fish Street Hill on Monument Street, The Monument was built to commemorate the Great Fire of London which broke out about 10:00 PM on September 2, 1666, at Mr. Faryner's bake shop on Pudding Lane. The street was named for the puddings and other offal of the beasts slaughtered by the butchers in the area.

The Monument is the tallest isolated stone column in the world. When Boswell climbed to the top in 1762, he found it:

> horrid to be so monstrous a way up in the air, so far above London and all its spires ... the shaking of the earth by wagons passing would make the tremendous pile tumble to the foundations.

A fluted roman Doric pillar of Portland stone is surmounted by a flaming gilded urn, and a female figure representing the City of London sitting mournfully on the ruins left by the fire. An exterior viewing balcony, reached by a winding staircase of 311 steps, provides the best view of St. Paul's Cathedral and of 28 of the remaining 60 churches for which Wren was the original architect.

Daniel Defoe described The Monument as "built in the form of a candle", the top making a "handsome gilt flame like that of a candle."

The Monument appears in Charles Dickens' *Martin Chuzzlewit* where Tom Pinch loses his way and finds himself at last by the Monument. Gazing at the structure, he engages in some philosophical musings about a mythical "Man in the Monument".

Sir Christopher Wren and Robert Hooke, the City surveyor who was largely responsible for its construction, designed the Monument in 1671 and finished it in 1677 as an exercise in classical archeology.

Inscriptions on the Monument record the catastrophe which it commemorates and the fact that the structure itself is 202 feet high, the exact distance from the bake shop in Pudding Lane where the Great Fire broke out.

The Lord Mayor, when notified of the fire in the early hours of the morning, was contemptuous of the small blaze, saying "Pish! a woman might piss it out." Many of the locals must have agreed with the Lord Mayor for the Star Tavern across the street form the bake shop did a brisk business that evening.

The "small blaze", driven by a fierce wind through the densely packed wooden structures and the wharves loaded with coal and wood, destroyed most of the City's medieval heritage. When the fire finally halted after five days, it had consumed seven-eighths of the City within the walls, including the Guildhall, the Royal Exchange, the Customs House, 6 prisons, 44 City company halls, 87 parish churches, St. Paul's Cathedral and more than 13,000 homes.

Two distinguished eye witnesses lift their vivid impressions of the fire. John Evelyn wrote in his diary:

> The whole city is in dreadful flames, a resemblance of Sodome. God grant mine eye may never behold the like, who now saw above 10,000 houses all in one flame! The noise and cracking and thunder of the imperious flames, the shrieking of women and children, the hurry of people, the fall of towers, houses, and churches, was like a hideous storm; and the air was so hot and inflamed, that at last one was not able to approach it, so that they were forced to stand still, and let the blames burn on, which they did, for near two miles in length and one in breath .... London was, but is no more.

Samuel Pepys watched the awful conflagration from the Tower of London, from the steeple of All Hallows Barking (now called All Hallows by the Tower), from a boat on the Thames and from the south side of the river. He saw:

> ... the fire grow, and as it grew darker, appeared more and more, and in corners and upon steeples, and between churches and houses, as far as one could see up the hill of the City, in a most horrid malicious bloody flame ... as only one entire arch of fire from this to the other side of the bridge, and in a bow up the hill from an arch of the above a mile long.

> It made me weep to see it. The churches, houses, and all on fire, and flaming at once; and a horrid noise the flames made, and the crackling of houses at their ruine ... but Lord!

what a sad night it was by moonlight to see the whole City almost on fire. The saddest sight of desolation that I ever saw.

Pepys' own house in Seething Lane near the Tower, was in the path of the fire, but just barely escaped the flames. On September 3, in the pre-dawn hours, Pepys himself could have been seen in his dressing gown moving household goods, personal papers, silver plate and bags of gold in a cart to a friend's house in Bethnal Green.

OLDE WINE SHADES

A real feeling of antiquity is evident in this old drinking house, at No.8 Martin Lane, which dates from 1663. When you step inside, you suddenly find yourself transported to the Victorian period. Now a branch of El Vino's at No.47 Fleet Street, it may well lay claim to being the oldest wine house in London.

The following testimonial of 1840 is prominently displayed:

> According to Virgil, "The Shades" were divided
> Into two different regions where Spirits resided,
> Like ghost from the Styx we leave the streets' busy hum
> To revel in joy in "The Shades" best Elysium.

The Shades was a popular name for drinking places in the 18th and 19th centuries, which were usually underground or sheltered from the sun by an arcade.

PLOUGH COURT

Alexander Pope, the great satirist, was born on May 21, 1688, in Plough Court on Lombard Street. Across the street is the church of St. Edmund where his friend, Joseph Addison, entered into a disastrous marriage with Countess Dowager of Warwick in 1716. The house of his birth, which faced up the alley, was destroyed in 1872. Only the gloomy court remains.

Excluded from the universities and public office because of his Roman Catholic religion, he was largely self educated. When his enemies, chiefly minor poets, attacked him, he mercilessly ridiculed them in *The Dunciad* (1728-43). His brilliant *An Essay on Criticism* (1711) summed up his poetic neoclassical principles. His *Rape of the Lock* (1712-14) is one of the finest mock heroic poems in the English language. Pope's translation of Homer (1715-26) made him independently wealthy.

The most celebrated writer of his day, Pope died in 1744 at Twickenham on the Thames. Suffering from ill health all his life, he was the victim of a tuberculous infection that condemned him to be a hunchback not five feet tall. Tormented with excruciating headaches and other painful ailments, it is little wonder that he wrote:

This long disease, my life.

THE ROYAL EXCHANGE

The Royal Exchange, in the area between Threadneedle Street and Cornhill, opposite the Bank of England, was the earliest formal commercial building in London, and in which the Stock Exchange started business.

First established by Sir Thomas Gresham in 1568 and modeled after the Bourse at Antwerp, the Exchange provided space for London merchants and a large public square accommodating a hundred open air shops. After Queen Elizabeth I visited it in 1571, the word Royal was added to its name. A bell in the tower summoned the merchants at noon and again at six in the evening. Many stone grasshoppers, representing Gresham's crest, were placed around the square.

The present Exchange, opened by Queen Victoria in 1844, is the third structure, fire having destroyed the first two. Lloyd's, the famous insurance underwriters, occupied the Exchange from 1844 to 1928 when it moved to its new building on Leadenhall Street.

After World War I, brokers would assemble only two days a week to transact business. The meetings were discontinued in 1921 and when Lloyd's left, the Royal Exchange Assurance Corporation took over sole possession.

The Royal Exchange today is but a memento, interesting only because of its past. The courtyard still attracts visitors and provides a pleasant area for City clerks to enjoy their lunch hour.

SOUTH SEA HOUSE

On the north side of Threadneedle Street, almost at its intersection with Bishopsgate Street, the South Sea House, famous for the South Sea Scheme or South Sea Bubble, was built for the British South Sea Company in 1711.

In return for a monopoly of British trade in the south seas, the Company assumed the national debt and gave stock to creditors of the government in exchange for their claims. Misled by the support given to the Company by the government, the public indulged in wild dreams of fantastic profits from the high speculative project. The stock soared to a price of 1,000% of par in August 1720, whereupon the promoters sold out and the South Sea Bubble burst, ruining thousands of shareholders. The resulting panic almost brought down the government itself.

Curiously enough, the Company was not dissolved, but continued as a legitimate trading company engaged in whale fishing and Negro slave traffic. After 1750 it was no longer a trading company, but continued with its exclusive privileges in the south seas until 1807.

Charles Lamb (1775-1834) obtained a clerkship in the South Sea House in 1789, where his brother John was employed. Charles left for the East India House in 1792. One of Lamb's fellow clerks at South Sea House was an Italian named Ellia; he chose that name, spelled Elia, as his pen name.

Charles Lamb, in his essay *The South Sea House*, reached back into the recesses of his memory to nostalgically describe the place of his first employment:

> This was once a house of trade—a centre of busy interests. The throng of merchants was here .... Here are still to be seen stately porticoes, imposing staircases ... directors seated in form on solemn days ... at long worm-eaten tables, that have been mahogany, with tarnished gilt-leather coverings, supporting massy silver inkstands long since dry, the oaken wainscots ... dusty maps of Mexico ... long since dissipated, or scattered into air at the blast of the breaking of that famous BUBBLE.

Lamb continues on to gently describe the eccentricities of many of the clerks employed at that time. He concludes:

> Such is the SOUTH SEA HOUSE. At least such it was forty
> years ago, when I knew it—a magnificent relic.

After the South Sea House was demolished, the British Linen Bank was built over part of its site in 1902.

Abutting Threadneedle Street to the north lies Throgmorton Street where an interesting event occurred. Thomas Cromwell, Henry VIII's minister, had a home on that street. He was an arrogant and unpopular official against whom "no man durst argue" and was later beheaded by the same monarch he served. John Stow's father was a neighbor. Cromwell dug Stow's house out of the ground, placed it on rollers and moved it 20 feet away from its boundary so that Cromwell could extend his garden further down the street. The Drapers' Company Hall now occupies the site.

ST. CLEMENT, EASTCHEAP

The earliest mention of this church, on Clement Lane off King William Street, was in the 11th century. The saint to whom it is dedicated was one of St. Paul's followers mentioned in "The Letter of Paul to the Philippians" of the *New Testament*:

> ... help these women, for they have labored side by side with me in the gospel together with Clement and the rest of my fellow workers, whose names are in the book of life.

Clement suffered martyrdom about 100 A.D. when he was thrown into the sea with an anchor tied around his neck. He became the patron saint of seamen.

St. Clement was the first City church to be destroyed by the Great Fire of 1666. Sir Christopher Wren rebuilt the church in 1686. He designed the new church without a single right angled corner.

A brass tablet of 1878 commemorates Thomas Fuller (1608-61), the quaint writer beloved of Charles Lamb, and minister of the Queen's Chapel of the Savoy. In his *The History of the Worthies of England*, full of interesting facts and fancies, Fuller describes the wit-combats between Shakespeare and Ben Jonson.

In the Middle Ages, Spanish barges used to dock at London Bridge and sell their oranges within the shadow of this church. That has given rise to the church's claim that it is the one referred to in the nursery rhyme, *Oranges and Lemons*:

> Oranges and lemons
> Say the bells of St. Clement's.
> When will you pay me?
> Say the bells of Old Bailey.
> When I grow rich,
> Say the bells of Shoreditch.
> Here comes a candle to light you to bed.
> Here comes a chopper to chop off your head.

ST. MAGNUS THE MARTYR

This church on Lower Thames Street, with a grand tower and octagonal lantern below a clock and a lead dome, was Sir Christopher Wren's welcome to the City for people coming over the old London Bridge. The clock was a gift to the church by the Lord Mayor in 1709 to commemorate the loss of his first job because he was late for a meeting with his prospective employer on London Bridge. He had been too poor to afford a timepiece and there were no clocks in the area. He vowed that if he became rich, he would prevent anyone else from experiencing the same unfortunate situation.

T. S. Eliot, the Nobel prize winning poet, felt that the church had "one of the finest among Wren's interiors" and that "the walls of Magnus Martyr hold inexplicable splendour of Ionian white and gold."

The earliest reference to the church was contained in a grant by William the Conqueror dated 1067. Miles Coverdale was rector from 1563 to 1566 and author of the first translation of the Bible in English in 1535. It was authorized for general use in 1539. His version of the Psalms in the Prayer Book has been used since the 1547 to 1553 reign of Edward VI. Coverdale died in 1569 and his remains were transferred in 1840 from the original burial place to this church. A memorial was placed south of the sanctuary.

A recently discovered register entry of 1594 reads: "Benjamine Johnson and Anne Lewis Marryed." As a resident of the area, this probably refers to the noted dramatist, Ben Jonson.

Fish Street, now called Fish Street Hill, was once the main street to London Bridge from Eastcheap to Lower Thames Street. In Shakespeare's *Henry VI, Part 2*, Jack Cade cries to his rabble:

Up Fish Street! Down St. Magnus corner!
Kill and knock down! Throw them into the Thames!

The Vestry of St. Michaels, Crooked Lane (demolished in 1831), used to meet in the famous Boar's Head Tavern, which belonged to the church in medieval times. An Elizabethan drinking cup, 11¾ inches high and weighing 15 ounces, was used at their meetings. Washington Irving was shown the cup in 1818 and associated it with a remarkable passage in *Henry IV, Part2* in which Dame Quickly says to Falstaff:

Thou didst swear to me upon a parcel-gilt goblet, sitting in
my Dolphin-chamber ... to marry me, and make me my
lady, they wife.

An iron tobacco box, its cover purportedly painted by William
Hogarth of the exterior of the Boar's Head Inn and showing Falstaff
and Prince Hal, was also used at the Vestry meetings. Both the goblet
and the tobacco box are in the possession of the church.

Another link between the Boar's Head Tavern and the church
may be found in the churchyard. Against the wall is this headstone,
attesting to the temperate virtues of one Robert Preston:

> Here lieth the Body of Robert Preston,
> late Drawer at the Boars-head Tavern,
> in Great Eastcheap, who departed this life
> March the 16, Anno Dom 1730
> Aged 27 years.

> Bacchus, to give the Toping World surprize
> Produc'd one Sober Son, and here he lies.
> Tho' nurs'd among full Hogsheads, he defy'd
> The charms of Wine, and ev'ry vice beside.
> O Reader! if to Justice thou'rt inclin'd,
> Keep Honest Preston daily in thy mind.
> He drew good Wine, took care to fill his Pots,
> Had sundry virtues that out weigh'd his faults.
> You that on Bacchus have the like dependence,
> Pray copy Bob in Measure and Attendance.

After John Salter, a respected member of the church, died in
1605, a service was held in accordance with his will. Each person in
procession was required to knock upon his tomb with a stick and
shouted three times:

> How do you do, Brother Salter?
> I hope you are well.

There is no record of any reply.

ST. MARGARET PATTENS

This church, on Rood Lane off Eastcheap, is dedicated to St. Margaret of Antioch, a Christian martyr of the 3rd to 4th centuries. Pattens were shoes with metal attached to the soles to protect the wearer from muddy roads; they were once made and sold in the lane. The church vestibule exhibits a reproduction of an old church notice to its parishioners: "Will the women leave their pattens before entering the church and men wipe shoes on mat." There was probably some association between the pattens and William Shakespeare's imagination when he wrote The Merchant of Venice:

> ... look, how the floor of heaven
> Is thick inlaid with patines of bright gold.

In a glass case are two pairs of pattens, one over 100 years old, the other made in a Salford factory in 1928. The Patten-Maker's Company has held its annual service here in the octave of Epiphany since 1911.

Nothing is known of the first church on this site, but the date 1067 is inscribed on the church porch. The original was rebuilt in 1530, repaired during 1614-32, and finally destroyed in the Great Fire of 1666. The present church was built by Sir Christopher Wren in 1687. The 200 foot spire gives the church a more medieval appearance than any of Wren's other conceptions.

The church possesses a communion cup from 1543 made of silver gilt and considered to be the oldest in the City. The baptismal register goes back to 1559. A beautiful glazed Della Robbia plaque was purchased in Florence and presented to the church by the congregation. The original Beadle's pew and a low punishment bench stand north of the altar.

Two canopied pews, unique in the City churches, stand at the back of the church. One of the pews has a carved lion, the other a unicorn. Wren regularly worshipped here and the north pew possesses his monogram in inlaid wood.

ST. MARY-AT-HILL

Hidden away among cobbled alleys, paved passages and brick walls, overhung by a plane tree, stands the church of St. Mary-at-Hill on Lovat Lane off Eastcheap, containing the least spoiled and most gorgeous interior of any church in the City.

The earliest reference to a church on this site was about 1190. Destroyed in the Great Fire of 1666, it was reconstructed by Sir Christopher Wren in 1672-77, but the old tower and several of the walls were left standing. Twenty years later, the west wall was rebuilt in yellow brick. Eighty years later the side walls were re-erected. The tower was replaced in 1780.

Wren designed the church as almost a square with the dome resting on four free-standing columns to the Byzantine quincunx architectural plan.

A tablet to the memory of Reverend John Brand (d. 1806) "for 22 years the faithful rector of this, and the united parish of St. Andrew Hubbard", and the author of *Observations on Popular Antiquities* (1777), is on the east wall. Edward Young, author of the noted poem, *Night Thoughts*, was married to Lady Elizabeth Lee in this church in 1731.

The organ was built by the famous Father Smith during the reign of Charles II (1660-85), but the color of the keys was reversed; the normally black keys were made of ivory and the normally white keys of ebony. Father Smith also made the organs in St. Paul's Cathedral and Westminster Abbey. In the vestibule is a relic of the Great Fire, a piece of a carving representing the resurrection and second coming of Christ. The dark, richly carved woodwork of the box pews and the beautiful carved staircase give the church a Dickensian atmosphere.

ST. MICHAEL, CORNHILL

The earliest mention of this church, on Cornhill at Gracechurch Street, was in 1055. The great-grandfather, grandfather and father of John Stow, the antiquarian, were all buried in the church. The grandfather, who died in 1527, directed that his body "be buried in a little green churchyard of St. Michael's, Cornhill, nigh the wall as may be by my father and mother." The secluded little green garden may still be visited although it is not directly accessible from the church. It may be reached through the archway on the Southwest side of the church tower, or via St. Michael's Alley.

The old church was destroyed by the Great Fire of 1666 and rebuilt by Sir Christopher Wren in 1672. The tower was left in its damaged state until 1722 when Wren reconstructed it in his 90th year, one year before his death. The tower, modeled after the one at Magdalen College Oxford, was probably Wren's last design.

When coffee was introduced into England in 1657, coffee houses sprung up like mushrooms, with several of the most important ones clustered around St. Michael's. They played an integral part in the social life of 17th and 18th century London as meeting places for the wits and men of fashion, as well as merchants and politicians. One of the oldest and most historic of the coffee houses was Garraway's in Change Alley, just below the church.

Garraway's stood preeminent among the coffee houses for over 200 years until finally demolished in 1921. Such literary personages as Sir Richard Steele (1672-1729), Jonathan Swift (1667-1745), Daniel Defoe (1659-1731) and Charles Dickens (1812-1870) introduced the famous coffee house in their novels. In the essay, "City of the Absent" in *The Uncommercial Traveller*, Dickens gives us a revealing picture of the affection in which Garraway's was held by so many Londoners:

> … here is Garraway's, bolted and shuttered hard and fast! … imagination is unable to pursue the men who never come. When they are forcibly put out of Garraway's on Saturday night—which they must be, for they never would go out of their own accord—where do they vanish until Monday morning?

In the "Poor Relations Story" of *Christmas Stories*, the narrator relates how he used to sit in Garraway's Coffee House in the City to pass the time until dinner, after which he returns to his lodging for the evening. The most interesting of the references is contained in Mr. Pickwick's note to Mrs. Bardell in *Pickwick Papers*:

> Garraway's, twelve o'clock, Dear Mrs. B.
> Chops and Tomato Sauce. Yours, Pickwick.

Thomas Gray, the poet, was born on December 26, 1716, just a few yards south of St. Michael's at No.39 Cornhill (a plaque commemorates the event) and baptized in the church. He was the only one of 12 children in the family to have survived infancy and became the most famous poet in London upon publication of his *Elegy Written in a Country Churchyard* in 1751. Presumed to be a description of the churchyard at Stoke Poges, it is a sincere and tranquil affirmation of the virtues of the life of the poor in the small country villages of England. The verses are still familiar and the philosophy is as valid today as it was over 200 years ago. In fact, many of the phrases are in common use today and have provided many writers with titles for their stories.

A couple of the 29 verses preceding *The Epitaph* will serve to illustrate the emotional appeal of Gray's imagery and artless language:

> Let not Ambition mock their useful toil,
>   Their homely joys, and destiny obscure;
> Nor Grandeur hear with a disdainful smile
>   The short and simple annals of the poor,
>
> •   •   •   •   •   •
>
> Far from the madding crowd's ignoble strife
>   Their sober wishes never learn'd to stray;
> Along the cool sequester'd vale of life
>   They kept the noiseless tenor of their way.

Gray died in 1771 and was buried in the churchyard at Stoke Poges; a monument commemorating him is in the Poets' Corner at Westminster Abbey. It is remarkable that in the history of English literature, no one who published as little as Thomas Gray holds so high a place. A walking stick that belonged to Gray is kept in a glass case at St. Michael's.

Carved panels on a door at No.32 Cornhill commemorate the arrival of Charlotte and Anne Brontës in 1848 for their first meeting with Thackeray and to prove to their publisher, Smith Elder & Co., that their pseudonyms, Currer and Acton Bell, where actually the two sisters. Another panel shows Garraway's Coffee House, established in 1670, at No.3 Exchange Alley off Cornhill.

In addition to Gray's walking stick, the church possesses an unusual poor box which is inscribed "The poor cannot recompense thee, but thou shall be recompensed at the resurrection of the just." A piece of the Roman wall found under the church; a copy of *The Book of Martyrs by Mr. Fox*, which was stolen in 1607 but retrieved in the following year; and a 1775 wooden sculpture of an enormous wooden pelican feeding its young are all preserved in St. Michael's.

ST. PETER, CORNHILL

Destroyed in the Great Fire of 1666, St. Peter on Gracechurch Street was rebuilt by Sir Christopher Wren in 1677-81. A tablet in the vestry claims it to be the oldest foundation in London, having been established during the reign of King Lucius in 179 A.D. William Makepeace Thackeray (1811-63), the novelist and editor of *Cornhill Magazine*, added substance to this claim in his *Roundabout Papers*:

> I had occasion to pass a week in the autumn in the little old
> town of Coire or Chur, in the Grisons, where lies buried that
> very ancient British king, saint, and martyr, Lucius, who
> founded the Church of St. Peter, on Cornhill.

The original organ keyboard, built by Father Smith, has been carefully preserved in the vestry. Felix Mendelssohn played on it in 1840; his autograph rests beside it. The carved wooden choir screen is the only survivor of the two known to be by Wren. The other, at All Hallows the Great, was consumed by the Great Fire. Also on display is a copy of Jerome's *Vulgate*, a fourth century translation of the Old and New Testaments into Latin. The copy was made in 1290 by a scribe of St. Peter's Church.

George Barrow, the novelist, married Mrs. Mary Clarke in this church on April 23, 1840.

The churchyard, which may also be the oldest in London, is reached from Gracechurch Street through St. Peter's Alley. Here are the tombstones which Charles Dickens wrote about in Our Mutual Friend (1864):

> Here ... were the dead and the tombstones, some of the lat-
> ter droopingly inclined from the perpendicular, as if they
> were ashamed of the lies they told.

It was also here, in the same novel, where Bradley Headstone, the schoolmaster, makes his futile declaration of love to Lizzie Hexham.

THE STOCK EXCHANGE

The issuance of stocks and shares to provide capital for business began as long ago as the 17th century. The brokers had their first headquarters at the Royal Exchange, later moving to the nearby coffee houses.

The first Stock Exchange Building was erected in 1773 at the corner of Threadneedle Street and Sweetings Alley. It was replaced by another building in 1801, and then by the present building in 1971 on the same site at No.8 Throgmorton Street.

The trading floor may be viewed from the Visitors' Gallery, reached via the public entrance on Threadneedle Street.

AREA I

TOWER OF LONDON

AND

ALL HALLOWS

AREA I ATTRACTIONS

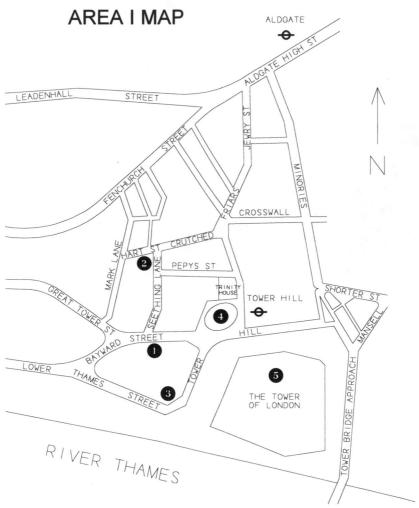

AREA I MAP

ALDGATE

ALDGATE HIGH ST

LEADENHALL   STREET

FENCHURCH   STREET

JEWRY ST

MINORIES

CROSSWALL

MARK LANE

HART ST   CRUTCHED

SEETHING LANE

FRIARS

2

PEPYS ST

TRINITY HOUSE

TOWER HILL

SHORTER ST

GREAT TOWER ST

4

HILL

MANSELL

BAYWARD   STREET

1

TOWER

LOWER   THAMES   STREET

3

5

THE TOWER OF LONDON

TOWER BRIDGE APPROACH

RIVER THAMES

N

⊖ UNDERGROUND STATION

```
          200 m
 |----|----|
 0        200 Yds
                        1/4 km
 |-------------------|
 0                  1/4 mi
```

ALL HALLOWS BY THE TOWER

The history of this medieval parish church goes back to 675 AD when it was in the possession of the Abbess of a nunnery at Barking. The first church was destroyed by fire in 1087 and rebuilt while the Tower of London was being erected. Richard I founded a Lady Chapel in the church in the 12th century. Subsequent additions to the church and tower were made in the 17th century.

As the church nearest to the Tower of London, it was the temporary place of internment for some of the Tower's victims. In 1535 Bishop Fisher was buried there for a short time until his body was removed to a permanent plot in St. Peter ad Vincula in the Tower of London. The remains of Henry Howard, Earl of Surrey, the poet who helped introduce the sonnet into England from Italy, lay in the church from 1547 to 1614 until he was finally taken to Framlingham, in Suffolk, for final internment. Archbishop Laud's body was in the church from 1645 to 1663 when it was moved to St. John's College at Oxford University, where he had been president.

Bishop Lancelot Andrewes, scholar and divine, was baptized in the church in 1555. William Penn, English Quaker and founder of the colony of Pennsylvania, USA, was baptized on October 23, 1644. His father, Admiral Penn, helped the church survived the Great Fire of 1666 as Samuel Pepys recorded in his *Diary*:

Sept. 5th, 1666. At about two in the morning my wife calls me up and tells me of new cryes of fire, it being come to Barking Church which is at the bottom of our lane…. But going to the fire I find by the blowing up of our houses, and the great help given by the workmen out of the king's yard sent up by Sir W. Pen, there is a good stop given to it as well as at Mark Lane end as ours, it having burned only the dyall of Barking Church and part of the porch and was there quenched. I up to the top of Barking Steeple and there saw the saddest sight of desolation that I ever saw.

John Quincy Adams, who was destined to become President of the United States in 1824, was married to Louisa Johnson in the church in 1797.

Only the exterior walls and the brick tower of 1659, from which Pepys had watched the Great Fire of 1666, were left after repeated bombings in World War II. The church was repaired in 1947 and completely restored in 1957.

In a magnificent 15th century canopied stone tomb, in the Lady Chapel, is a casket containing the Toc H (Talbot House) lamp donated by the Prince of Wales in 1922 in memory of his fallen comrades in World War I. A beautiful bronze effigy of a soldier slain in that war lies near it. Toc H is a society devoted to continuing the comradeship of World War I and whose founder padre, Rev. P. B. Clayton, was vicar of this church. A new font was made out of limestone from the rock of Gibraltar.

The bombing of World War II revealed a capsule of London's history in the undercroft. Roman mosaic pavements, two extremely rare Saxon crosses and Saxon walls of the original church of 675 AD were uncovered. The church register, with the entries of significant baptisms, marriages and deaths, is proudly displayed.

A new memorial tablet to William Penn outside the north porch was unveiled on July 24, 1950. In an adjoining garden is a tablet with a Latin inscription, translated as:

> The ancient church of All Hallows,
> A.D. 675, Ethelburga founded me.
> 1666, Pepys from fire did ward me.
> 1940, German bombs wounded me.
> 1948, loving friends restored me.

ST. OLAVE, HART STREET

This church is probably of 15th century origin and now most closely associated with Samuel Pepys, the famous diarist. Long before it became known as Pepys' Church, it had interesting historical connections. In 1585 Queen Elizabeth I stood as godmother for Sir Philip Sidney's first child, named after the Queen, and attended the christening ceremonies at St. Olave's.

The church registers from 1563 to 1893 recorded 9,818 baptisms, 3,179 marriages and 11,533 burials with the letter P after a long list of the names to indicate that they had died of the Plague. There is a record that a Mother Goose was buried her on September 14, 1586. Mary Ramsay, who is said to have brought the Great Plague to London, was interred in the churchyard on July 24, 1665.

Pepys referred to the churchyard many times in connection with the Plague burials of 1665. He wrote: "It frightened me to see so many graves lie so high upon the churchyard where people had been buried of the plague." The churchyard was probably much larger then.

Charles Dickens referred to it in his essay in *The Uncommercial Traveler*, entitled "The City of the Absent":

One of my best beloved churchyards, I call the churchyard of Saint Ghastly Grim; touching what men in general call it, I have no information. It lies at the heart of the City, and the Blackwall Railway shrieks at it daily. It is a small churchyard, with a ferocious strong spiked iron gate, like a jail. This gate is ornamented with skulls and crossbones, larger than life, wrought in stone; but it likewise came into the mind of Saint Ghastly Grim, that to stick iron spikes a-top of the stone skulls, as though they were impaled, would be a pleasant device. Therefore the skulls grin aloft horribly, thrust through and through with iron spears. Hence there is attraction of repulsion for me in Saint Ghastly Grim ....

Samuel Pepys and his wife Elizabeth worshipped here when they lived in adjacent Seething Lane and he worked as Secretary of the Admiralty at the Navy office on Hart Street's extension, Crutched Friars. He referred to St. Olave as "our own church". Pews were installed in 1660 in a gallery on the south side for the use of the officials of the Navy Office. The principal occupants of the gallery were Sir William Batten, Admiral Sir William Penn and Samuel Pepys. The galleries were removed in 1853, but the monument to Pepys marks the place.

When Elizabeth Pepys died in 1669, she was buried in the church and her husband erected a marble monument to her on the north end of the chancel. He drew up a long Latin inscription which says that Elizabeth bore no children because she could bear none worthy of herself. It was placed where he could look at it from the Navy gallery. Samuel was buried in the same grave as his wife when he died in 1703. A memorial in his honor is on the south side of the nave. His brother is also buried in the church, in the middle aisle "just under my mother's pew".

John Betjeman, poet and authority on English architecture, said of St. Olave's: "It stands today like a country church in the world of Seething Lane."

THE TIGER TAVERN

This modern pub at No.1 Tower Hill replaces the original 14th century inn. A previous reconstruction unearthed a tunnel, believed to run all the way to the Tower of London. Inside the tunnel were the mummified remains of a cat and several rats.

Legend has it that when Queen Mary confined Elizabeth, the future queen, the young princess often used the tunnel, to play with the cat at the inn. The mummified cat and rats are displayed in the pub.

TOWER HILL

From 1388 to 1747, Tower Hill was the principal place of execution of prisoners brought from the Tower of London. Even before a permanent scaffold was erected at the western end of what is now Trinity Square Gardens, Wat Tyler and his Kentish rebels broke into the Tower, seized four of Richard II's ministers and beheaded them on Tower Hill in 1381.

The scaffold, of rough planks, was about five feet high with wooden steps at one end, draped in black and surrounded by a railing . Straw covered the deck and a basket half filled with sawdust was placed by the block to receive the severed head. The gruesome site where at least 75 victims, innocent and guilty, were beheaded is marked by a stone in the pavement. Several plaques commemorate many of the famous persons who met their deaths on the scaffold.

The first recorded execution was that of Sir Simon Burley in 1388, tutor to King Richard II. Other prominent figures followed, such as John Fisher, Bishop of Rochester and Sir Thomas More, Lord Chancellor, in 1535. Both had been imprisoned in the Bell Tower for their opposition to the royal supremacy and Henry VIII's divorce from Catherine of Aragon.

While in the Tower, Bishop Fisher wrote a pitiful letter to Thomas Cromwell, Henry VIII's minister, who met the same fate five years later:

> I beseech you to be good Master, unto me in my necessity;
> for I have neither shirt nor suit, nor yet other clothes that are
> necessary for me to wear, but that be ragged and rent so
> shamefully. Notwithstanding I mighte easily suffer that, if
> they would keep my body warm. But my diet also, God
> knoweth how slender it is at times, and now in mine age my
> stomach may not away with but a few kinds of meats, which
> if I want, I decay forthwith, and fall into cough and diseases
> of my body, and cannot keep myself in health.

By 1535 Bishop Fisher was so weak that he had to be carried to the scaffold.

Two weeks later, Sir Thomas More followed Fisher to his death. When More stumbled on the steps of the scaffold, he humorously remarked to the executioner:

> I pray you, Master Lieutenant, see me safe up, and for my coming down, let me shift for myself.

He continued to reassure him by saying:

> Pluck up thy spirits, man, and be not afraid to do thy office; my neck is very short; take heed therefore thou strike not awry for the saving of thine honesty.

More also asked him to wait until his beard was moved aside for "it had never committed treason."

More's head was impaled on a spike on London Bridge until blown down in a storm and retrieved by his daughter, who kept it hidden away until her death in 1544. The head was then interred in the Roper family vault at St. Dunstan's Church in Canterbury. More's headless body lies in the Chapel of St. Peter ad Vincula at the Tower of London.

Among the others who fell victim to the headman's axe were: Thomas Cromwell in 1540; The Duke of Somerset, Lord Protector in the reign of Edward VI, for plotting to overthrow John Dudley, Duke of Northumberland, in 1552; the same John Dudley for attempting to usurp the right of Princess Mary to the throne in 1553; Thomas Wentworth, Earl of Stafford, principal adviser to King Charles I, for high treason in 1641; and William Laud, Archbishop of Canterbury, for two attempts to convert the Scottish church to Episcopalianism.

Samuel Pepys describes an execution of June 14, 1662 in his *Diary* which seems to indicate that such incidents were almost commonplace:

> About 11 o'clock ... we all went out to Tower-hill, and there, over against the scaffold, made on purpose this day, saw Sir Henry Vane brought. A very great press of people ... then he prayed, and so fitted himself, and received the blow; but the scaffold was so crowded that we could not see it done .... So to the office a little, and to the Trinity-house, and there all of us to dinner ...

The dramatist, Thomas Otway, died on Tower Hill, but not from the axe. He received so little money from his greatest work, *Venice Preserved*, that he was reduced to begging on Tower Hill. The story goes that one day a man who recognized him was so distressed by Otway's miserable condition that he gave him a guinea. Otway, close to starvation, ordered an enormous meal at the nearest restaurant—and choked to death.

The Duke of Monmouth was beheaded in 1685 for treason. In 1716 the Jacobite Robert, Earl of Kenmure, and an English sympathizer, the Earl of Derwentwater, were beheaded. Over the next few years many more Jacobites were beheaded for attempting to restore the Stuarts. After the Jacobite defeat at Culloden in 1746, the Lords Kilmarnock and Balmerino were executed on Tower Hill.

The last man beheaded on Tower Hill was another Jacobite, Simon Fraser, Lord Lovat, in 1747. After that date, hanging replaced beheading. The last people executed on Tower Hill were two prostitutes and a one-armed soldier arrested during the Gordon Riots of 1780 for leading an attack by a drunken mob on the tavern of a foreign Roman Catholic.

THE TOWER OF LONDON

The pageant of English history has unfolded in the Tower in the worst manifestations of the human spirit—terror, tragedy and murder—within those cold stone walls.

The history of the Tower began with William the Conqueror who constructed the great keep, known as the White Tower, about 1078 at the corner section of a wall on the Thames where the Romans had built a fort. The name may have been derived form the white Caen stone used, from the White Hill on which it stood, or from the white-washing by Henry III in 1240.

William created the White Tower for protection from foreign attack by way of the Thames. Vikings and Normans had previously used th river route for their raiding forays. Undoubtedly, the Tower was also intended to discourage any Londoners who might want to challenge his conquest. For the most recalcitrant, he included a dark unventilated cell four feet square where the prisoner could neither stand nor sit down, appropriately called Little Ease.

Succeeding monarchs over the next 400 years added 13 towers within the inner walls and six more in the outer walls, the whole covering nearly 18 acres. The last fortifications were added to the northwest and northeast corners by Henry VIII between 1509 and 1547.

Over the centuries, the Tower served not only as a fortress, but as a prison, royal palace, menagerie, the Royal Mint, the Public Records Office and the Royal Observatory, as well as the repository of the Crown Jewels. With the exception of Elizabeth I, who hated and feared it, the Tower served as the residence of every English monarch until James I died in 1625. It was even used as a bank by merchants, until Charles I in 1640 "borrowed" the deposits totaling £130,000.

But the Tower is best known as a prison and execution ground for the innumerable victims of over reaching ambition and insensate pride. Of the vast number of the unfortunates who sojourned here on their inexorable way to internment or death, many are deserving of special notice:

12th CENTURY

The first prisoner of record, Ralph Flambard, Bishop of Durham, was seized in 1100 for selling ecclesiastical offices. After first having made his guards drunk, he attempted to escape using a rope smuggled to him in a cask of wine. Although he fell from a window 65 feet above ground he was unhurt, but he failed to escape. After his eventual release, he lived to a ripe old age. Griffin, the son of the Prince of Wales, tried the same trick but was not as fortunate—the rope snapped and he died of a broken neck.

13th CENTURY

In 1278 some 600 Jews were thrown into the dungeons, accused of adulterating the King's coins. Few survived the damp rat infested quarters; 267 were hanged and the rest banished. In 1296 John Baliol, King of the Scots, rebelled against Edward I's authority and was imprisoned in the Tower. He was freed in 1299.

14th CENTURY

The population of the Tower increased dramatically in 1303 when Richard de Podlicote, keeper of the Palace of Westminster, and 48 monks were arrested for robbing the Royal Treasury in Westminster Abbey. After a long trial, all the monks were released, but Podlicote was hanged. The valuables were recovered.

Sir William Wallace, Scottish hero and patriot, organized strong resistance to Edward I in his resolve to liberate Scotland form the English yoke. After a victory over the English forces at Stirling Bridge in 1297, Wallace was proclaimed "governor of Scotland in the name of King John", John Baliol being then a captive in the Tower. Wallace was betrayed by a countryman and captured on August 5, 1305 and lodged in the Tower until his execution at Smithfield. A favorite hero of the Scots, Wallace has been celebrated by such Scottish poets as Robert Burns in *Bannockburn*:

> Scots, who hae wi' Wallace bled,
> Scots, whom Bruce has often led,
> Welcome to your gory bed,
>   Or to victorie!

Roger Mortimer, a rebellious Welsh baron, was imprisoned in the Tower in 1322. He escaped two years later with the help of his lover, Edward II's Queen, Isabella of France. He and the Queen raised an army in 1326 and seized the Tower, releasing all the prisoners. The following year after Edward II was murdered, Mortimer and Isabella governed the country while Edward III, a minor of 14 years, was held a virtual prisoner in the Tower. However, before he was 18, Edward gained the support of the Barons and had Mortimer arrested and executed, and banished Isabella to Castle Rising in Norfolk.

King David II of Scotland, after several unsuccessful raids into England, was taken prisoner in 1346 and confined to the Tower. He was later moved to other quarters and finally freed in 1357.

King John II of France, captured at the battle of Poitiers in 1356, was imprisoned in the Tower. He was released after the Treaty of Brétigny was signed in 1360 by Edward III giving up his claim to the throne of France.

In 1381 Simon Sudbury, Archbishop of Canterbury, was seized by Wat Tyler's rebels while at prayer in the chapel and executed on Tower Hill.

Thomas Beauchamp, Earl of Warwick, was imprisoned for treason in the Tower by Richard II in 1397. Richard was deposed in 1399 and Warwick was then restored to liberty and honor by Henry IV. He later took a prominent part in suppressing the Welsh Chieftain Glendower's rebellion against Henry IV. The Beauchamp Tower is named after this distinguished person.

The last year of the century reveals the abdication of King Richard II and the assumption of the crown by his cousin, Henry Bolingbroke of Lancaster, as Henry IV. After confinement for a short time in the Tower, Richard was moved to Pontefract Castle. As he prepares to cast aside his kingdom, Shakespeare in *King Richard The Second* has him saying:

> For God's sake, let us sit upon the ground,
> And tell sad stories of the death of kings:—
> How some have been depos'd; some slain in war;

Some haunted by the ghosts they have depos'd;
Some poison'd by their wives; some sleeping kill'd;
All murder'd:—for within the hollow crown
That rounds the mortal temples of a king
Keeps Death his court ...

15th CENTURY

To begin this century, the body of Richard II, who had been murdered at Pontefract Castle, rested for a night in the Tower chapel. After being exposed to public view for three days at St. Paul's Cathedral,
he was then obscurely buried in Hertfordshire. In 1413 his body was
disinterred by Henry V's order and buried in Westminster Abbey in the
tomb of his first wife, Anne.

James I, Prince of Scotland, was sent to France by his father,
King Robert III, in 1406 to escape the plots of the Duke of Albany.
He was captured by English sailors while on the high seas and imprisoned in the Tower by order of Henry IV. Upon his father's death that
same year, James was proclaimed King of Scotland. A prisoner in the
Tower for two years, he was then moved to Nottingham for another 16
years until his ransom was paid in 1423. He was crowned at Scone in
the following year. In 1437 he was assassinated at Perth by Sir Robert
Grahame in a conspiracy devised by the Earl of Atholl.

Sir John Oldcastle, Shakespeare's Falstaff, under sentence of
death, escaped from the Tower in 1414, was recaptured and found
guilty of heresy and treachery. He was hanged in St. Giles' Fields.

The Tower was the involuntary home of Prince Charles of Orleans, father of Louis XII, for 12 years beginning in 1415. He had
been taken prisoner by Henry V at the battle of Agincourt. He was
released in 1427 after his ransom of 300,000 Crowns had been paid.
The richly illuminated manuscript, *Poesies de Charles duc d'Orleans*,
which he wrote during his long detention is now in the British Museum.

Sir Thomas Mallory, author of *Le Morte d'Arthur*, the first ambi-
tious effort in English prose, was lodged in the Tower in 1455. He
was transferred to Newgate Prison in 1457, and found himself in and
out of prisons until his death in 1471.

King Henry VI became king in 1422 before his first birthday. By the time of his death in 1471, he had lost two kingdoms, his only son and his sanity. During the period of his insanity, from 1453 to 1455, Richard, Duke of York, ruled in his stead. When Henry's sanity returned, Richard was reluctant to lose his power and the Wars of the Roses began.

Henry VI became a prisoner in the Tower twice, the first time in 1464 and the last in 1471. On May 2, 1471 he was murdered while at prayer in the little chapel in the Wakefield Tower. According to the historians, the murderer was Richard of Gloster, who later became King Richard III. Shakespeare dramatized the occasion in Act V of *The Third Part of King Henry The Sixth*, foreshadowing the Machiavellian arch villain Richard III:

<u>King Henry</u>

And thus I prophesy,—that many a thousand,

•   •   •   •   •   •

Shall rue the hour that ever thou wast born.

•   •   •   •   •   •

Thy mother felt more than a mother's pain,
And yet brought forth less than a mother's hope,—
An indigested and deformed lump,
Not like the fruit of such a goodly tree

<u>Gloster</u>

I'll hear no more: die, prophet, in thy speech:
(Stabs him)

•   •   •   •   •   •

If any spark of life be yet remaining,
Down, down to hell; and say I sent thee thither,
(Stabs him again)

Every year on May 21, the anniversary of Henry VI's murder, lilies from Eton College and white roses from Kings College, Cambridge, both of which he founded, are placed in the chapel in Wakefield Tower. The lilies are tied together with blue ribbons. The flowers are deposited in the oratory in the chapel at 6 P.M. and burned the next day.

In 1478 George, Duke of Clarence, was drowned in a keg of malmsey wine in the Bowyer Tower by order of Richard of Gloucester, his brother and future king. This inspired an unforgettable scene in Shakespeare's *Richard III*, the "false, fleeting, perjured" Duke dreamed that he was drowning in the English Channel:

> Lord, Lord! methought, what pain it was to drown!
> What dreadful noise of water in mine ears!
> What ugly sight of death within mine eyes!

King Edward IV died in 1483 and, on his death bed, appointed Richard of Gloucester as Lord Protector of his two young sons, heirs to the throne. According to Shakespeare, Richard is determined to eliminate all who stand in his way and orders the deaths of the two boys, Edward, Prince of Wales and Richard, Duke of York. Sir James Tyrrel, for "whom corrupting gold would tempt into a close exploit of death", is bribed to commit the murders. The deed is believed to have been done in the Bloody Tower with a secret burial by the chaplain of the Tower in an unknown location.

One of the most remarkable survivors of the Tower's suffocating embrace was Sir Henry Wyatt. Imprisoned in 1483 by Richard III, he was kept alive by one of the Tower cats. The cat slept with him at night, keeping him from freezing to death in his damp cellar. During the day, the cat brought him the pigeons she caught and kept him from starvation. This symbiotic relationship continued for two years until Richard's bloody reign ended with his death in 1584 at Bosworth field. For the next 52 years of his life, Sir Henry never forgot the cat. Indeed, he commissioned a painting of the cat in the act of delivering a pigeon for his daily dinner.

The century ended with the strange case of Perkin Warbeck who had been touring the royal courts of Europe, passing himself off as the younger of King Edward IV's two princes, who had been murdered in the Tower by Richard III. Warbeck gathered an army of about 6,000 local followers who were taken in by his impersonation, and headed an attack against King Henry VIII. His army, defeated at Exeter, melted away as he tried to reach the coast and safety on the Continent. He was captured and sent to the Tower where, after an unsuccessful attempt to escape, he was executed in 1499.

16th CENTURY

This was a very busy period in the Tower. Beginning in 1503, Elizabeth of York, consort of King Henry VII, died in childbirth in the Tower. The body lay in state with 500 tapers and candle sticks abound her bier.

Upon the death of Henry VII in 1509, Henry VIII became king. With his accession, harsh treatment of prisoners in the Tower became almost regular policy. In that same year, 1509, Henry VIII married Catherine of Aragon, widow of his brother Arthur. Henry VII's despised tax collectors were sent to the Tower and executed in the following year, along with Dudley, Henry VII's minister.

In 1512, the venerable chapel of St. Peter ad Vincula was destroyed by fire and rebuilt three years later.

The opposition of the Bishop of Rochester and Sir Thomas More, Lord Chancellor, to the royal supremacy and Henry VIII's divorce landed them in the Tower in 1534. They were both executed on Tower Hill in the following year. John Fisher, nearly starved, had to be carried to the scaffold.

In 1536 Henry, aided by his unscrupulous secretary, Thomas Cromwell (who was also to die by the axe four years later), charged Anne Boleyn, his second wife, with five unproved adulteries. Anne's uncle, the Duke of Norfolk, presided over the judgment of 26 peers and wept as he pronounced the death sentence on her, her brother Lord Rochford, a court musician and three courtiers accused of adulterous conduct.

Three years to the day after her coronation, Anne Boleyn was executed on Tower Green outside Waterloo Barracks. A brass plate marks the site of the scaffold. All five of her alleged lovers were executed on Tower Hill. A few days afterwards, Henry married Jane Seymour.

Beauchamp Tower contains 91 inscriptions on its walls. Number 66 is the carving of a bell with the letter A, representing Thomas Abel. He was domestic chaplain to Queen Catherine of Aragon and had advocated her cause during the divorce proceedings; in addition, he denied the king's supremacy. Henry VIII was not pleased and had Abel arrested and executed in 1540.

Thomas Cromwell, Earl of Essex, Henry's secretary, who had devised the strategy enabling the king to condemn Anne to death for adultery, was himself arrested and executed in the same year.

When the question of divorce was first raised by Henry VIII, the Archbishop of Canterbury, Reginald Pole, seemed willing to approve it, but later changed his mind. After strongly disapproving the proposed divorce, he fled to the Continent. The spiteful Henry could not reach the Archbishop, so in 1541 he condemned his mother Margaret, Countess of Salisbury, governess to Henry's first daughter Mary, to death.

Margaret refused to place her head on the block and the 71 year old matriarch, last of the Plantagenet family, ran round and round the scaffold with the executioner in hot pursuit, axe in hand. He missed her with the first three blows but finally threw her down and brutally hacked off her head in a bizarre dance of death.

In the same year, 1541, Sir Thomas Wyatt was arrested and imprisoned in the Tower on the capital charge of treason. King Henry VIII not only forgave him but added to his land holdings. However, the condition of his release required that Sir Thomas resume living with his wife from whom he had been separated for 15 years.

The following year, 1542, saw Katherine Howard, Henry VIII's fourth wife, brought to the Tower, accused of infidelity. As she passed over London Bridge, she saw the heads of her lovers, Culpepper and Dereham, impaled on the spikes. She was executed on February 13, along with Jane, Viscountess Richford, for supporting Katherine.

Henry Howard, Earl of Surrey, one of the pioneers in the development of English poetry, was arrested on December 12, 1546, on a trumped up charge of treason and other unfounded allegations such as: affecting foreign dress and employing a foreign jester. The Privy council took these charges seriously and he was ordered to the Tower. He sealed his fate when he rashly demanded a new coat of arms including those of Edward the Confessor. This was strictly forbidden by the Royal College of Arms. Howard was found guilty and beheaded on Tower Hill on January 19, 1547. A plaque marks the spot.

Thomas Cranmer, Archbishop of Canterbury, was a tool of Henry VIII's. He declared the king's marriage to Catherine of Aragon null and void, and performed and dissolved the marriages of Anne Boleyn, Anne of Cleves and Catherine Howard. He supported Henry's supremacy over the Church of England. After the death of Edward VI, successor to Henry VIII, he made the fatal mistake of approving Lady Jane Grey's claim to the throne.

Lady Jane Grey, the Nine Days Queen was a granddaughter of Henry VII's younger daughter Mary and the daughter of Henry Grey and Lady Frances Brandon, whose father allied himself to the Duke of Northumberland, Lord Protector of Edward VI. The Duke, determined to retain his power, compelled Jane to marry his son, Lord Guilford Dudley, and upon the death of Edward VI had her proclaimed queen in London on July 10, 1553.

Mary Tudor (Bloody Mary) acted quickly. She had Lady Jane Grey and her husband Lord Guilford Dudley, Thomas Cranmer, the Duke of Northumberland and Hugh Latimer, Bishop of London, confined in the Tower of London. Northumberland was sentenced to death for treason and executed on Tower Hill. Lady Jane Grey and her husband were tried at the Guildhall and found guilty of treason. They were allowed to live separately in comparative comfort in the Tower.

Although Cranmer was found guilty of treason, he was spared by the Queen; however, he was convicted of heresy and stripped of his Episcopal offices. Cranmer and Latimer were burned at the stake in Oxford in 1555. As the fire grew, Latimer said, "We shall this day light such a candle as I trust shall never be put out." Cranmer stuck his right hand in the flames as punishment for signing a document embracing Catholicism, and saying, "This hath offended. Oh, this unworthy hand!"

In the following year, Mary ushered in an official return to Catholicism. When she announced that she would marry Philip of Spain, rebellion broke out throughout England. Thomas Wyatt with a force of 3,000 men reached London, but was quickly defeated and Wyatt captured. Under torture in the Tower, Wyatt incriminated Princess Elizabeth; she was arrested and brought to the Tower.

It was too dangerous now to keep Lady Jane Grey and her husband Guilford Dudley alive. Dudley was beheaded in the morning of February 12th on Tower Hill. His headless body was brought back to the Tower on a cart in full view of his despairing widow. In the afternoon Jane was executed on Tower Green in a sad display of cruel and heartless punishment. Only 17 years old, her frail body was convulsed by shivers of fear as she stumbled around the scaffold, blindfolded, trying desperately to find the beheading block.

From March 18, when Elizabeth was taken to the Bell Tower, Mass was held in her cell every day in an unsuccessful attempt to convert her to Roman Catholicism. To relieve her close confinement which was affecting her health, she was allowed to walk in the Lieutenant's garden and on the section of rampart between the Bell and the Beauchamp Towers. It is still called Princess Elizabeth's Walk. On May 19th Elizabeth was released; no evidence of any complicity in the plots had been found.

In 1556 John Daniell attempted to rob the treasury. He was arrested and imprisoned in the Tower and not only hanged but also beheaded on Tower Hill.

When Mary died in 1558, Elizabeth rode to the Tower, patted the earth and said:

> Some have fallen from being princes of this land to be prisoners in this place. I am raised from being prisoner in this place to be the prince of the land.

During Queen Elizabeth's reign from 1558 to 1603, a number of attempts were made to wrest the throne from her and bestow it on the Catholic Mary, Queen of Scots. In 1572 the Duke of Norfolk was clapped into the Tower for intriguing in favor of Mary. He was quickly beheaded.

The most dangerous conspiracy occurred in 1586 when John Ballard, a Jesuit priest, and Anthony Babington, an 18 year old poet, conceived a plan, known as the Babington Plot, for a general uprising of Catholics, the murder of Queen Elizabeth and the accession of Mary, Queen of Scots, to the throne. All 14 of the plotters were arrested and held in the Tower. They were executed in the most diabolical manner on successive days in Lincoln's Inn Fields, where they had planned their ill fated scheme.

James Froude, the English historian, describes the executions:

> They were hanged but for a moment, according to the letter of the sentence, taken down while the susceptibility of agony was unimpaired, and cut in pieces afterwards with due precautions for the protraction of the pain.

Queen Elizabeth was horrified by such barbarism and forbade its repetition.

In that same year the surprising escape of one Father Gerard was a topic of considerable interest. Housed in the Cradle Tower, the priest attached a leaden weight to a long thin string and threw it to friends waiting outside the wall. They caught it and attached a stout rope which the priest fastened to a turret of the tower, worked his way down into a boat and got away.

In 1590 Lady Clifford, Margaret, Countess of Derby, cousin to Queen Elizabeth I, was accused of witchcraft and imprisoned in the Tower. She was eventually released with the proviso that she was not to approach the court, or to live with her husband.

The following year saw Sir Walter Raleigh secretly married to Elizabeth Throckmorton, one of Queen Elizabeth's maids of honor, and already carrying his child. When the Queen discovered the secret, she was furious and imprisoned both of them in the Tower. Eventually her ire subsided and they were released, but this did not prove to be Sir Walter's only confinement in the Tower; there would be two more times, the last one fatal.

Thomas Howard, Duke of Norfolk, spent ten years in the Tower and died in his chambers in the Beauchamp Tower in 1595.

17th CENTURY

The beginning of the century saw what was to become high drama. Young Robert Devereux, Earl of Essex, was one of the most colorful and important courtiers in the Court, and the chief favorite of Queen Elizabeth I. When he was only 30 years old his expeditions to Cadiz in 1596 and the Azores in 1597 did much to strengthen England's control of the seas, and also further the cause of Protestantism in Europe.

In 1599 he became lieutenant of Ireland and the country's hero. Shakespeare's prologue to Act V of *Henry V* reflects the public's patriotic adulation:

> ... the general of our gracious empress—
> As in good time he may—from Ireland coming,
> Bringing rebellion broached on his sword.

Essex's downfall from power and favor was as rapid as his rise. His disastrous campaign in Ireland, and his impulsive and inept at-

tempt to incite a riot against the Queen in 1601, resulted in his arrest
and imprisonment in the Devereux Tower. He was tried, Francis Bacon being the prosecutor, and received the death sentence. After a
great deal of hesitation, Elizabeth made the heart breaking decision to
sign his death warrant. Essex was executed on Tower Green on February 25, 1601.

Shakespeare may have been reflecting his own emotions over the
fearful downfall of Essex in Ophelia's description of Hamlet's disinte-
gration:

> O, what a noble mind is here o'erthrown!
> The courtier's, soldier's, scholar's eye, tongue, sword;
> Th' expectancy and rose of the fair state,
> The glass of fashion and the mould of form,
> Th' observ'd of all observers,—quite, quite down!

Legend has it that if Essex had sent her the ring she had given
him earlier, the Queen would have pardoned him out of her great love
for him. The ring never reached Elizabeth. It is not known whether
Essex was too proud to beg for her favor, or if he did send the ring but
his enemies prevented it from reaching her.

This emotional dilemma was to form the climax of Maxwell
Anderson's 1930 play, *Elizabeth the Queen*. Written in blank verse
and poetic prose, it was Anderson's version of the love story of Elizabeth and Essex. In the final scene, the day set for the execution,
Elizabeth cannot see him die without giving Essex a chance to ask for
his life:

> ... I have waited late at night
> Thinking, tonight the ring will come, he will never
> Hold out against me so long, but the nights went by
> Somehow, like the days, and it never came,
> Till the last day came, and here it is the last morning
> And the chimes beating out the hours.

In the play, Essex cannot plead for mercy because he knows that
once free he would again reach for the power of the throne. Even as
Elizabeth begs him to ask her pardon, he goes off to die.

A gold ring, with a sardonyx cameo and a carved portrait of
Queen Elizabeth I, is in the possession of the Westminster Abbey Mu-

seum. The ring is reputed to be the one Elizabeth gave Essex in the expectation that he would sent it to her to ask for a pardon.

After Queen Elizabeth's death in 1603, another one of her gallant courtiers was sent for the second time to the Tower by her successor, King James I. Under the new monarch, Sir Walter Raleigh had fallen into disfavor and was deprived of his office as captain of the guard. He increased James' animosity by advocating war with Spain and, on slender charges of complicity in a plot against the king, was tried for high treason.

Found guilty and condemned to death, Raleigh was reprieved, but not pardoned, and remained a prisoner for 13 years in the Bloody Tower. The passage outside his room, where he took his daily walk, is still known as Raleigh Walk. He passed the time by writing a number of books, the most important being the *History of the World*, as well as a considerable body of fine poetry. A copy of the *History of the World*, is preserved in a glass case in the Tower.

The Gunpowder Plot was the most exciting event of 1605. A conspiracy to blow up the Houses of Parliament on November 5, 1605, when King James would open Parliament in person, was hatched by one Robert Catesby. The conspirators rented a cellar immediately below the House of Lords in which they stored casks of gunpowder.

A little before midnight on November 4, the cellar was stormed by the authorities, acting upon secret information, and Guy Fawkes had the bad luck to be in the cellar at that time. Fawkes was one of the plotters, but joined the plot after it was underway; he had had no part in its planning. Several of the gang, including Catesby, were killed in the ensuing battle. The rest, including Fawkes, were taken prisoners and lodged in the Tower to await trial.

Guy Fawkes was confined, tied by his ankles and wrists to a ring in the floor, in a cell in the subcrypt of St. John's Chapel in the White Tower. He was tortured until he signed a confession of his part in the plot. Fawkes, Winter, Rookwood and Keys were hanged in Palace Yard, Westminster.

The Gunpowder Plot is commemorated in the annual search of the cellars below the Houses of Parliament at the opening of each session. Guy Fawkes Day, November 5, corresponding roughly to our Halloween, is celebrated with scarecrow effigies of Fawkes paraded through the streets by processions of boys requesting donations. The effigies are then tossed into a great bonfire to mark the end of the celebration—and of Guy Fawkes.

Arabella Stuart, Scottish noblewoman and granddaughter of James V of Scotland, was in the line of succession to the English throne after James I. She was, as a result, the center of many political intrigues. When, in 1610, she married Sir William Seymour, a representative of the Suffolk branch of the royal family, she became doubly dangerous to James I.

King James imprisoned his unfortunate cousin and her husband in the Bell Tower. In the following year, 1611, Seymour escaped from the Tower. Disguised as a driver in a smock and rough wig, he drove a cart full of branches and yard debris out of the Tower to freedom. He found refuge in France, but his wife Arabella remained a prisoner in the Tower until she died in 1615, insane and broken hearted.

One of the most tragic figures of the period was Sir Thomas Overbury, a poet and courtier who belonged to a distinguished political family. Overbury was secretary and adviser to Robert Carr, Earl of Somerset, one of the king's favorites. He disapproved of the Earl's prospective marriage to the notorious Lady Frances Howard, Countess of Essex. As a result of her machinations, Lady Howard persuaded Carr to have Overbury imprisoned in the Bloody Tower in 1613, after which the marriage took place.

Lady Howard, still consumed by enmity toward Overbury for his disapproval of her marriage, was determined to put him out of the way. She replaced the Lieutenant of the Tower with her own lackey and a personally loyal jailer. She then began a systematic and slow poisoning of Overbury with arsenic and mercury. On September 15, Sir Thomas finally died and was hurriedly buried, wrapped only in a sheet, on the same day in the chapel of St. Peter ad Vincula.

A year later an inquiry resulted in all parties involved being found guilty of murder. The four accomplices were hanged, but the Earl and his Countess escaped the gallows by the king's pardon. They were, however, ordered to live together in the Tower for seven years before being released. By that time they hated each other.

King James, in need of money, released Sir Walter Raleigh in 1616, after 13 years of imprisonment—but still without a pardon—to head an expedition to Guiana to search for gold and silver. The trip was a failure and Raleigh's son was killed during the expedition. Sir Walter was rearrested on his return in June 1618, imprisoned in a small cell in the White Tower for the third time, and condemned to death.

Sir Walter spent the last night before his execution on October 29 in the Gate House Prison in Old Palace Yard where he wrote:

> Even such is time which takes in trust
> Our youth, our joys, and all we have,
> And pays us but with age and dust;
> Who in the dark and silent grave
> When we have wandered all our ways
> Shuts up the story of our days.
> And from which earth and grave and dust
> The Lord shall raise me up I trust.

When Sir Walter mounted the scaffold, the executioner objected to the placement of his head on the block. Raleigh made his famous reply, "What matter how the head lie, so long the heart be right?" His body was buried in the chancel of St. Margaret's Church, marked by a tablet. His head was preserved by his widow.

So died Sir Walter Raleigh, poet, philosopher, adventurer, historian, cavalier—the very embodiment of the Elizabethan Age. The quality of this quintessential Renaissance Man may be found evident in this excerpt from his *The Pilgrimage*:

> Give me my scallop-shell of quiet,
> My staff of faith to walk upon,
> My scrip of joy, immortal diet,
> My bottle of salvation,
> My gown of glory, hope's true gage
> And thus I'll take my pilgrimage.

Sir Francis Bacon, one of the most influential men of his time—lawyer, courtier, statesman, philosopher, essayist, Lord Chancellor—was imprisoned in the Tower in 1621, charged with two counts of bribery. His stay in the Tower lasted just a few days when the king issued a provisional pardon prohibiting Bacon from coming within 12 miles of the Court. This restriction was relaxed in the following year, but Bacon never received a full pardon.

In 1629, nine Members of Parliament were imprisoned for harsh attacks on the Duke of Buckingham, Charles I's favorite. The conditions under which they lived in the Tower were so squalid that Sir John Eliot, one of the prisoners, contracted tuberculosis and died three years later.

William Laud, Archbishop of Canterbury, Bishop of London, Chancellor of Oxford University and the University of Dublin, had great influence in the Star Chamber Courts and in the High Commission. In his unsuccessful attempts to suppress Puritanism with his insistence on absolute conformity to the English liturgy and all church regulations, he made many powerful enemies. The Puritans, of course, were very hostile but Parliament and the people in general disliked him.

Laud failed in two attempts to convert the church in Scotland to Episcopalianism and finally, in 1641, the House of Commons ordered his arrest and imprisonment in the Tower. He was charged with endeavoring to overthrow the Protestant religion. In 1643 he was acquitted by the House of Lords. Nevertheless, the House of Commons sentenced him to death and the House of Lords finally conceded. Although Laud was pardoned by the King, Parliament was able to exercise its powers and had Laud beheaded in January 1645.

Edmund Waller, poet and Member of Parliament, became involved in what is known as Waller's Plot, which was a scheme to secure London for King Charles I. The plot was leaked to Parliament and he and others arrested on May 31, 1643. After his trial at Guildhall where he was found guilty, he was thrown into the Tower. On November 11, 1644, Parliament agreed to accept a £10,000 fine in lieu of execution. Waller was then banished form the realm until 1651 when he was permitted to return to London and resume his political career.

Weller is probably best remembered for his poetry, particularly:

Go, Lovely Rose

> Go, lovely Rose!
> Tell her that wastes her time and me
> That now she knows,
> When I resemble her to thee,
> How sweet and fair she seems to be.

and

On A Girdle

That which her slender waist confined,
Shall now my joyful temples bind;
No monarch but would give his crown,
His arms might do what this has done.

Sir William Davenant, said to be the natural son of William Shakespeare by the wife of an Oxford innkeeper, attached himself to the Court, succeeded Ben Jonson as poet laureate in 1638 and was knighted in 1643. He fought in the royalist army during the civil war; when Cromwell was victorious, Davenant had to seek refuge in France.

In 1650 he headed a royalist colonizing expedition planning to sail to Virginia. The ship was apprehended before it was able to clear the English Channel and Davenant was imprisoned in the Tower. John Milton, then Latin Secretary to the Commonwealth, intervened and secured his release from the gallows in 1652.

Devenant wrote and produced a number of masques and plays, and was responsible for many innovations in theater craft. He was the first to produce an English opera, to introduce painted stage sets and full-scale moveable scenery and to recruit an English woman to act upon the stage for the first time.

William Penn, founder of the colony of Pennsylvania, USA, joined the Quaker faith early in his life and remained essentially a Quaker preacher, traveling among members of the faith in England, the Continent and the Colonies. Although somewhat inconsistent with what is supposed to be Quaker doctrine, Penn took part in politics and spent a great deal of his time at court using his influence and abilities to secure the release of sect members from prison.

Penn became a controversial writer of classics of Quaker doctrine. In 1668-69 he was imprisoned in the Tower for publishing his books in which he supposedly attacked the doctrine of the trinity. Even while in prison he wrote a pamphlet, *No Cross, No Crown*, which is still read today.

Sir William Covernty, at one time Secretary of the Navy, became a prisoner in the Tower in 1669 for challenging the Duke of Buckingham to a duel. Samuel Pepys, who had a close relationship with Sir William because of his service in the Navy, visited him, according to his *Diary*, on March 9, 1669, and told him his closely guarded secret that he also kept a Diary:

> Up, and to the Tower; and there find Sir William Coventry alone, writing down his Journal, which, he tells me, he now keeps of the material things; upon which I told him, and he is the only man I ever told it to, I think, that I kept it most strictly these eight or ten years; and I am sorry almost that I told it to him, it not being necessary, nor may be convenient, to have it known.

The Tower of London was built to guard against attack from outside, not from within. But that is what happened in 1671 when Colonel Blood stole the Crown Jewels from the basement of the Martin Tower.

Thomas Blood, an Irish adventurer usually called Colonel Blood, had a long history of dangerous undertakings. In 1663 he plotted to surprise Dublin Castle and seize the lord lieutenant. Later, in 1670, he attempted to abduct and hang the Duke of Ormonde.

Blood disguised himself as a clergyman to gain the confidence of the Jewel House Keeper. The unsuspecting man invited Blood and his supposedly wealthy nephew to supper, hoping that the nephew would take a fancy to his daughter. During the evening Blood wheedled the Keeper to sell him his pair of his pistols which he affected to admire. The Keeper was thus rendered unarmed.

The next morning, Blood arrived with some friends to view the jewels; once inside they gagged and bound the Keeper and seized the jewels. He and three of his accomplices were captured, the jewels were recovered and the thieves thrown into one of the dungeons in the White Tower. Blood refused to answer any questions or to speak to anyone but the king. Taken before the king, Charles II, Blood's Irish charm and impudence made such an impression on the king that he not only pardoned Blood and his accomplices, but gave him estates in Ireland and a pension of £500 a year.

Excavations at the foot of a Tower staircase in 1674 disclosed the bones of two young boys. King Charles II believed them to be royal remains and ordered that they be interred in Westminster Abbey. A marble urn for this purpose was designed by Sir Christopher Wren and it rests in the north aisle of Henry VII's Chapel. A Latin inscription provides a history of the tragic deed; the English translation reads:

Here lie the Reliques of Edward the Fifth, King of England, and Richard Duke of York. These brothers being confined in the Tower, and there stifled with Pillows, were privately and meanly buried by order of their perfidious Uncle Richard the usurper; whose bones, long enquired after and wished for, after two hundred and one years in the rubbish of the stairs [those leading to the Chapel of the White Tower] were on the 17th day of July 1674, by undoubted proofs discovered, being buried deep in that place. Charles the Second, a most compassionate Prince, pitying their severe fate, ordered these unhappy Princes to be laid amongst the monuments of their predecessors, Anno Dom. 1678, in the 30th year of his reign.

Samuel Pepys, the famous diarist and secretary of the Admiralty, was arrested and committed to the Tower on May 22, 1679. He had been accused by Titus Oates, a perjured conspirator, of giving naval secrets to the French. Pepys came extremely close to execution for treason. He was released on bail in August 1679, but the proceedings were not dropped until June 1680 when he was exonerated and restored to his office.

James, Duke of Monmouth, believed to be the illegitimate son of King Charles II, was implicated in the Rye House Plot, a plan to assassinate Charles II and his brother as they passed Rye House on the London-Newmarket Road in April 1683. The Duke was then to be placed on the throne.

The plot was discovered and the principals hustled to the Tower and executed. The Duke of Monmouth, however, was pardoned and fled to Holland. He returned in 1695 to lead a rebellion against James II, who succeeded to the throne upon the death of Charles II, to assert his right to the throne. The rebellion was suppressed at the battle of Sedgemoor on July 6 and Monmouth was imprisoned in the Tower. This time no pardon was forthcoming and Monmouth was executed on Tower Hill on July 15. The axe was dull and after the first blow, Monmouth got up and rebuked the executioner, John Ketch. After two more attempts, Ketch had to resort to a knife.

In a strange stoke of irony, one man found protection form arrest within the Tower of London. Daniel Defoe, author of *Robinson Crusoe* and *Moll Flanders*, was a dissenter and no stranger to prisons. In 1692 he went bankrupt and fled to the Mint which was then located in the Tower. The Mint was one of the places in London where the right of sanctuary still applied (it was repealed in 1697) and Defoe was legally safe from arrest for one month. By that time, he had escaped to Bristol, where he remained until arrangements were made to repay his debts and he could return to England.

18th CENTURY

The flight of James II and the accession of William and Mary in 1689 represented more than a mere change of rulers. The supremacy of Parliament was now guaranteed, the theory of divine right disappeared and the liberty of the press and pulpit was secured. The Crown was surrounded by constitutional checks, and its power to arrest and execute persons without due process had vanished. As a result, the Tower's occupancy was greatly reduced and it became less a prison than a show piece of English history as a reminder of the excesses and cruelty of those monarchs who ruled by divine right, rather than by citizens' rights.

In 1716 the most daring escape in the Tower's history took place. William Maxwell, Earl of Nithsdale, had been condemned to death for his part in the Scottish uprising. He was awaiting execution in the Tower.

On the eve of his execution, his wife Winifred visited him in his room, accompanied by two other women. The two women left first, each leaving some wearing apparel behind. Shortly afterwards, Lord Nithsdale, disguised in the clothing, wearing a wig smuggled in by his wife, and crying into a large handkerchief to hide his red beard, was led to the main gate on his wife's arm. Lady Nithsdale returned to her husband's room and carried on a simulated conversation by imitating his voice. Upon leaving, she met a servant on his way to the room and asked him not to disturb her husband because he was at his prayers.

Lord Nithsdale fled to Rome with his wife and lived there until his death 28 years later in 1744. His two fellow conspirators in the uprising, Robert Earl of Kenmure, and the Earl of Derwentwater were executed. The escape is the subject of a play by Clifford Bax, titled *The Immortal Lady*.

The term, Power Play, never had greater meaning than the stratagem practiced by Dr. Richard Mead in 1723. It all began with the imprisonment in the Tower of Francis Atterbury, Dean of Westminster and the Bishop of Rochester, as the first player. He was accused of conspiring to place the Old Pretender, James Stuart, son of the deposed king James II, on the throne. He was found guilty, deprived of his offices and condemned to perpetual exile.

At the same time, Dr. John Freind, an eminent physicist and scholar, and the second player in the game, was also imprisoned in the Tower due to his intimacy with Dean Atterbury: guilt by association.

Now the third and leading player enters the picture: Dr. Richard Mead, physician to King George II. When Sir Robert Walpole, the Prime Minister, fell ill during Dr. Freind's incarceration, he sent for Dr. Mead to cure him. Mead refused to prescribe or perform medical treatment of Sir Walpole until his close friend, Dr. Freind, was released from the Tower. The Prime Minister, whether from fear or favor, thereupon freed Dr. Freind and never troubled him again.

Simon Fraser Lovat, 12th Baron, has the distinction of in 1747 being the last person to be beheaded on Tower Hill. A Scottish intriguer, Simon Fraser became Lord Lovat upon his father's death in 1699. The family of the 10th Lord, his cousin, presented a rival claim to the title including extensive land holdings. Lovat forced his cousin's widow to marry him, and for this he was banished form the realm in 1701.

Lord Lovat returned to Scotland in 1714 as a Jacobite clan leader. For his services in supporting the English government, he was given a pardon. In 1745 he resumed his Jacobite intrigues. When the forces of Bonnie Prince Charlie were defeated at Culloden on April 16, 1746, Lovat was captured, condemned for treason and imprisoned in the Tower. Lord Lovat, along with two other members of the Scottish nobility, the Earl of Kilmarnock and Lord Balmerino, were beheaded on Tower Hill.

John Wilkes had a long history of political service. Elected four times as a Member of Parliament, twice expelled from the House of Commons and a member of the Cogers Debating Society, he was well known as a political agitator and reformer. He was imprisoned in the Tower in 1763 on a charge of seditious libel of the court and the government (he criticized a speech by King George III). After a week's detention, he was discharged by the judges as a Member of Parliament, but then expelled by the House of Commons and banished from England.

Wilkes lived on the Continent until 1768 when he returned to England in defiance of his banishment. He was at once elected a Member of Parliament, but again expelled and imprisoned from 1768 to 1770 in the Marshalsea Prison for libel. In 1774 he was reelected to Parliament, serving until 1790, and elected Lord Mayor of London in the same year. Wilkes' epitaph on his burial vault in Grosvenor Chapel reads: "a friend of liberty".

In 1780, a madman almost brought down the government. Lord George Gordon, son of the third Duke of Gordon, assembled a mob on June 2, 1780 to protest the removal of restrictions on Roman Catholics. The mob became violent and uncontrolled, referred to as the No Popery Riots. The rioters held London in terror for 13 days and destroyed nearly a million pounds worth of property.

Lord Gordon was arrested, sent to the Tower and tried for high treason. Acquitted on the grounds of insanity, he died insane some 12 years later in Newgate Prison. Two women and a drunken sailor were hanged for complicity in the riots. A vivid description of the Gordon riots is furnished in Charles Dickens' *Barnaby Rudge*.

James Turnbull, a worker in the Mint located in the Tower, held up the employees in 1798 and made off with 2,804 newly minted guineas. He was captured after nine days and executed. The Mint was moved to Little Tower Hill some 12 years later.

19th CENTURY

The Tower held very few prisoners during this century as its bloody history wound down. The most important prisoner was Arthur Thistlewood, leader of the Cato Street Conspirators.

Thistlewood was a former estate agent and army officer. Meeting in Cato Street quarters, the conspirators planned to murder the entire Cabinet at a dinner to be given by Lord Harrowby in Grosvenor Square on February 23, 1820. The elaborate plan was to kill all the Ministers and remove the heads of Lord Sidmouth, the Home Secretary and Lord Castlereagh. Afterwards, they were to assault Coutts' Bank and Gray's Inn, capture the cannon in the Artillery Ground, seize the Mansion House, the Bank of England and the Tower. Then a provisional government would be proclaimed.

The conspirators were betrayed by one of their own. On the appointed day, just before the dinner was to be held, the authorities raided the headquarters of the group in the stable loft at No.6 (now No.1A) Cato Street. Eleven of the conspirators escaped, but a large number were captured and imprisoned in the Tower. On May 1, 1820, the five ringleaders, including Thistlewood, were hanged at Newgate Prison, another five were exiled. A blue plaque on the loft describes what happened there on the evening of February 23, 1820.

On January 24, 1885, the Fenians planted a bomb on the second floor of the White Tower. The resultant explosion occurred almost simultaneously with others in the Houses of Parliament and Westminster Hall. Fortunately no one was killed by the terrorist actions of the Irish revolutionaries, although several people were severely injured.

20th CENTURY

For 100 years after the Cato Street Conspirators were hanged for high treason, no one else was executed for this offense. The two World Wars, however, added to the legendary history of the Tower.

Robert David Casement, Irish rebel, joined the British Consular Service in 1895. His distinguished services earned him a knighthood; he retired in Ireland in 1913.

During world War I Casement became an active agitator for Irish independence. He organized Irish soldiers to fight against Britain, and traveled secretly to Germany for consultations. Upon his return to Ireland in a German submarine, he was arrested and imprisoned in the Tower From April 25 to May 15, 1916, during which time he was found guilty of conspiring with the Germans in planning the Easter uprising. Transferred to Pentonville Prison, he was hanged as a traitor on August 3, 1916.

During World War II, eleven spies were shot in the miniature rifle range outside Martin Tower. They were buried in Brixton Prison.

In World War II the Tower was used to hold prisoners of war. These included Herr Gerlach, German Consul in Iceland, confined for three and a half months, and Herr Rudolf Hess, deputy Führer, who was held in the Tower for four days. One spy was shot within the Tower walls.

Also during World War II, fifteen enemy bombs fell near the White Tower, killing 23 people.

The last execution within the Tower took place on August 14, 1941. A pathetic German spy named Josef Jakobs had been dropped by parachute in England, carrying only a slice of a frankfurter to sustain himself on his mission. He broke an ankle on landing and was unable to avoid immediate capture. Because of his injury, he was afforded the choice of remaining seated while he was shot.

THE CHAPEL OF ST. JOHN

The Chapel of St. John the Evangelist in the White Tower is a perfect specimen of Norman architecture. Except for some minor changes made by Sir Christopher Wren in the 17th century, the small stone chapel, 55½ feet long with thick and squat columns and sturdy arches, is much the same as in 1080 when it was built.

Medieval monarchs passed the night in the chapel before their coronation in Westminster Abbey. It was in this chapel that the body of the murdered Henry VI lay in state in 1471, Lady Jane Grey prayed before her execution in 1554, and where the Order of the Bath, the second of the great Orders of Chivalry, was founded in 1399 by Henry IV.

Annually on May 21, the anniversary of Henry VI's death, lilies from Eaton College and white Roses from Kings College, Cambridge, both of which he founded, are placed in the chapel.

THE CHAPEL ROYAL OF ST. PETER AD VINCULA

St. Peter's Chapel on Tower Green is probably the most ignominious testimonial to the admonition that "the paths of glory lead but to the grave." Westminster Abbey and St. Paul's Cathedral celebrate life's successes; St. Peter's buries its failures, the just with the unjust.

The chapel was built in the 11th century, in Henry I's reign, and rebuilt in 1515 after being destroyed by fire in 1512. The dedication, ad Vincula—in chains—refers to the miraculous release of the disciple from his first imprisonment in Jerusalem.

Inscribed on a memorial tablet near the entrance is a "List of Remarkable Persons Buried in this Chapel", consisting of over 30 names. Anne Boleyn was buried here in a common oak chest in 1536. Others buried her include: Duke of Northumberland (1535), Bishop Fisher (1535), Sir Thomas More (1535), Thomas Cromwell, Earl of Essex (1540), Katherine Howard (1542), Thomas, Lord Seymour (1549),

Protector Somerset (1552), Lady Jane Grey, Lord Guilford Dudley (1554), Robert Devereux, Earl of Essex (1601), Sir Thomas Overbury (1613), Duke of Monmouth (1685), and Jacobite Lords of the 1745 Rebellion.

Lord Macaulay expressed deep sorrow and compassion for these victims of the cruel lust for power that was so much a part of England's history:

> In truth there is no sadder spot on the earth than that little cemetery. Death is there associated ... with whatever is darkest in human nature and in human destiny, with the savage triumph of implacable enemies, with the inconstancy, the ingratitude, the cowardice of friends, with all the miseries of fallen greatness and of blighted fame. Thither have been carried ... the bleeding relics of men who had been the captains of armies, the leaders of parties, the oracles of senates, and the ornaments of courts.

TRAITORS' GATE

The great water gate under St. Thomas' Tower, erected by Henry III in honor of St. Thomas à Becket, was the principal entrance to the Tower when the Thames was London's main thoroughfare. So many illustrious figures accused of crimes against the Crown were rowed through the river entrance that the name Traitors' Gate became common usage.

"To the water side I must conduct your grace", says Sir Thomas Lovell in Shakespeare's *Henry VIII* to Edward, Duke of Buckingham, prior to his execution in 1521. Others who followed to find death on the other side of the archway include: Bishop Fisher and Sir Thomas More in 1534, Anne Boleyn in 1536, Thomas Cromwell, Earl of Essex, in 1540, Katherine Howard in 1542, Lady Jane Grey in 1554, Robert Devereux, Earl of Essex in 1601 and James, Duke of Monmouth in 1685.

The Princess Elizabeth was ushered through this gateway in 1554; she did not die, but lived to become Queen Elizabeth I in 1558.

EPILOGUE

For me, three of the loveliest and most strangely touching sights of London are the stars shining very high in the blue and very quietly when you look up at them from the roaring depths of a crowded, naphtha-flaring, poverty-stricken market street; a sunrise brightening over the Thames below London Bridge, while the barges are still asleep with the gleam of their lamps showing pale in the dawn; and the blurred lights and ghostly buildings of a long city road that is clothed in mystery and transfigured by a brooding, dream-haunted fog. Perhaps this is only because of the dim feeling one has that the wasting centuries have not changed; and the fog that blots out today makes it easier to realise that yesterday and the life of yesterday are close about us still, and that we might see them with our waking eyes, even as we see them in our dreams, if the darkness would but lift.

—A. St. John Adcock
Famous Houses and Literary Shrines of London

My purpose has been to bring life to the dry dust of history by enabling the reader to vicariously participate in events which have receded into the past. We may thus, as Shakespeare suggested, "satisfy our eyes with the memorials and things of fame that do renown this city."

These reminders of past history helps us understand the enduring values, that not only belong to the past, but to the present and future as well. Malcolm Muggeridge said, "In England time softens everything."

The City is so miraculously haunted, that it often becomes difficult to separate the real form the unreal, to distinguish between those characters who never existed and those who have ceased to exist. Falstaff, Mr. Pickwick, Moll Flanders, David Copperfield, to name but a few, seem as real today as any of their contemporaries who once walked the streets of the City.

For all those who would seek out the people and places of the City's past, Christopher Fry takes them by the hand and whispers these words from his *Curtmantle*:

> Time walks by our side, ma'am,
> Unwilling to pass.

INDEX

Each index entry includes the attraction's area letter and number, followed by the page(s) containing the explanatory text. For example: Punch Tavern D17, 124 indicates that Punch Tavern is the No.17 attraction of area D and is discussed on page 124.

ORDER FORM

P.O. Box 725
Snoqualmie, WA 98065
U.S.A.

Please send _____ copies of **London's City. A Guide Through the Historic Square Mile** to:

Name: _____

Street: _____

City, State: _____

Phone: _____ Zip: _____

Enclosed is: $15.95/book = _____

Shipping (see below) + _____

Sales Tax (if applicable) + _____

Total = _____

Ship Via: ❏ Book Rate   ❏ Priority Mail

Shipping: Books are normally shipped via Parcel Post, Book Rate. Please allow two or three weeks for delivery. For faster service, we ship via Priority Mail.

Book Rate: $2.00 first book, $1.00 for each additional book.

Priority Mail: $3.50 per book.

Sales Tax: Orders shipped to Washington state addresses <u>only</u>, please add $1.31 to your order (for 8.2% sales tax).

Canada: If sending Canadian funds; please use the following prices:

Price per book: $22.50 Can   Postage: $3.00 Can

Please make your check or money order payable to **Marmot Publishing**. **Thank you for your order!**